Fodor's 94
Las Vegas,
Reno, Tahoe

D1711280

Fodor's Travel Publications, Inc.
New York • Toronto • London • Sydney • Auckland

ISBN 0–679–02524–3

Fodor's Las Vegas, Reno, Tahoe

Editor: Edie Jarolim
Editorial Contributors: Deke Castleman, Jefferson Graham, Elliot Krane, Valerie Martone, Marcy Pritchard
Creative Director: Fabrizio La Rocca
Cartographer: David Lindroth
Illustrator: Karl Tanner
Cover Photograph: R. Llewellyn/Superstock, Inc.

Design: Vignelli Associates

Special Sales

Contents

Foreword

With nine of the world's ten largest resort hotels, Las Vegas accommodates more than 24 million tourists a year, attracted by the grand hotels and theme parks, the large variety of gambling opportunities, the inexpensive rooms and food, the world-class entertainment, the neon lights of the city, and the spectacular scenery of the American Southwest surrounding it all.

These are the renowned enticements of Las Vegas, but there are other, more subtle ones. There's the twisting of time, noticeable, for example, in coffee shops, when at any hour some people are having breakfast, others lunch or dinner, and still others snacks or coffee. There's the unmistakable air—sounds, smells, sights—of a casino. And there's the phenomenon of a city that never closes or seems to sleep, that galvanizes and emblazons the familiar activities of daily life.

This year's edition of *Fodor's Las Vegas, Reno, Tahoe* will help prepare you for the casinos and suggest other activities and excursions to tear you away from the slot and video-poker machines. But it will also attune you to the essence of Las Vegas, which is often obscured by the steamrolling stimulation of the town.

Many thanks go to the following Las Vegans for their help, direct or indirect, with the preparation of this book: Myram Borders, Bethany Coffey, Anthony Curtis, June Flowers, Katie and Jacob Hawkins, Dave Krzyzopolski, Dennis McBride, Blair Rodman, Ira D. Sternberg, and Stanford Wong.

While every care has been taken to ensure the accuracy of the information in this guide, the passage of time will always bring change, and consequently the publisher cannot accept responsibility for errors that may occur.

All prices and opening times quoted here are based on information supplied to us at press time. Hours and admission fees may change, however, and the prudent traveler will avoid inconvenience by calling ahead.

Fodor's wants to hear about your travel experiences, both pleasant and unpleasant. When a hotel or restaurant fails to live up to its billing, let us know, and we will investigate the complaint and revise our entries where the facts warrant it.

Send your letters to the editors of Fodor's Travel Publications, 201 E. 50th Street, New York, NY 10022.

Highlights'94 and Fodor's Choice

Highlights '94

Las Vegas has been a boomtown on and off for the past 40 years, but all the booms combined probably can't match the noise of 1993–1994. Circus Circus's 55-acre **Grand Slam Canyon amusement park,** with its roller coaster, flume, and gondola leading to the casino, opened in August 1993. Mirage Resorts' 3,000-room **Treasure Island,** with its life-size pirate schooner battling a navy frigate on a South Seas bay within splashing distance of the Strip, made its debut in November 1993, as did Circus Circus' 2,500-room **Luxor pyramid,** Las Vegas's tribute to ancient Egypt, boasting 29 million cubic feet of open space. Bob Stupak's **Stratosphere Tower,** when completed in early 1994, will loom 70 stories higher than any other building on the Strip. And the magnificent 5,000-room **MGM Grand and 33-acre theme park** will provide an appropriate climax to the latest Las Vegas cannonade when it opens its doors in February 1994.

But that's not all. Far from it. The **Flamingo Hilton** is putting the finishing touches on its 18-year expansion program with a $104 million tower, bringing the hotel's room count to 4,000, and a 15-acre pool complex. The **Dunes,** which closed in early 1993, is scheduled to be razed in early 1994 to make way for a 3,000-room hotel and 14-acre lake. **Hard Rock Cafe** has announced Las Vegas's first rock 'n' roll hotel, slated to open in late 1994. And Denver developers have teamed up with the Jackson family (including Michael), to build the 400-room Desert Winds hotel-casino, with the world's largest bingo hall and a recording studio.

The Nevada state demographer calculates that 10 permanent residents are gained for every new hotel room added: Thus the nearly 12,000 accommodations added between late 1993 and early 1994 should bring 120,000 settlers to town. Though its growth has slowed slightly in the past few years (from 6% to 4% annually), Las Vegas is still the fastest-growing city in the country in the fastest-growing state. Clark County's population, now at 850,000, will reach the 1 million mark as early as 1997.

Las Vegas is also an expanding retirement destination. The 80,000 houses of **Summerlin,** rising on 22,000 acres near the western rim of Las Vegas Valley, won't be completed until the year 2015, but more people are signing on to this master-plan community than to any other in the United States. Just north of Summerlin is **Sun City,** a 1,900-acre age-restricted adult community with a 36-acre world-class golf course.

Other new additions to the Las Vegas landscape include the new main hall at the **Las Vegas Convention Center,** which replaces the 35-year-old rotunda; the **Lied Discovery**

Children's Museum and Las Vegas library complex, just north of downtown; an expanded and revamped citywide bus system called **CAT;** a statue of **Benny Binion** astride a trusty steed in back of the Horseshoe Hotel; and triangular billboards that rotate on their axes, displaying three different signs.

Amid all this change, however, one thing about Las Vegas remains the same. The people keep coming, and they keep gambling. This year, 24 million of them are expected to visit Las Vegas. They'll gamble $25 billion and lose $5 billion. And they'll spend another $5 billion on activities not related to games of chance.

Fodor's Choice

No two people will agree on what makes a perfect vacation, but it's fun and helpful to know what others think. We hope you'll have a chance to experience some of Fodor's Choices yourself while visiting Las Vegas, Reno, and Tahoe. For detailed information about each entry, refer to the appropriate chapters in this guidebook.

Activities

Rockin' and rollin' on Merlin's Magic Motion Machine at Excalibur

Ice-skating at the Santa Fe Hotel

People-watching at the Forum Shops at Caesars

Moments

First glimpse of the MGM Grand and Luxor

First coffee shop comp for two after a couple of hours at a $5 blackjack table

The audience bell-ringing episode in Cirque du Soleil

Sights

The neon extravaganza along Fremont Street downtown

Hoover Dam

Valley of Fire

The volcano in front of the Mirage Hotel

Snacks

Shrimp cocktail at the Golden Gate downtown

Strawberry shortcake at the Westward Ho

Free popcorn at Slots-A-Fun

Hotels

Caesars Palace (*Very Expensive*)

Sands (*Moderate*)

Gold Spike Hotel and Casino (*Inexpensive*)

Restaurants

Primavera (*Very Expensive*)

Le Montrachet (*Expensive*)

The Steak House (*Moderate*)

The Tillerman (*Moderate*)

The Rio Suites' buffet (*Inexpensive*)

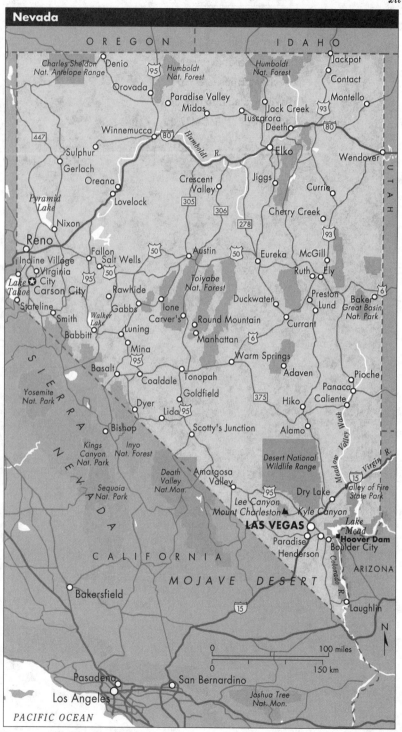

Nevada

OREGON · IDAHO

Charles Sheldon Nat. Antelope Range
Denio
95
Humboldt Nat. Forest
Jackpot
Contact
Montello
Orovada
Paradise Valley
Midas
Jack Creek
Tuscarora
Deeth
93
80
Humboldt Nat. Forest
Winnemucca
80
Humboldt R.
Elko
Wendover
447
Sulphur
Gerlach
Oreana
Crescent Valley
Jiggs
Currie
Pyramid Lake
Lovelock
305
306
278
Cherry Creek
93
Nixon
Reno
Fallon
Salt Wells
50
Austin
50
Eureka
McGill
Ruth
Ely
Incline Village
Virginia City
95
50
Toiyabe Nat. Forest
Duckwater
Preston
Lund
Baker
Great Basin Nat. Park
6
Lake Tahoe
Carson City
Rawhide
Gabbs
Ione
Carver's
Round Mountain
Currant
Stateline
Smith
Walker Lake
Luning
Manhattan
6
Babbitt
Mina
Warm Springs
Adaven
Pioche
95
Basalt
Coaldale
Tonopah
Panaca
Caliente
S I E R R A
Goldfield
375
Hiko
Yosemite Nat. Park
Dyer
Lida
95
Scotty's Junction
Alamo
Meadow Valley Wash
Bishop
Kings Canyon Nat. Park
Inyo Nat. Forest
Desert National Wildlife Range
Virgin R.
N E V A D A
Sequoia Nat. Park
Death Valley Nat. Mon.
Amargosa Valley
95
Dry Lake
15
Valley of Fire State Park
Lee Canyon
Mount Charleston ▲
Kyle Canyon
LAS VEGAS
Lake Mead
Hoover Dam
Boulder City
Paradise
Henderson
Colorado R.
C A L I F O R N I A
ARIZONA
M O J A V E   D E S E R T
Bakersfield
15
Laughlin
Pasadena
San Bernardino
Joshua Tree Nat. Mon.
Los Angeles

N

0   100 miles
0   150 km

PACIFIC OCEAN

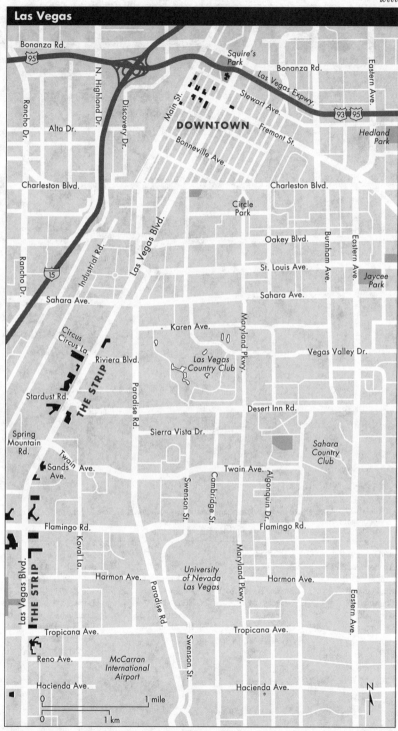

World Time Zones

Numbers below vertical bands relate each zone to Greenwich Mean Time (0 hrs.).
Local times frequently differ from these general indications,
as indicated by light-face numbers on map.

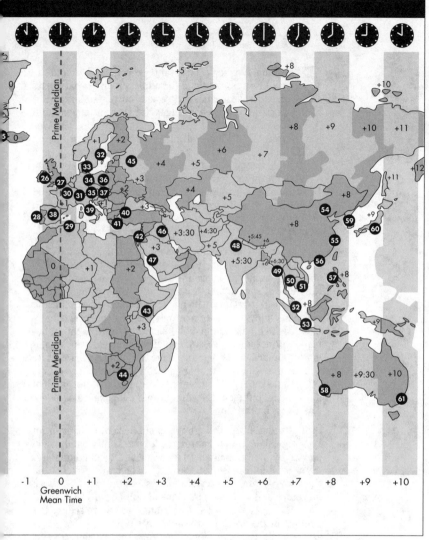

Introduction

The name Las Vegas is instantly recognized around the world as a fantasyland for adults, a place that exists for one reason and one reason only: gambling. But Las Vegas is currently changing faster than its image's ability to keep pace, as this traditionally X-rated city strives for the big "G" of general admittance, trying to attract adults, children, friends, babysitters, grandparents, and nongamblers, and nonsmokers—in short, everybody. Fabulous theme hotels such as Excalibur, Treasure Island, and Luxor, and amusement parks such as Wet 'n' Wild, Grand Slam Canyon, and the MGM Grand backlot all provide a minivacation's worth of excitement—without visitors ever having to step up to a slot machine or blackjack table.

Why is Las Vegas seemingly abandoning its adult-only image in favor of appealing to a wholesome family market? For one thing, gambling is proliferating around the country and the world at such a furious pace that Las Vegas must broaden its appeal to maintain its edge. And the demographically powerful baby boomers are now having their own baby bulge, which has changed the shape of their vacation demands. Finally, Las Vegas, which remains only the second most popular tourist destination in the country, has cast its wanton gaze toward number one, Disney World. And everything that Las Vegas has ever desired, from ridding itself of underworld influence to hosting the National Finals Rodeo, Las Vegas has attained.

Still, a substantial, though underpublicized, contingent of Las Vegas boosters is content to let the family bandwagon parade by, and continues to embrace adults and gamblers. After all, Las Vegas hasn't exactly been transformed. Yes, there are pyramids and water slides and towers, along with museums and galleries, but tens of millions of visitors still come to Las Vegas for the traditional reason, to seduce the goddess of chance. You are constantly reminded of this fact as you walk or drive along the Strip or Fremont Street. There are no supermarkets, post offices, movie theaters, or other familiar businesses of everyday life, only places where you can buy a hamburger or a souvenir, get married, and lay a bet.

The Las Vegas of the Strip and downtown is Dolly, Frank, Rodney, and Diana. It's cards, dice, roulette wheels, and slots. It's harried keno runners and leggy cocktail waitresses, grizzled pit bosses and nervous break-in dealers. It's cab and limo drivers, valets and bellmen. Las Vegas is show girls with smiles as white as spotlights and headwear as big and bright as fireworks. It's a place where thousands of people earn their living counting billions in chips, change, bills, checks, and markers. The big bosses in this town, which has never had a widely known political leader, have always been the flamboyant casino owners: Moe Dalitz of the Desert Inn; Kirk Kerkorian of the MGM Grand; Steve Wynn of the Golden Nugget, Mirage, and Treasure Island; Jackie Gaughan of the Plaza and El Cortez; Michael Gaughan of the Barbary Coast and Gold Coast; Bob Stupak of Vegas World; Sam Boyd of the Fremont, California, and Stardust; and the late Benny Binion of the Horseshoe.

While the Strip and downtown are the best known and principal tourist areas of the city, 850,000 people live—and lead "normal" lives—within 10 miles of them. Endless subdivisions enclose rows and rows of pink-stuccoed and red-tiled, three-bedroom and two-bath houses, most of them less than five years old and occupied by recent transplants hoping to cash in on the fulsome boom. "Lost Wages" is a city of dreamers: gamblers hoping to beat the odds and get rich; dancers, singers, magicians, acrobats, and comedians praying to make it in the Entertainment Capital of the World; realtors, supermarket cashiers, shoe salesmen, librarians, seeking a better way of life.

F or all the local talk about Las Vegas citizens being average people who just happen to live and work in an unusual city, living here is undeniably different. For example, three out of every four locals have a connection to the hospitality industry; the town is full of people whose jobs are to cater to strangers 24 hours a day, 365 days a year. Las Vegas probably has the largest graveyard shift in the world. And the notion that locals never gamble and rarely see a show or eat at a buffet is also largely mythic. Las Vegas residents are a large and active part of the total market that indulges in 99¢ breakfasts and $9 king crab legs, slot clubs and gambling promotions. Indeed, the casinos that cater primarily to locals (Palace Station, the Rio, Gold Coast, Santa Fe, and Arizona Charlie's) are among the most successful in town. Surprisingly, Las Vegas is also a religious town—about a third of the 450 congregations here are Latter-day Saint (Mormon)—which adds a somewhat incongruous conservative dimension to local politics and morals.

Gambling and tourism are not the only games in town. Nellis Air Force Base employs 8,000 people, and 10,000 more work at the Nevada Test Site. The construction industry is huge, and the warehousing business is major. Large corporations and small manufacturing firms frequently relocate to southern Nevada, which offers tax incentives as well as a lower cost of living. But local life is merely a curiosity to the tens of millions of tourists whose primary concern is choosing among 50 major hotel-casinos, several dozen shows, a mind-boggling variety of gambling options, limitless dining, and spectacular day-trips.

The largest city in Nevada, Las Vegas is 2,030 feet above sea level. It's one of the most remote large cities in the country: The nearest major population center to the west is Barstow, California, two and a half hours away; St. George, Utah, is two hours to the east. Over the years, Las Vegas has wrested the political and economic power in the state away from Reno, 448 miles to the northwest, the city where legalized gambling first became popular and where the early casinos were built.

Las Vegas is surrounded by the Mojave Desert, and Las Vegas Valley is flanked by mountain ranges. Among them are the Spring Mountains, including Mt. Charleston (11,918 feet), which features downhill skiing, and Red Rock Canyon, characterized by stunning Southwest sandstone. The Las Vegas Wash drains the valley to the southeast into Lake Mead and the Colorado River system.

Average high temperatures in Las Vegas rise to 105 degrees in July and August; lows drop to 30 degrees in January and February. The heat is dry and saunalike throughout the summer, except during electrical storms that can dump an inch of rain an hour and cause dangerous flash floods. Heavy rains any time of year exacerbate two of Las Vegas's major problems: lack of water drainage and surplus of traffic. The summer blaze often makes it very uncomfortable to be outside for any length of time. Winters can be surprisingly cold during the day, and especially chilly after the sun goes down. The weather doesn't get any better here than in September and October, and April and May, also relatively uncrowded months.

To get the full impact of the neon spectacle, it's best to drive into Las Vegas at night. Fifty miles out, the great desert glow is discernible; 30 miles away, it begins to resolve into pinpoints of light. In another 10 miles you can start to make out the skyline, surrounded by the brilliance of a billion bulbs. Ten miles from Las Vegas you're finally in it: amber streetlights, harsh like the desert. If you stop, get out of the car, and listen, you can hear the hum of the shine.

Las Vegas is the largest United States city founded in the 20th century—1905 to be exact. Some might argue that the significant year was 1946, when Bugsy Siegel's Fabulous Flamingo opened for business. But the beginnings of modern Las Vegas can be traced back to 1829, when Antonio Armijo led a party of 60 on the Old Spanish Trail to Los Angeles. While his caravan camped about 100 miles northeast of the present site of Las Vegas, a scouting party set out to look for water. Rafael Rivera, a young Mexican scout who left the main party and headed due west over the unexplored desert, discovered an oasis. The abundance of artesian spring water here shortened the Spanish trail to Los Angeles by allowing travelers to go directly through, rather than around, the desert and eased the rigors of travel for the Spanish traders who used the route. They named the oasis Las Vegas, Spanish for "the Meadows."

The next major visitor to the Las Vegas Springs was John C. Fremont, who in 1844 led one of his many explorations of the Far West. Today he is remembered in the name of the principal downtown thoroughfare.

Ten years later, a group of Mormon settlers were sent by Brigham Young from Salt Lake City to colonize the valley. They built a 150-square-foot, adobe-brick fort, a small remnant of which still stands today; it's one of the oldest buildings in Nevada. The Mormons spent two years growing crops, mining lead, and converting the local Paiute Indians, but the rigors of the desert defeated their ambitions and by 1857 the fort was abandoned.

Things didn't start hopping here until 1904, when the San Pedro, Los Angeles, and Salt Lake Railroad laid its tracks through Las Vegas Valley, purchased the prime land and water rights from the handful of homesteaders, and surveyed a town site for its railroad servicing and repair facilities. In April 1905, the railroad held an auction and sold 700 lots. Las Vegas became a dusty railroad watering stop with a few downtown hotels and stores, a saloon and red-light district known as Block 16, and a few thousand residents— and remained just that for the next 23 years. It all changed, however, in 1928, when the Boulder Canyon Project Act was signed into law, appropriating $165 million for the building of the world's largest antigravity dam 40 miles from Las Vegas.

Construction of the dam began in 1931, a historic year for Nevada. This was the year Governor Fred Balzar approved the "wide-open" gambling bill that had been introduced by a Winnemucca rancher, Assemblyman Phil Tobin. Gambling had been outlawed several times since Nevada became a state in 1864, but it had never been completely eliminated. Backroom gambling, brothels, and easy divorces continued regardless of laws that attempted to curtail these activities. Tobin maintained that controlled gaming would be good for tourism and the state's economy; people were going to gamble anyway, so why shouldn't the state tax the profits? Thus, he was able to convince lawmakers to make gambling permanently legal.

The early 1930s marked the height of the Depression and Prohibition. The construction of the dam on the Colorado River (bordering Arizona and Nevada) brought thousands of job seekers to southern Nevada. Because the federal government didn't want dam workers to be distracted by the temptations of Las Vegas, it created a separate government town, Boulder City—still the only community in the state where gambling is illegal.

At this time, Nevada's political and economic power resided in the northern part of the state: The capital is Carson City and the major casinos (notably Harold's Club and Harrah's) were in Reno. But the completion of the dam in 1935 turned southern Nevada into a magnet for federal appropriations, thousands of tourists and new residents, and a seemingly inexhaustible supply of electricity and water. In addition, as the country mobilized for World War II, tens of thousands of pilots and gunners trained at the Las Vegas Aerial Gunnery School, opened by the federal government on 3 million acres just north of town. Today, this property is home to Nellis Air Force Base and the Nevada Test Site.

By the early 1940s, downtown Las Vegas boasted several luxury hotels and a dozen small but successful gambling clubs. In 1941, Thomas Hull, who owned a chain of California motor inns, decided to build a place on a plot of land in the desert just outside the city limits on Highway 91 from Los Angeles. El Rancho Vegas opened with 100 motel rooms, a western-motif casino, and, right off the highway, a large parking lot with an inviting swimming pool in the middle. El Rancho's quick success led to the opening a year later of the Last Frontier Hotel, a mile down the road. Thus the Las Vegas Strip was founded.

Benjamin "Bugsy" Siegel, who ran the New York mob's activities on the West Coast, began to see the incredible potential of a remote oasis where land was cheap and gambling was legal. He visualized a swank resort showplace with Hollywood entertainment, neon, palm trees, and a big bright casino. He struggled for two years to build his Fabulous Flamingo down the highway from the Last Frontier, alienating both his local partners and silent investors with his lavish overspending. He opened the joint prematurely, on a rainy night, the day after Christmas 1946. Although movie stars attended and headliners Jimmy Durante, Xavier Cugat, and Rose Marie performed, the Flamingo flopped; the casino paid out more money than it took in. This made Siegel's partners very unhappy, and six months later, Bugsy was dead. Ironically, once he had been bumped off, business at the Flamingo boomed. Siegel's gangland assassination had made front-page news across the country, and people flocked to see the house that Bugsy built.

The success of the Flamingo paved the way for gamblers and gangsters from all over the country to invest in Las Vegas hotel-casinos, one after another. The Desert Inn, Horseshoe, Sands, Sahara, Riviera, Dunes, Fremont, Tropicana, and Stardust were all financed with mob money at first. Every new hotel came on like a theme park opening for the summer with a new ride. Each was bigger, better, more unusual than the last. The Sahara had the tallest free-standing neon sign. The Riviera was the first high-rise building in town. The Stardust had 1,000 rooms and the world's largest swimming pool.

That the underworld owned and ran the big joints was a proverbially worst-kept secret, but only added to the allure of Las Vegas. And the town's great boom in the 1950s couldn't have happened without the mob's access to millions of dollars in cash. Under the circumstances, no bank, corporation, or legitimate investor would have touched the gambling business.

In time, however, the state began to take steps to weed out the most visible undesirables. The federal government assisted in the crackdown, using its considerable resources to hound the gangsters out of business. And, finally, an old man arrived on a train and soon revolutionized the nation's image of Las Vegas.

Howard Hughes had just sold TWA for $546 million and he either had to spend some of the money or turn it in as taxes. During a four-year stay in Las Vegas, he bought the Desert Inn, Frontier, Landmark, and Silver Slipper hotels, a television station, and an airfield. His presence in Las Vegas gave gambling its first positive image: As a former pilot and aviation pioneer, Hollywood mogul, and American folk hero, Hughes could in no way be connected with gangsters.

Hughes' presence also opened the door to corporate ownership of hotel-casinos. In 1971, Hilton Corporation purchased the International (now the Las Vegas Hilton) and the Flamingo, becoming the first major hotel chain to step onto the Las Vegas playing field. Ramada, Holiday Inn, Hyatt, MGM, and others have since followed suit.

Las Vegas felt the effects of both the legalization of gambling in Atlantic City in the late 1970s and of the national recession of the early 1980s—but not for very long. Over the years, the city has carved a secure niche for itself as a destination for national and international tourists, a winter sojourn for snowbirds from the north, and a weekend getaway for gamblers and families from California, Arizona, and Utah. Las Vegas has expanded at a ferocious pace for the past seven or eight years, during which upwards of 35,000 hotel rooms have been added and 300,000 people have moved in.

And why not? Room costs are 50% to 90% lower than in any other major city. Restaurant and buffet dining here can be cheaper than buying and preparing a meal. Entertainment is abundant and reasonably priced. Las Vegas is possibly the easiest place in the world to receive freebies—the ubiquitous "comps." And best of all, gambling promotions such as coupons, bonus payoffs, slot clubs, and relaxed rules provide a fighting chance to win in the casino. In the back of everyone's mind is the idea that a trip to Las Vegas can be free or even a money-making vacation. That kind of thinking keeps the Las Vegas bosses smiling as they add the finishing touches to their new multimillion-dollar hotels.

1 Essential Information

Before You Go

Visitor Information

For general information and brochures, contact the **Las Vegas Convention and Visitors Authority** (3150 Paradise Rd., Las Vegas, NV 89109, tel. 702/892–0711) or the **Las Vegas Chamber of Commerce** (711 E. Desert Inn Rd., Las Vegas, NV 89109, tel. 702/737–2011). For maps and brochures on Las Vegas and the rest of Nevada, contact the **Nevada Commission on Tourism** (Capitol Complex, Carson City, NV 89710, tel. 800/237–0774).

Tours and Packages

Should you buy your travel arrangements to Las Vegas packaged or make them yourself? There are advantages either way. Packaged arrangements save you money, particularly if you find a program that includes exactly the features you want. You also get an idea of what your trip will cost from the outset. Generally, you have two options: independent packages and fully escorted tours (though those available here include Las Vegas as part of a longer Arizona or West Coast itinerary). Escorted tours are most often via motorcoach, with a tour director in charge. They're ideal if you don't mind having limited free time and traveling with strangers. Your baggage is handled, your time rigorously scheduled, and most meals planned. Escorted tours are therefore the most hassle-free way to see a destination, as well as usually the least expensive. Independent packages allow plenty of flexibility. They generally include airline travel and hotels, with certain options available, such as sightseeing, car rental, and excursions. Independent packages are usually more expensive than escorted tours, but your time is your own.

While you can book directly through tour operators, you will pay no more to go through a travel agent, who will be able to tell you about tours and packages from a number of operators. Whatever program you ultimately choose, be sure to find out exactly what is included: taxes, tips, transfers, meals, baggage handling, ground transportation, entertainment, excursions, sports or recreation (and rental equipment if necessary). Ask about the level of hotel used, its location, the size of its rooms, the kind of beds, and its amenities, such as pool, room service, or programs for children, if they're important to you. Find out the operator's cancellation penalties. Nearly everyone charges them, and the only way to avoid them is to buy trip-cancellation insurance. Also ask about the single supplement, a surcharge assessed to solo travelers. Some operators do not make you pay it if you agree to be matched up with a roommate of the same sex, even if one is not found by departure time. Remember that a program that has features you won't use, whether for rental sporting equipment or discounted museum admissions, may not be the most cost-wise choice for you.

Fully Escorted Tours
Escorted tours are usually sold in three categories: deluxe, first class, and tourist or budget class. The most important differences are the price, of course, and the level of accommodations. Some operators specialize in one category, while others offer a range.

Most packages to Las Vegas are in the first-class category. Operators include **Brendan Tours** (15137 Califa St., Van Nuys, CA 91411, tel. 800/421–8446 or 818/785–9696), **Brennan Tours** (1402 3rd Ave., Suite 717, Seattle, WA 98101, tel. 800/237–7249 or 206/622–9155), **Caravan Tours** (401 N. Michigan Ave., Chicago, IL 60611, tel. 800/227–2826 or 312/321–9800), **Domenico Tours** (751 Broadway, Bayonne, NJ 07002, tel. 800/554–8687 or 201/823–8687), **Globus-Gateway** (95–25 Queens Blvd., Rego Park, NY 11374, tel. 800/221–0090 or 718/268–7000), and **Mayflower Tours** (1225 Warren Ave., Downers Grove, IL 60515, tel. 800/323–7604 or 708/960–3430). Try Globus's sister operator, **Cosmos** (at the same address), in the budget category.

Most itineraries are jam-packed with sightseeing to give you a lot in a short amount of time (usually one place per day). To judge just how fast-paced the tour is, review the itinerary carefully. If you are in a different hotel each night, you will be getting up early each day to head out, travel to your next destination, do some sightseeing, have dinner, and go to bed; then you'll start all over again. If you want some free time, make sure it's mentioned in the tour brochure; if you want to be escorted to every meal, confirm that any tour you consider does that. Also, when comparing programs, be sure to find out if the motorcoach is air-conditioned and has a restroom on board. Make your selection based on price and stops on the itinerary.

Independent Packages
Independent packages are offered by airlines, tour operators who may also do escorted programs, and any number of other companies from large, established firms to small, new entrepreneurs.

Airlines offering packages to Las Vegas include **America West** (tel. 800/356–6611), **American Airlines Fly AAway Vacations** (tel 800/321–2121), **Continental Airlines' Grand Destinations** (tel. 800/634–5555), **Delta Dream Vacations** (tel. 800/872–7786), and **United Airlines' Vacation Planning Center** (tel. 800/328–7786). Other operators include **Affordable Las Vegas Vacations** (400 W. Sahara Ave., Las Vegas, NV 89102, tel. 800/352–3500 or 702/384–0026), **American Express Vacations** (300 Pinnacle Way, Norcross, GA 30093, tel. 800/241–1700), **Gogo Tours** (book through your travel agent), and **Supercities** (7855 Haskell Ave., Van Nuys, CA 91406, tel. 800/333–1234 or 818/988–7844).

Their programs come in a wide range of prices based on levels of luxury and options—in addition to hotel and airfare, sightseeing, car rental, transfers, admission to local attractions, and other extras. Note when you price different packages that it sometimes pays to purchase the same arrangements separately, as when a rock-bottom promotional airfare is being offered, for example. Again, base your choice on what's available at your budget for the destinations you want to visit.

Tips for British Travelers

Government Tourist Office Contact the **United States Travel and Tourism Administration** (Box 1EN, London W1A 1EN, tel. 071/495–4466).

Passports and Visas British subjects need a valid 10-year passport. A visa is not necessary unless (1) you are planning to stay more than 90 days; (2) your trip is for purposes other than vacation; (3) you have at some time been refused a visa or admission to the United States, or have been required to leave by the U.S. Immigration and Naturalization Service; or (4) you do not have a return or onward ticket. You will need to fill out the Visa Waiver Form 1–94W, supplied by the airline.

To apply for a visa or for more information, call the U.S. Embassy's Visa Information Line (tel. 0891/200–290; calls cost 48p per minute or 36p per minute cheap rate). If you qualify for visa-free travel but want a visa anyway, you must apply in writing, enclosing an SAE, to the U.S. Embassy's Visa Branch (5 Upper Grosvenor St., London W1A 2JB), or, for residents of Northern Ireland, to the U.S. Consulate General (Queen's House, Queen St., Belfast BT1 6EO). Submit a completed Nonimmigrant Visa Application (Form 156), a valid passport, a photograph, and evidence of your intended departure from the United States after a temporary visit. If you require a visa, call 0891/234–224 to schedule an interview.

Customs British visitors aged 21 or over may import the following into the United States: 200 cigarettes or 50 cigars or 2 kilograms of tobacco; one U.S. liter of alcohol; gifts to the value of $100. Restricted items include meat products, seeds, plants, and fruits. Never carry illegal drugs.

Insurance Most tour operators, travel agents, and insurance agents sell specialized policies covering accident, medical expenses, personal liability, trip cancellation, and loss or theft of personal property. Some policies include coverage for delayed departure and legal expenses, winter sports, accidents, or motoring abroad. You can also purchase an annual travel-insurance policy valid for every trip you make during the year in which it's purchased (usually only trips of less than 90 days). Before you leave, make sure you will be covered if you have a preexisting medical condition or are pregnant; your insurers may not pay for routine or continuing treatment, or may require a note from your doctor certifying your fitness to travel.

The **Association of British Insurers,** a trade association representing 450 insurance companies, advises extra medical coverage for visitors to the United States. For advice by phone or a free booklet, "Holiday Insurance," that sets out what to expect from a holiday-insurance policy and gives price guidelines, contact the Association of British Insurers (51 Gresham St., London EC2V 7HQ, tel. 071/600–3333; 30 Gordon St., Glasgow G1 3PU, tel. 041/226–3905; Scottish Provincial Bldg., Donegall Sq. W, Belfast BT1 6JE, tel. 0232/249176; call for other locations).

Tour Operators The on-again, off-again price battle over transatlantic fares has meant that most tour operators now offer excellent budget packages to Las Vegas, usually in conjunction with tours to other U.S. cities. Among those companies you might consider as you plan your trip are: **Albany Travel (Manchester) Ltd.** (Royal London House, 196 Deansgate, Manchester M3 3NF, tel. 061/833–0202), **British Airways Holidays** (Atlantic House, Hazelwick Ave., Three Bridges, Crawley, W. Sussex RH10 1NP, tel. 0293/518022), **Cosmosair** (Ground floor, Dale House, Tiviot Dale, Stockport, Cheshire SK1 1TB, tel. 061/480–5799), **Jetsave** (Sussex House, London Rd., East Grinstead, Sussex RH19 1LD, tel. 0342/312033), **Key to America** (15 Feltham Rd., Ashford, Middlesex TW15 1DQ, tel. 0784/248777), and **Kuoni Travel** (Kuoni House, Dorking, Surrey RH5 4AZ, tel. 0306/742222).

Airfares There is no direct service between Great Britain and Las Vegas; American and United Airlines fly to hub cities in the U.S., where you can connect with flights to McCarran International Airport.

Thomas Cook Ltd. can often book you on very inexpensive flights. Ring the Cook branch nearest you and ask to be put through to the Airfare Warehouse. Be sure to ring at least 21 days in advance of when you want to travel. Also check out the small ads in the Sunday newspapers and in magazines such as *Time Out*.

Travelers with Main information sources include the **Royal Association for**
Disabilities **Disability and Rehabilitation** (RADAR, 25 Mortimer St., London W1N 8AB, tel. 071/637–5400), which publishes travel information for the disabled in Britain, and **Mobility International** (228 Borough High St., London SE1 1JX, tel. 071/403–5688), the headquarters of an international membership organization that serves as a clearinghouse of travel information for people with disabilities.

When to Go

Las Vegas is a year-round destination. Except for the first three weeks in December and the months of July and August, you can assume that Las Vegas will be running at full bore. Weekends, always crowded, are especially jam-packed for the Super Bowl, Valentine's Day, the NCAA Final Four, Easter, the week between Christmas and New Year's, and three- and four-day holidays. Nearly 50 conventions of more than 10,000 participants are held here every year; prices skyrocket, availability plummets, and the hordes fill every open space. Sporting events, such as boxing matches, golf tournaments, and the National Finals Rodeo, also have a major impact on the crowd situation. It's a good idea to call the Las Vegas Convention and Visitors Authority (tel. 702/892–0711) to find out who or what will be in town at the time you're planning to visit.

During a "normal" week—no conventions, holidays, title fights, or local events—the weekdays, Sunday through Thursday, are uncrowded, inexpensive, and relatively stress-free. During even a routine weekend, however, traffic jams, along with competition for rooms, restaurants, and show reservations and for spots at the slots or tables, can be ferocious.

Weatherwise, the most comfortable times to be in Las Vegas are the spring and fall. In April and May, daytime temperatures are delightful, in the 70s and 80s. The Las Vegas you see pictured in the ads—women lying by the pools, saxophone players performing on the street, visitors dressed in shorts and T-shirts, but not sweating like pigs—begins when the pools open in the spring.

In September, October, and November, the summer crowds and heat have abated, and the pools remain open.

Winter is a distinctly different season, with snowcapped mountains in the distance, windy and chilly days, and surprisingly cold nights. The two weeks before Christmas find Las Vegas nearly deserted, with rooms going for bargain rates, and hardly a traffic jam on the Strip.

Summer is a time of dry, uncomfortably hot weather (sometimes literally 110 degrees in the shade), when lounging at an outdoor pool requires protection from the relentless desert sun. You'll probably find yourself thirstier than you can remember ever being. At the height of the heat, however, hotels offer their lowest rates.

Climate The following are average daily maximum and minimum temperatures for Las Vegas.

Jan.	60F	16C	May	89F	32C	Sept.	95F	35C
	28	-2		51	11		57	14
Feb.	66F	19C	June	98F	37C	Oct.	84F	29C
	33	1		60	16		46	8
Mar.	71F	22C	July	102F	39C	Nov.	71F	22C
	39	4		68	20		35	2
Apr.	80F	27C	Aug.	102F	39C	Dec.	60F	16C
	44	7		66	19		30	-1

Information   For current weather conditions for cities in the United
Sources   States and abroad, plus the local time and helpful travel
tips, call the **Weather Channel Connection** (tel. 900/932–
8437; 95¢ per minute) from a touch-tone phone.

Festivals and Seasonal Events

Las Vegas is not known for specific celebrations—the Strip
is the venue for a never-ending parade. Still, a number of
annual events do attract wide attention.

Mar.: The LPGA Invitational golf tournament draws top
women golfers who compete for a money prize. *Tel. 702/733–
4653.*

Apr.: Clark County Fair takes place 60 miles north of Las
Vegas in Logandale. *Tel. 702/398–3247.*

Apr. or May: World Series of Poker draws crowds to the
Binion's Horseshoe casino to watch the poker faces of players from around the world, each investing $10,000 and play-
ing for 22 days (or until their luck runs out) in the biggest
poker game in the world. *Tel. 702/366–7397.*

Early May: Over-50s gather at the Desert Inn for the four-
day Senior Classic golf tournament, started in 1985. *Tel.
702/733–GOLF.*

June: Helldorado Days and Rodeo celebrates the Old West
with parades, contests, Western costumes, and a championship rodeo at the Thomas and Mack Center. *Tel. 702/870–
1221.*

Mid-Sept.: Football season begins at the University of Nevada, Las Vegas. *Tel. 702/739–FANS.*

Mid-Oct.: Las Vegas Invitational golf tournament, a five-
day event, is played on three courses, with television coverage. *Tel. 702/382–6616.*

Mid-Oct.: The U.S. Triathlon Series national championships and world invitational draws top competitors from
around the globe. *Tel. 702/731–2115.*

Early Dec.: National Finals Rodeo brings together 15 final-
ists to compete in each of seven events; there are 10 performances in nine days at the Thomas and Mack Center. When
the rodeo comes to town, the showrooms all feature country
music, and it seems as though everyone on the street is
wearing jeans, boots, and a cowboy hat. *Tel. 702/731–2115.*

Dec. 31: New Year's Eve is celebrated with fireworks over
Fremont Street in downtown Las Vegas, televised nationally. *Tel. 702/382–6397.*

What to Pack

Clothing   Ever since the Last Frontier opened on the Los Angeles
highway, which later became the Strip, visitors have been
invited to "Come As You Are." The warm weather and informal character of Las Vegas render casual clothing appropriate day and night. Some people like to spruce up for the
evening—the women wearing cocktail dresses and the men

donning jacket and tie. But only a handful of the fanciest restaurants in town require such attire. Shorts and sundresses can be worn from April through October. November through March, it's sweaters and overcoats.

Comfortable shoes for walking are a must; no matter what your intentions may be, you'll find yourself covering a lot of ground on foot. If you pack light you'll avoid long waits for the transfer of luggage to and from hotel rooms on arrival and departure.

Miscellaneous Bring an extra pair of eyeglasses or contact lenses. If you have a health problem that may require you to purchase a prescription drug, pack enough to last the duration of the trip. And don't forget to pack a list of the addresses of offices that supply refunds for lost or stolen traveler's checks.

Luggage Free baggage allowances on an airline depend on the air-
Regulations line, the route, and the class of your ticket. In general, on domestic flights you are entitled to check two bags—neither exceeding 62 inches, or 158 centimeters (length + width + height), or weighing more than 70 pounds (32 kilograms). A third piece may be brought aboard as a carryon; its total dimensions are generally limited to less than 45 inches (114 centimeters), so it will fit easily under the seat in front of you or in the overhead compartment. There are variations, so ask in advance. The single rule, a Federal Aviation Administration safety regulation that pertains to carry-on baggage on U.S. airlines, requires only that carryons be properly stowed and permits the airline to limit allowances and tailor them to different aircraft and operational conditions. Charges for excess, oversize, or overweight pieces vary, so inquire before you pack.

Safeguarding Your Before leaving home, itemize your bags' contents and their
Luggage worth; this list will help you estimate the extent of your loss if your bags go astray. To minimize that risk, tag them inside and out with your name, address, and phone number. (If you use your home address, cover it so that potential thieves can't see it.) At check-in, make sure that the tag attached by baggage handlers bears the correct three-letter code for your destination. If your bags do not arrive with you, or if you detect damage, do not leave the airport until you've filed a written report with the airline.

Insurance In the event of loss, damage, or theft on domestic flights, airlines limit their liability to $1,250 per passenger. Excess-valuation insurance can be bought directly from the airline at check-in but leaves your bags vulnerable on the ground. Your own homeowner's policy may fill the gap; or you may want special luggage insurance. Sources include **The Travelers Companies** (1 Tower Sq., Hartford, CT 06183, tel. 203/277–0111 or 800/243–3174) and **Wallach and Company, Inc.** (107 W. Federal St., Box 480, Middleburg, VA 22117, tel. 703/687–3166 or 800/237–6615).

Traveler's Checks

Although you will want plenty of cash when visiting rural areas, traveler's checks are usually preferable. The most widely recognized are **American Express, Barclay's, Thomas Cook,** and those issued by major commercial banks such as **Citibank** and **Bank of America.** American Express also issues *Traveler's Cheques for Two*, which can be signed and used by you or your traveling companion. Some checks are free; usually the issuing company or the bank at which you make your purchase charges 1% of the checks' face value as a fee. Always record the numbers of checks as you spend them, and keep this list separate from the checks.

Getting Money From Home

Cash Machines Automated-teller machines (ATMs) are proliferating; many are tied to international networks such as **Cirrus** and **Plus.** You can use your bank card at ATMs away from home to withdraw money from an account and get cash advances on a credit-card account (providing your card has been programmed with a personal identification number, or PIN). Check in advance on limits on withdrawals and cash advances within specified periods. Remember that on cash advances you are charged interest from the day you get the money from ATMs as well as from tellers. And note that transaction fees for ATM withdrawals outside your home turf will probably be higher than for withdrawals at home.

For specific Cirrus locations in the United States and Canada, call 800/424–7787 (for U.S. Plus locations, 800/843–7587) and press the area code and first three digits of the number you're calling from (or the calling area where you want an ATM).

American Express Cardholder Services The company's **Express Cash** system lets you withdraw cash and/or traveler's checks from a worldwide network of 57,000 American Express dispensers and participating bank ATMs. You must *enroll first* (call 800/227–4669 for a form and allow two weeks for processing). Withdrawals are charged not to your card but to a designated bank account. You can withdraw up to $1,000 per seven-day period on the basic card, more if your card is gold or platinum. There is a 2% fee (minimum $2.50, maximum $10) for each cash transaction, and a 1% fee for traveler's checks (except for the platinum card), which are available only from American Express dispensers.

At AmEx offices, cardholders can also cash personal checks for up to $1,000 in any seven-day period; of this $200 can be in cash, more if available, with the balance paid in traveler's checks, for which all but platinum cardholders pay a 1% fee. Higher limits apply to the gold and platinum cards.

Wiring Money You don't have to be a cardholder to send or receive an **American Express MoneyGram** for up to $10,000. To send one, go to an American Express MoneyGram agent, pay up to $1,000 with a credit card and anything over that in cash, and phone a transaction reference number to your intended recipient, who needs only present identification and the reference number to the nearest MoneyGram agent to pick up the cash. There are MoneyGram agents in more than 60 countries (call 800/543–4080 for locations). Fees range from 5% to 10%, depending on the amount and how you pay. You can't use American Express, which is really a convenience card—only Discover, MasterCard, and Visa credit cards.

You can also use **Western Union.** To wire money, take either cash or a check to the nearest office. (Or you can call and use a credit card.) Fees are roughly 5%–10%. Money sent from the United States or Canada will be available for pick up at agent locations in Las Vegas within minutes. There are approximately 20,000 agents worldwide (call 800/325–6000 for locations).

Traveling with Cameras, Camcorders, and Laptops

About Film and Cameras   If your camera is new or if you haven't used it for a while, shoot and develop a few rolls of film before leaving home. Pack some lens tissue and an extra battery for your built-in light meter, and invest in an inexpensive skylight filter, to both protect your lens and provide some definition in hazy shots. Store film in a cool, dry place—never in the car's glove compartment or on the shelf under the rear window.

Films above ISO 400 are more sensitive to damage from airport security X-rays than others; very high speed films, ISO 1,000 and above, are exceedingly vulnerable. To protect your film, don't put it in checked luggage; carry it with you in a plastic bag and ask for a hand inspection. Such requests are honored at American airports. Don't depend on a lead-lined bag to protect film in checked luggage—the airline may very well turn up the dosage of radiation to see what you've got in there. Airport metal detectors do not harm film, although you'll set off the alarm if you walk through one with a roll in your pocket. Call the Kodak Information Center (tel. 800/242–2424) for details.

About Camcorders   Before your trip, put new or long-unused camcorders through their paces, and practice panning and zooming. Invest in a skylight filter to protect the lens, and check the lithium battery that lights up the LCD (liquid crystal display) modes. As for the rechargeable nickel-cadmium batteries that are the camera's power source, take along an extra pair, so while you're using your camcorder you'll have one battery ready and another recharging.

About Videotape   Unlike still-camera film, videotape is not damaged by X-rays. However, it may well be harmed by the magnetic field of a walk-through metal detector. Airport security personnel may want you to turn the camcorder on to prove that

that's what it is, so make sure the battery is charged when you get to the airport.

About Laptops Security X-rays do not harm hard-disk or floppy-disk storage. Most airlines allow you to use your laptop aloft but request that you turn it off during takeoff and landing so as not to interfere with navigation equipment. Make sure the battery is charged when you arrive at the airport, because you may be asked to turn on the computer at security checkpoints to prove that it is what it appears to be. If you're a heavy computer user, consider traveling with a backup battery.

Car Rentals

All major car-rental companies are represented in Las Vegas, including **Avis** (tel. 800/331–1212, 800/879–2847 in Canada); **Budget** (tel. 800/527–0700); **Dollar** (tel. 800/800–4000); **Hertz** (tel. 800/654–3131, 800/263-0600 in Canada); and **National** (tel. 800/227–7368). **Alamo** (tel. 800/327–9633) also rents in Las Vegas. Unlimited-mileage rates range from about $20 per day for an economy car to $43 for a large car; weekly unlimited-mileage rates range from $109 to $250.

Extra Charges Picking up the car in one city and leaving it in another may entail drop-off charges or one-way service fees, which can be substantial. The cost of a collision or loss-damage waiver (*see below*) can be high, also.

Cutting Costs If you know you will want a car for more than a day or two, you can save by planning ahead. Major international companies have programs that discount their standard rates by 15%–30% if you make the reservation before departure (anywhere from two to 14 days), rent for a minimum number of days (typically three or four), and prepay the rental. Ask about these advance-purchase schemes when you call for information. More economical rentals are those that come as part of fly/drive or other packages, even those as bare-bones as the rental plus an airline ticket (*see* Tours and Packages, *above*).

Other sources of savings are the companies that operate as wholesalers—companies that do not own their own fleets but rent in bulk from those that do and offer advantageous rates to their customers. Rentals through such companies must be arranged and paid for in advance. Among them is **Auto Europe** (Box 1097, Camden, ME 04843, tel. 207/236–8235 or 800/223–5555, 800/458–9503 in Canada). These wholesalers' deals are even better in summer, when business travel is down. Always ask if unlimited mileage is available. Find out about any required deposits, cancellation penalties, and drop-off charges, and confirm the cost of the CDW.

One last tip: Remember to fill the tank when you turn in the vehicle, to avoid being charged for refueling at what you'll swear is the most expensive pump in town.

Insurance and Collision Damage Waiver The standard rental contract includes liability coverage (for damage to public property, injury to pedestrians, etc.) and coverage for the car against fire, theft, and collision damage with a deductible—most commonly $2,000–$3,000, occasionally more. In case of an accident, you are responsible for the deductible amount unless you've purchased the collision damage waiver (CDW), which costs an average $12 a day, although this varies depending on what you've rented, where, and from whom.

Because this adds up quickly, you may be inclined to say "no thanks"—and that's certainly your option, although the rental agent may not tell you so. Planning ahead will help you make the right decision. By all means, find out if your own insurance covers damage to a rental car while traveling (not simply a car to drive when yours is in for repairs). Check also whether charging car rentals to any of your credit cards will get you a CDW at no charge. Note before you decline that deductibles are occasionally high enough that totaling a car would make you responsible for its full value. In many states, laws mandate that renters be told what the CDW costs, that it's optional, and that their own auto insurance may provide the same protection.

Traveling with Children

Publications
Newsletter **Family Travel Times,** published 10 times a year by **Travel With Your Children** (TWYCH, 45 W. 18th St., 7th Floor Tower, New York, NY 10011, tel. 212/206–0688; annual subscription $55), covers destinations, types of vacations, and modes of travel.

Books *Great Vacations with Your Kids,* by Dorothy Jordon and Marjorie Cohen ($13; Penguin USA, 120 Woodbine St., Bergenfield, NJ 07621, tel. 800/253–6476) and *Traveling with Children—And Enjoying It,* by Arlene K. Butler ($11.95 plus $3 shipping per book; Globe Pequot Press, Box 833, Old Saybrook, CT 06475, tel. 800/243–0495, or 800/962–0973 in CT), both help plan your trip with children, from toddlers to teens.

Tour Operators **GrandTravel** (6900 Wisconsin Ave., Suite 706, Chevy Chase, MD 20815, tel. 301/986–0790 or 800/247–7651) offers international and domestic tours for grandparents traveling with their grandchildren. The catalogue, as charmingly written and illustrated as a children's book, positively invites armchair traveling with lap-sitters aboard. **Rascals in Paradise** (650 5th St., Suite 505, San Francisco, CA 94107, tel. 415/978–9800, or 800/872–7225) specializes in programs for families.

Getting There
Air Fares On domestic flights, children under 2 not occupying a seat travel free, and older children currently travel on the "lowest applicable" adult fare.

Baggage The adult baggage allowance applies for children paying half or more of the adult fare. Check with the airline for particulars.

Safety Seats The FAA recommends the use of safety seats aloft and details approved models in the free leaflet **"Child/Infant Safety Seats Recommended for Use in Aircraft"** (available from the Federal Aviation Administration, APA–200, 800 Independence Ave. SW, Washington, DC 20591, tel. 202/267–3479). Airline policy varies. U.S. carriers must allow FAA-approved models, but because these seats are strapped into a regular passenger seat, they may require that parents buy a ticket even for an infant under 2 who would otherwise ride free.

Facilities Aloft Airlines do provide other facilities and services for children, such as children's meals and freestanding bassinets (to those sitting in seats on the bulkhead, where there's enough legroom to accommodate them). Make your request when reserving. The annual February/March issue of *Family Travel Times* gives details of the children's services of dozens of airlines ($10; *see above*). "Kids and Teens in Flight" (free from the U.S. Department of Transportation, tel. 202/366–2220) offers tips for children flying alone.

Hotels In addition to offering family discounts and special rates for children (for example, some large hotel chains don't charge extra for children under 12 when they stay in their parents' room), many hotels and resorts arrange for baby-sitting services and run a variety of special children's programs. Check with your travel agent for more information, or ask a hotel representative about children's programs when you make your reservations. The Nevada Commission on Tourism's accommodation guide lists Las Vegas hotels that have a children's game room (Capitol Complex, Carson City, NV 89710, tel. 800/237–0774).

Children's Programs Many Las Vegas hotels such as Circus Circus and Excalibur offer activities to keep children occupied while their parents play their own games, but an especially comprehensive child care program can be found at the **Las Vegas Hilton's Youth Hotel** (3000 W. Paradise Rd., tel. 702/732–5111). If you're a guest at the Flamingo or Las Vegas Hiltons, your kids (ages 3–18) play, snack, and eat meals with counselors in a special dorm, where they can also spend the night. During the day, kids can take part in fencing, tumbling, arts and crafts, table tennis, dance, basketball, tennis, volleyball, and magic shows. Rates are $4 per child per hour and $25 per child for overnight stays (midnight–8 AM).

Baby-sitting Services Make your child-care arrangements with the hotel concierge or front desk. Independent local agencies typically charge $6 to $7 an hour (4-hour minimum).

Hints for Travelers with Disabilities

Organizations   Several local organizations provide information to visitors
with disabilities. **HELP of Southern Nevada** (tel. 702/369–
4357) refers callers to the proper social agency. **Nevada Association for the Handicapped** (6200 W. Oakey Blvd., Las
Vegas 89102, tel. 702/870–7050) refers callers to agencies
serving the disabled. **Southern Nevada Sightless** (1001 N.
Bruce St., Las Vegas 89101, tel. 702/642–0100) provides
general information and transportation assistance.

Several organizations provide travel information for people
with disabilities, usually for a membership fee, and some
publish newsletters and bulletins. Among them are the **Information Center for Individuals with Disabilities** (Fort
Point Pl., 27–43 Wormwood St., Boston, MA 02210, tel.
617/727–5540 or 800/462–5015 in MA between 11 and 4, or
leave message; TDD/TTY tel. 617/345–9743); **Mobility International USA** (Box 3551, Eugene, OR 97403, voice and
TDD tel. 503/343–1284); **MossRehab Hospital Travel Information Service** (1200 W. Tabor Rd., Philadelphia, PA
19141, tel. 215/456–9603, TDD tel. 215/456–9602); the **Society for the Advancement of Travel for the Handicapped**
(SATH, 347 5th Ave., Suite 610, New York, NY 10016, tel.
212/447–7284, fax 212/725–8253); the **Travel Industry and
Disabled Exchange** (TIDE, 5435 Donna Ave., Tarzana, CA
91356, tel. 818/368–5648); and **Travelin' Talk** (Box 3534,
Clarksville, TN 37043, tel. 615/552–6670).

Travel Agencies   **Directions Unlimited** (720 N. Bedford Rd., Bedford Hills,
and Tour   NY 10507, tel. 914/241–1700), a travel agency, has exper-
Operators   tise in tours and cruises for the disabled. **Evergreen Travel
Service** (4114 198th St. SW, Suite 13, Lynnwood, WA 98036,
tel. 206/776–1184 or 800/435–2288) operates tours for those
in wheelchairs, for the blind, and for the deaf, and makes
group and independent arrangements for travelers with
any disability. **Flying Wheels Travel** (143 W. Bridge St.,
Box 382, Owatonna, MN 55060, tel. 800/535–6790 or 800/
722–9351 in MN), a tour operator and travel agency, arranges international tours, cruises, and independent travel
itineraries for people with mobility disabilities.

Publications   In addition to the fact sheets, newsletters, and books mentioned above are several free publications available from
the Consumer Information Center (Pueblo, CO 81009):
"New Horizons for the Air Traveler with a Disability," a
U.S. Department of Transportation booklet describing
changes resulting from the 1986 Air Carrier Access Act and
those still to come from the 1990 Americans with Disabilities Act (include Department 608Y in the address), and the
Airport Operators Council's *Access Travel: Airports*
(Dept. 5804), which describes facilities and services for the
disabled at more than 500 airports worldwide.

Twin Peaks Press (Box 129, Vancouver, WA 98666, tel. 206/
694–2462 or 800/637–2256) publishes the *Directory of Trav-*

el Agencies for the Disabled ($19.95), listing more than 370 agencies worldwide; *Travel for the Disabled* ($19.95), listing some 500 access guides and accessible places worldwide; the *Directory of Accessible Van Rentals* ($9.95) for campers and RV travelers worldwide; and *Wheelchair Vagabond* ($14.95), a collection of personal travel tips. Add $2 per book for shipping. The Sierra Club publishes *Easy Access to National Parks* ($16 plus $3 shipping; 730 Polk St., San Francisco, CA 94109, tel. 415/776–2211).

Accommodations Generally, the layouts of most hotels and casinos require that you walk long distances to get around in them. The following hotels take into account the special needs of the physically disabled with wheelchair-accessible accommodations: Bally's Casino Resort (3645 Las Vegas Blvd. S, tel. 702/739–4111), Barbary Coast Hotel and Casino (3595 Las Vegas Blvd. S, tel. 702/737–7111), Caesars Palace (3570 Las Vegas Blvd. S, tel. 702/731–7110), Excalibur (3850 Las Vegas Blvd. S, tel. 702/597–7777), The Flamingo Hilton and Tower (3555 Las Vegas Blvd. S, tel. 702/733–3111), Four Queens Hotel and Casino (202 E. Fremont St., tel. 702/385–4011), Golden Nugget Hotel and Casino (129 E. Fremont St., tel. 702/385–7111), Hacienda Hotel and Casino (3950 Las Vegas Blvd. S, tel. 702/739–8911), Lady Luck Casino and Hotel (206 N. 3rd St., tel. 702/447–3000), Las Vegas Club Hotel and Casino (18 E. Fremont St., tel. 702/385–1664), Las Vegas Hilton (3000 W. Paradise Rd., tel. 702/732–5111), Sam's Town Hotel and Casino (5111 W. Boulder Hwy., tel. 702/456–7777), and the Plaza Hotel (1 Main St., tel. 702/386–2110). The Imperial Palace (3535 Las Vegas Blvd. S, tel 702/731–3311) has the most facilities for accommodating the mobility impaired, including a hydraulic lift at the pool, an Amigo chair in the pit, and over 100 accessible rooms, many of which feature roll-in showers and transfer chairs.

Hints for Older Travelers

Organizations The **American Association of Retired Persons** (AARP, 601 E St. NW, Washington, DC 20049, tel. 202/434–2277) provides independent travelers the Purchase Privilege Program, which offers discounts on hotels, car rentals, and sightseeing, and the AARP Motoring Plan, with Amoco, which furnishes domestic trip-routing information and emergency road-service aid for an annual fee of $39.95 per person or couple ($59.95 for a premium version). AARP also arranges group tours, cruises, and apartment living through AARP Travel Experience from American Express (400 Pinnacle Way, Suite 450, Norcross, GA 30071, tel. 800/927–0111); these can be booked through travel agents, except for the cruises, which must be booked directly (tel. 800/745–4567). AARP membership is open to those 50 and over; annual dues are $8 per person or couple.

Two other membership organizations offer discounts on lodgings, car rentals, and other travel products, along with such nontravel perks as magazines and newsletters. The **National Council of Senior Citizens** (1331 F St. NW, Washington, DC 20004, tel. 202/347–8800) is a nonprofit advocacy group with some 5,000 local clubs across the United States; membership costs $12 per person or couple annually. **Mature Outlook** (6001 N. Clark St., Chicago, IL 60660, tel. 800/336–6330), a Sears Roebuck & Co. subsidiary with 800,000 members, charges $9.95 for an annual membership.

Note: When using any senior-citizen identification card for reduced hotel rates, mention it when booking, not when checking out. At restaurants, show your card before you're seated; discounts may be limited to certain menus, days, or hours. If you are renting a car, ask about promotional rates that might improve on your senior-citizen discount.

Educational Travel **Elderhostel** (75 Federal St., 3rd floor, Boston, MA 02110, tel. 617/426–8056) is a nonprofit organization that has had inexpensive study programs for people 60 and older since 1975. Programs take place at more than 1,800 educational institutions in the United States, Canada, and 45 countries overseas, and courses cover everything from marine science to Greek myths and cowboy poetry. Participants generally attend lectures in the morning and spend the afternoon sightseeing or on field trips; they live in dorms on the host campuses. Fees for programs in the United States and Canada, which usually last one week, run about $300, not including transportation.

Tour Operators **Saga International Holidays** (222 Berkeley St., Boston, MA 02116, tel. 800/343–0273), which specializes in group travel for people over 60, offers a selection of variously priced tours and cruises covering five continents. If you want to take your grandchildren, look into **GrandTravel** (*see* Traveling with Children, *above*).

Further Reading

Hunter S. Thompson's *Fear and Loathing in Las Vegas* is probably the most notorious book ever written about the city. In it, Thompson, the creator of "gonzo journalism," chronicles his trip from Los Angeles to Las Vegas—in a drug-filled red Cadillac convertible, with a 300-pound Samoan attorney—to cover the Mint 400 desert motorcycle race.

Mario Puzo's novel *The Godfather* describes the building of Las Vegas in the 1940s by the mob and the Corleone family's rub-out of Moe Green, the character modeled on Bugsy Siegel.

Ovid Demaris and Ed Reid's *The Green Felt Jungle* shocked the nation in the early 1960s with its account of how the mob built Las Vegas and had a hand in virtually every hotel and casino built during the 1940s and 1950s.

Omar Garrison's *Howard Hughes in Las Vegas* tells the story of one of the city's most enterprising residents, the man who legitimized corporate investment in gambling—-and who lived for four years on the ninth floor of the Desert Inn, refusing to leave or to be seen in public.

Newsletter The *Las Vegas Advisor* (5280 S. Valley View, Suite B-3F, Las Vegas, NV 89118, tel. 702/597–1884), a 12-page monthly newsletter, keeps up-to-the-minute track of the constantly changing Las Vegas landscapes of gambling, accommodations, dining, entertainment, Top Ten Values, complimentaries, and more. Indispensable for any Las Vegas visitor. Send $5 for a sample issue.

Arriving and Departing

By Plane

Flights are either nonstop, direct, or connecting. A **nonstop** flight requires no change of plane and makes no stops. A **direct** flight stops at least once and can involve a change of plane, although the flight number remains the same; if the first leg is late, the second waits. This is not the case with a **connecting** flight, which involves a different plane and a different flight number.

Airports and Airlines McCarran International Airport (tel. 702/261–5743), a large, modern facility, is situated 5 miles south of the business district and immediately east of the southern end of the Strip on Las Vegas Boulevard. The principal approach to McCarran is Paradise Road (from the northeast), while the air-charter terminal is reached from Las Vegas Boulevard. Slot machines in the main terminal allow eager travelers to get right to work, but the airport slots don't return as much money as do those slots in the casinos.

The principal airlines serving Las Vegas are Air Nevada (tel. 702/736–8900 or 800/634–6377), American (tel. 800/433–7300), America West (tel. 800/247–5692), Continental (tel. 702/383–8291 or 800/231–0856), Delta (tel. 800/221–1212), Northwest (tel. 800/225–2525), Southwest (tel. 702/435–9792), TWA (tel. 702/385–1000 or 800/438–2929), United (tel. 800/241–6522), and USAir (tel. 800/428–4322).

Cutting Flight Costs The Sunday travel section of most newspapers is a good source of deals. When booking, particularly through an unfamiliar company, call the Better Business Bureau to find out whether any complaints have been registered against the company, pay with a credit card if you can, and consider trip-cancellation and default insurance (*see* Insurance, *above*).

Promotional   All the less expensive fares, called promotional or discount
Airfares   fares, are round-trip and involve restrictions. The exact nature of the restrictions depends on the airline, the route,
and the season and on whether travel is domestic or international, but you must usually buy the ticket—commonly
called an APEX (advance purchase excursion) when it's for
international travel—in advance (seven, 14, or 21 days are
usual). You must also respect certain minimum- and maxi-
mum-stay requirements (for instance, over a Saturday
night or at least seven and no more than 30, 45, or 90 days),
and you must be willing to pay penalties for changes. Airlines generally allow some changes for a fee. But the cheaper the fare, the more likely the ticket is nonrefundable; it
would take a death in the family for the airline to give you
any of your money back if you had to cancel. The cheapest
fares are also subject to availability; because only a certain
percentage of the plane's total seats will be sold at that
price, they may go quickly.

Consolidators   Consolidators or bulk-fare operators—also known as bucket shops—buy blocks of seats on scheduled flights that airlines anticipate they won't be able to sell. They pay
wholesale prices, add a markup, and resell the seats to
travel agents or directly to the public at prices that still un-
dercut the airline's promotional or discount fares. You pay
more than on a charter but ordinarily less than for an APEX
ticket, and, even when there is not much of a price difference, the ticket usually comes without the advance-purchase restriction. Moreover, although tickets are marked
nonrefundable so you can't turn them in to the airline for a
full-fare refund, some consolidators sometimes give you
your money back. Carefully read the fine print detailing
penalties for changes and cancellations. If you doubt the re-
liability of a company, call the airline once you've made your
booking and confirm that you do, indeed, have a reservation
on the flight.

The biggest U.S. consolidator, C.L. Thomson Express,
sells only to travel agents. Well-established consolidators
selling to the public include **UniTravel** (Box 12485, St. Louis, MO 63132, tel. 314/569–0900 or 800/325–2222); **Council
Charter** (205 E. 42nd St., New York, NY 10017, tel. 212/
661–0311 or 800/800–8222), a division of the Council on International Educational Exchange and a longtime charter
operator now functioning more as a consolidator; and
Travac (989 6th Ave., New York, NY 10018, tel. 212/563–
3303 or 800/872–8800), also a former charterer.

Charter Flights   Charters usually have the lowest fares and the most restrictions. Departures are limited and seldom on time, and you
can lose all or most of your money if you cancel. (Generally,
the closer to departure you cancel, the more you lose, although sometimes you will be charged only a small fee if you
supply a substitute passenger.) The charterer, on the other
hand, may legally cancel the flight for any reason up to 10

days before departure; within 10 days of departure, the flight may be canceled only if it becomes physically impossible to operate it. The charterer may also revise the itinerary or increase the price after you have bought the ticket, but if the new arrangement constitutes a "major change," you have the right to a refund. Before buying a charter ticket, read the fine print for the company's refund policy and details on major changes. Money for charter flights is usually paid into a bank escrow account, the name of which should be on the contract. If you don't pay by credit card, make your check payable to the escrow account (unless you're dealing with a travel agent, in which case, his or her check should be payable to the escrow account). The Department of Transportation's Consumer Affairs Office (I–25, Washington, DC 20590, tel. 202/366–2220) can answer questions on charters and send you its "Plane Talk: Public Charter Flights" information sheet.

Charter operators may offer flights alone or with ground arrangements that constitute a charter package. Well-established charter operators include **Council Charter** (205 E. 42nd St., New York, NY 10017, tel. 212/661–0311 or 800/800–8222), now largely a consolidator, despite its name, and **Travel Charter** (1120 E. Long Lake Rd., Troy, MI 48098, tel. 313/528–3570 or 800/521–5267), with Midwestern departures. **DER Tours** (Box 1606, Des Plains, IL 60017, tel. 800/782–2424), a charterer and consolidator, sells through travel agents.

Discount Travel Clubs Travel clubs offer their members unsold space on airplanes, cruise ships, and package tours at nearly the last minute and at well below the original cost. Suppliers thus receive some revenue for their "leftovers," and members get a bargain. Membership generally includes a regular bulletin or access to a toll-free telephone hot line giving details of available trips departing anywhere from three or four days to several months in the future. Packages tend to be more common than flights alone, so if airfares are your only interest, read the literature before joining. Reductions on hotels are also available. Clubs include **Discount Travel International** (114 Forrest Ave., Suite 203, Narberth, PA 19072, tel. 215/668–7184; $45 annually, single or family), **Moment's Notice** (425 Madison Ave., New York, NY 10017, tel. 212/486–0503; $45 annually, single or family), **Travelers Advantage** (CUC Travel Service, 49 Music Sq. W, Nashville, TN 37203, tel. 800/548–1116; $49 annually, single or family), and **Worldwide Discount Travel Club** (1674 Meridian Ave., Miami Beach, FL 33139, tel. 305/534–2082; $50 annually for family, $40 single).

Smoking Since February 1990, smoking has been banned on all domestic flights of less than six hours' duration; the ban also applies to domestic segments of international flights aboard U.S. and foreign carriers.

Between the Airport and Hotels By Taxi Metered taxicab service awaits your arrival at the airport. The fare is $2.20 on the meter when you get in, plus $1.50 for every mile. The trip to most hotels on the Strip should cost less than $10; the trip downtown should be around $15.

By Limousine A limo from the airport to your hotel, shared with other riders, costs $3–$4 per person to the Strip, $4–$5 to downtown. The limos wait for passengers outside the terminal, along with the cabs. Private limousine service is available from Lucky 7 (tel. 702/739–6177), Bell Trans (tel. 702/739–7990), and Presidential (tel. 702/731–5577).

By Car

Approximately half of the visitors to Las Vegas arrive by automobile. The principal highway is I–15, which brings motorists from southern California in the southwest and Utah in the northeast. U.S. 93 (Boulder Highway and Fremont Street in Las Vegas) extends into Arizona in the southeast, where it connects with I–40. U.S. 95 brings traffic from northern California, Reno, and I–80 in the northwest.

Drivers en route to Las Vegas should keep in mind, when there's an opportunity to fill up, that the next gas station can be an hour away.

By Train

Amtrak (tel. 800/USA–7245) offers nationwide service to Las Vegas's Union Station (1 N. Main St., tel. 702/386–6896), a railway station within a casino, where you can leave the train and head straight for the crap tables. Some trains travel overnight, and you can sleep in your seat or book a roomette at additional cost. When available, excursion fares may save you up to half the round-trip fare.

Los Angeles is eight hours from Las Vegas by train.

By Bus

Greyhound/Trailways Lines (200 S. Main St., tel. 702/382–2640), one block south of the Plaza Hotel, has nationwide service.

Staying in Las Vegas

Important Addresses and Numbers

Tourist Information Las Vegas Convention and Visitors Authority (3150 Paradise Rd., tel. 702/892–0711), next door to the Las Vegas Hilton, can provide brochures and general information.

Hotels and gift shops on the Strip have maps, brochures, pamphlets, and free events magazines—*What's On in Las*

Vegas, Fun and Gaming, and *Tourguide*—that list shows and buffets and offer discounts to area attractions.

Emergencies Police, fire, ambulance (tel. 911).

Hospital Emergency Rooms **University Medical Center** (1800 W. Charleston Blvd. at Shadow La., tel. 702/383–2000) has a 24-hour emergency service with outpatient and trauma-care facilities.

Humana Hospital Sunrise (3186 S. Maryland Pkwy. near Desert Inn Rd., tel. 702/731–8000) has an emergency room.

Doctors **Clark County Medical Society** (tel. 702/739–9989) will make referrals.

Dentists **Clark County Dental Society** (tel. 702/435–7767) offers referral service.

Late-night Pharmacies **White Cross Drug** (1700 Las Vegas Blvd. S, tel. 702/382–1733) is near the Vegas World hotel on the Strip and is open 24 hours a day.

Opening and Closing Times

Banks are generally open Monday to Friday 10–3.

Most stores are open Monday to Friday 10–9, Saturday 9–6, and Sunday 11–6. The very expensive gift shops on the Strip remain open until midnight.

Getting Around Las Vegas

The best way to experience Las Vegas may be to drive it. A car gives you easy access to the attractions of the Strip as well as to those that are several blocks away, it lets you make excursions to Lake Mead and elsewhere at your leisure, and it gives you the chance to cruise the Strip and bask in its neon glow.

By Car Las Vegas is an easy city to drive in, even for those who are terrible navigators. The principal north-south artery is Las Vegas Boulevard (I–15 runs roughly parallel to it, less than a mile to the west). A 3½-mile stretch of Las Vegas Boulevard South is the Strip, where a majority of the city's hotels and casinos are clustered. Many of the major streets running east–west (Tropicana Avenue, Flamingo Road, Desert Inn Road, Sahara Avenue) are named for the casinos built on them, often at their intersection with the Strip.

Free parking is available at virtually every hotel although the parking area is usually far to the rear of the property and you may have to hunt for a space. To avoid this, simply make use of valet parking. You can't park anywhere on the Strip itself, and parking spaces on Fremont Street downtown are nearly always taken. Parking in the high-rise structures downtown is free, as long as you validate your ticket at the casino cashier.

Because the capacity of the streets of Las Vegas has not kept pace with the city's incredible growth, traffic can be heavy in the late afternoons, in the evenings, and on the weekends. At those times, you may prefer to drive the streets that parallel Las Vegas Boulevard: Paradise Road and Maryland Parkway to the east, and Industrial Road to the west. The Industrial Road shortcut (from Tropicana Avenue almost all the way to downtown) will save you an enormous amount of time. You can enter the parking lots at Caesars Palace, the Mirage, Treasure Island, the Stardust, and Circus Circus from Industrial Road (but there's no intersection with West Flamingo Avenue).

By Taxi Desert Cab (tel. 702/736–2687), Whittlesea Blue Cab (tel. 702/384–6111), and Yellow and Checker Cab (tel. 702/873–2000) are the principal taxi operators in Las Vegas. You'll find cabs waiting at the airport and at every hotel in town (*see* the By Taxi section in Between the Airport and Hotels, *above*, for rates). If you take a cab to a restaurant off the Strip, the restaurant will call a taxi to take you home.

By Bus and The municipally operated **Citizen Area Transit** (tel. 702/228-
Trolley 7433) runs local buses up and down the Strip, between the Hacienda Hotel and the Downtown Transportation Center, stopping at all the major hotels every 15 minutes 24 hours a day. An express Strip service stops at Circus Circus and Caesars Palace southbound, Harrah's and the Riviera northbound between 5:30 AM and 1 AM. The fare for both is $1 (exact change required). If you plan to get on and off the bus, buy a discounted commuter card from the driver. Other routes serve the Meadows and Boulevard shopping malls, and Sam's Town Hotel and Casino and the Western Emporium gift shop on Boulder Highway.

The private **Las Vegas Transit** (tel. 702/384–3540) runs essentially the same Strip route, but the fare is $1.25 (exact change required).

From 9:30 AM to 2 AM, the **Las Vegas Strip Trolley** (tel. 702/382–1404) travels every 30 minutes among Strip hotels, with stops at Fashion Show Mall and Wet 'N Wild. An exact fare of $1 is required.

Guided Tours

General Interest **Gray Line** (1550 S. Industrial Rd., tel. 702/384–1234 or 800/634–6579) offers a variety of bus tours of Las Vegas and its environs. Itineraries include the Strip, Hoover Dam, Mt. Charleston, Bryce Canyon, and the Grand Canyon. Vegas tours last from 2 hours to 6½ hours; tours beyond the area are all-day affairs. Gray Line will pick you up at your hotel and return you to it at the end of the tour. Tours run from $17.50 to $160 (Grand Canyon); city area tours average $27. Reservations can be made by telephone at any hour.

Ray and Ross Transport Inc. (300 W. Owens Ave., tel.702/ 646–4661) has city tours for $20.85. Hotel pickup and return are included.

Key Tours (3305 W. Spring Mountain, tel. 702/362–9355) offers tours from Las Vegas to Laughlin, a gambling town that is about 85 miles from Las Vegas on the Colorado River at the Arizona state line, from $5 a person; a sunset cruise of Lake Mead for $27.50 a person; a Hoover Dam tour for $14.50; and a Hoover Dam plus the city and desert tour for $28.

Special-Interest Tours

Helicopter Tours

Helicop-Tours (135 E. Reno Ave., tel. 702/736–0606) has a 10-minute helicopter tour of the Las Vegas Strip for $45 per person.

Cruises

Lake Mead Cruises (Lake Mead Marina, tel. 702/293–6180) offers narrated tours of the lower portion of the lake and the Hoover Dam on a 250-passenger sternwheeler, the *Desert Princess*. Cruises last 1½ to 3 hours; some are sightseeing only, while others include breakfast, dinner, or dinner and live entertainment. Prices range from $12 to $32.50 for adults, $5 to $10.50 for children 3–12.

2 Playing the Games

By Jack Ryder

*Jack Ryder is a
free-lance writer
and gambling
expert who lives in
Reno.*

Over the past 50 years, the name Las Vegas has become
synonymous with gambling. Nine out of 10 visitors gamble
while they're in town. It would be practically perverse to
visit Las Vegas and *not* gamble. But while overly high ex-
pectations can lead to disappointment—or worse, as in the
loss of a lot of money—the key to having a good time is to
approach the casinos with the idea that, contrary to popular
opinion, you *can* win or, at the very least, get much more
than your money's worth of playing time. Your success depends less on luck and more on being familiar with the rules
of the games, being aware of the concepts *behind* the
games, and being conversant with the strategies that en-
able you to play, not only with confidence, but also with a
fair shot at winning.

Casino Strategy

The House Advantage

The first important concept to understand about gambling
in Las Vegas is that the odds for all the games provide an
advantage for the casino ("house"), generally known, appropriately enough, as the "house advantage," "edge," or
"vigorish." The casino is a business, and wagering is its
product. Since the house establishes the rules, procedures,
and payoffs on every game, it builds an automatic commission into every bet to ensure a profit margin.

Here's how it works. Let's pretend that I'm the house and
you're the customer and we're betting on a series of coin
flips. The deal that I make with you is that every time the
coin lands heads up, I win and you pay me a dollar. Every
time the coin lands tails up, you win—-but I only pay you
90¢. The law of averages maintains that out of every hundred coin tosses, heads will win 50 times and tails will win
the other 50. If I take a dime out of every one of your winning payoffs, the longer you play, the more dimes will wind
up in my pocket. If you started with a $50 bankroll, after
1,000 tosses, *even if you win half of them*, you'd be busted
out.

In this example, you're at a 10% disadvantage, meaning
that you can expect to lose 10¢ on every winning wager.
Thus, the house advantage, or your "negative expectation," for our coin-toss game is 10%.

The second important gambling concept is known as
"short-term fluctuation" (or "variance"). In plain English,
we're talking about "luck." Looking at our coin-toss game
through the lens of averages, if you and I flip a coin 1,000
times, it's reasonable to expect that the coin will land heads
up and tails up close to 500 times each. However, if we flip
the coin only 10 times, it's conceivable that the coin could
land heads up only twice or as many as eight times. Now

let's say that we made the same betting deal as above but we limited the number of tosses to 10. This would largely eliminate your 10% disadvantage and leave it up to "the luck of the toss" or, in other words, the short-term fluctuation. Thus, a short-term fluctuation in the law of averages eliminates the threat of the long-term negative expectation.

How do these concepts—the house advantage and negative expectation, as well as short-term fluctuation—apply to the choices that you make as a casino customer? Your decisions, based on these concepts, will determine not only what you play, but also how you play, how long you play, and, ultimately, how well you play.

Luck Versus the Edge

The average "bankroll" (cash carried for the sole purpose of gambling) of a Las Vegas visitor who plans to spend some time in the casino is roughly $500. This is a crucial statistic. The amount of your bankroll and your preferred style of "action" (how you risk your bankroll) define your relationship to luck and the house edge.

Basically, the parameters of gambling action are fast and slow. Some people, though they're in the minority, like their action fast and loose and high-risk; these are true "gamblers," in the old-fashioned sense of the word. The extreme version of this type of action is to take the whole $500 bankroll and lay it down on a single play—say, red or black on the roulette table. The odds are not quite even. The green 0 and 00 on the roulette table give the house an advantage of 5.26% (*see* Roulette, *below*). Still, even though the odds are less than fair, the short-term result will be the same: double or nothing.

Making one play eliminates both the law of averages and the long-term negative expectation; here you rely solely on the luck of the draw. If you want to go on a roller coaster ride of luck, with a minute or so of adrenaline-pumping, heart-pounding excitement, lay it all down at once. In a matter of moments, you'll either be rich or broke.

A less extreme version of this wild ride is to break your bankroll into two units, and make two bets. Here you can either double your money, lose it all, *or break even*. Similarly, if you separate your $500 bankroll into five units and make five bets, or 10 units and make 10 bets, your ride is lasting a little longer and your outcome is a little less black and white: you can double, bust out, break even, *or come out somewhat ahead or behind*. Still, the house advantage barely comes into play.

Luck can supersede the house advantage, but only in the short run. And though luck accounts for winners big and small, such as the California nurse who lines up four Megabucks symbols on the $3 payline for $9 million or the

$2 dice shooter who parlays a hot hand into a couple of hundred bucks, the lack of luck can obliterate a bankroll faster than a crooked S&L.

Besides, most people who come to Las Vegas like to gamble for as long as they can without running out of money. These people take their $500 bankrolls and split them into 100 units to make $5 bets, 250 units for $2 bets, 500 units for $1 bets, or even 2,000 units for 25¢ bets. This guarantees plenty of time for the law of averages to even out the short-term fluctuations. On the other hand, it puts the house advantage and the long-term negative expectation right back into the game.

So how do you play as long as you like without the certainty of the house advantage grinding your bankroll into dust?

The Good Bets

The first part of any viable casino strategy is to risk the most money on wagers that present the lowest edge for the house. Blackjack, craps, video poker, and baccarat are the most advantageous to the bettor in this regard (all the games are described in detail below). The two types of bets at baccarat have a house advantage of a little more than 1%. The basic line bets at craps, if backed up with full odds, can be as low as a half percent. Blackjack and video poker, at times, can not only put you even with the house (a true 50-50 proposition), but actually give you a slight long-term advantage.

How can a casino possibly provide you with a 50–50 or even a positive expectation at some of its games? First, because a vast number of suckers make the bad bets (those with a house advantage of 5%–35%, such as roulette, keno, and slots) day in and day out. Second, because the casino knows that very few people are aware of the opportunities to beat the odds. Third, because it takes skill—requiring study and practice—to be in a position to exploit these opportunities the casino presents. However, a mere hour or two spent learning strategies for the beatable games will put you light years ahead of the vast majority of visitors who give the gambling industry an average 12%–15% profit margin.

Comps, Clubs, and Coupons

Not only can you even out the odds to a certain extent, but you can also take advantage of the various attractive incentives casinos offer so that the suckers will stay and play— and, in the long run, lose, whether because of the house advantage or basic ignorance. These available, profitable, and somewhat prestigious incentives are known as "comps" (short for complimentaries) or freebies. The most common comps are free parking in downtown parking structures (all you have to do is walk into the casino and validate your ticket at the cashier window) and free cocktails (all you have to do is play at any table or machine). Other comps range from a "line pass" (the right to proceed directly into a showroom or restaurant without having to wait in line) all the way to a penthouse suite complete with private swimming pool, butler and chef, and round-trip airfare from anywhere in the world. It all depends on how much you're willing to risk: Comps are calculated by multiplying your average bet by the amount of time you play by the house advantage by the comp percentage.

Say, for example, you play blackjack at a $25 table for 8 hours. The casino expects you to participate in 60 hands an hour and lose at a rate of 2% (the house advantage). Sixty hands an hour times $25 a hand times 8 hours times 2% equals $240. Of that anticipated profit, the house is prepared to return up to half to you in complimentaries in order to "reward" you for your action. Thus, under the described circumstances, you'll qualify for $120 worth of comps, whether you win, lose, or break even.

To be eligible for comps, you have to get "rated" as a player. When you sit down to play, have the dealer call over the pit boss—the person who supervises the action on the gaming tables—and tell him that you'd like to have your play rated. The pit boss will fill out a rating card with your name, average bet, and length of play. These data are input into the marketing department computer; based on your "comp equivalency" (for example, the $120 you've qualified for), you'll be provided with your free food or room or perks. The kings of comps are the "high rollers," those willing to drop a lot of money at high-stakes games.

Slot clubs are another good way to reconcile the house advantage with playing for as long as you like. These clubs, introduced in the late 1980s to give slot players some high-roller status, are similar to frequent-flier programs offered by the airlines. It costs nothing to sign up for slot clubs and the benefits can be substantial. When you become a member, you're given a plastic credit card that you insert into the slot machine you're using; the card tracks your play and you receive points—and, eventually, comps—based on the amount of money you risk. Preferred slot-club members are often rewarded with free gifts, food, and rooms, invitations to special parties and slot tournaments, and VIP status. You can join slot clubs at as many casinos as you like, then play at the places that offer the best perks.

Finally, the best bet in any casino is one that is accompanied by a gambling coupon. These are most often found in hotel "funbooks," small coupon booklets given out free for the asking at casino "welcome centers"; generally all you need is a hotel room key and an out-of-state ID (this prevents locals from taking advantage of the valuable promotions). Most funbooks contain coupons that return 7 to 5, 3 to 2, even 2 to 1 on even-money wagers.

Playing with coupons gives you a decided advantage over the house. In our coin-toss example, you'd wager a dollar of your own and a coupon for another dollar. If you won, I'd pay you $2 (for a return of $3). That extra dollar, though it might not seem like much, would pay my commission on 10 additional coin tosses. Furthermore, since most of the major hotel-casinos distribute funbooks free, you and a partner can collect a dozen of them and then go on a "coupon run." You make even-money bets backed up by coupons, touring a number of casinos while you're at it. Done properly, you could conceivably fill up an entire Las Vegas visit making positive plays with casino coupons.

The Games

The following sections explain the rules, the plays, the odds, and the strategies for the most popular games in Las Vegas, Reno, and Lake Tahoe casinos. When you've decided on the kind of action you wish to pursue, you can choose a game that best suits your style. Then, if you take the time to learn the basics and fine points thoroughly, you'll be adequately prepared to play with as much of an edge as the game, combined with comps and coupons if possible, provides. In the meantime, good short-term fluctuation!

Blackjack

Blackjack is the most popular table game in the casino. It's easy to learn and fun to play. It involves skill, and therefore presents varying levels of challenge, from beginner to postgraduate. Blackjack also boasts one of the lowest house advantages. Furthermore, it's the game of choice when it comes to qualifying for comps: You can play for as long as you like, stand a real chance of breaking even or winning, *and* be treated like visiting royalty while you're at it.

Because blackjack is the only table game in the casino in which players can gain a long-term advantage over the house, it is the only game in the casino (other than, to a limited degree, video poker) that can be played professionally. And because blackjack can be played professionally, it is the most written-about and discussed casino game. Dozens of how-to books, trade journals, magazines, newsletters, computer programs, videos, theses, and novels are available on every aspect of blackjack, from how to add to 21 to how to play against a variety of shuffles, from when to stand or hit to the Level-Two Zen Count. Blackjack pros can spend hours debating whether the two-deck game at the Las Vegas Hilton has a starting house edge of .03 or .0275 due to the doubling-down-after-splitting option, or if the Hi-Opt II count system's 88% betting efficiency correlation makes it stronger than the unbalanced count's perfect insurance indicator. Of course, training someone to play blackjack professionally is beyond the scope of this

Blackjack Table

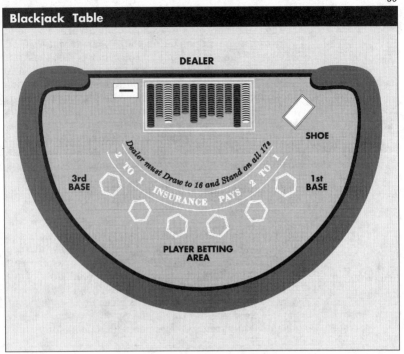

DEALER

SHOE

3rd
BASE

Dealer must Draw to 16 and Stand on all 17s
2 TO 1 *INSURANCE PAYS 2 TO 1*

1st
BASE

PLAYER BETTING
AREA

guide. Contact the Gambler's Book Club (tel. 702/382–7555) for a catalogue of gambling books, software, and videotape, including the largest selection on blackjack around.

The Rules Basically, here's how it works: You play blackjack against a dealer, and whichever of you comes closest to a card total of 21 is the winner. Number cards are worth their face value, picture cards are worth 10, and aces are worth either 1 or 11. (Hands with aces in them are known as "soft" hands. Always count the ace first as an 11; if you also have a 10, your total will be 21, not 11.) If the dealer has a 17 and you have a 16, you lose. If you have an 18 against a dealer's 17, you win (even money). If both you and the dealer have a 17, it's a tie (or "push") and no money changes hands. If you go over a total of 21 (or "bust"), you lose immediately, even if the dealer also busts later in the hand. If your first two cards add up to 21 (a "natural"), you're paid 3 to 2. However, if the dealer also has a natural, it's a push. A natural beats a total of 21 achieved with more than two cards.

You're dealt two cards, either face down or face up, depending on the local casino custom. The dealer also gives herself two cards, one face down and one face up (except in double-exposure blackjack, where both the dealer's cards are visible). Depending on your first two cards and the dealer's up card, you can:

stand pat, or refuse to take another card.

hit, or take as many cards as you need until you stand or bust.

double down, or double your bet and take one card.

split a like pair; if you're dealt two 8s, for example, you can double your bet and play the 8s as if they're two hands.

buy insurance if the dealer is showing an ace. Here you're wagering half your initial bet that the dealer *does* have a natural; if so, you lose your initial bet, but are paid 2 to 1 on the insurance (which means the whole thing is a push).

surrender half your initial bet if you're holding a bad hand (known as a "stiff") such as a 15 or 16 against a high-up card like a 9 or 10.

Buying In and Playing 21

First you must select a table to play at. A small sign in the left-hand corner of the "layout" (the diagram printed on the felt tabletop; *see* the Blackjack Table illustration *above*) indicates the table minimum and maximum, and often displays the house rules. You can be sure that the $2-minimum tables will be packed, the $5-minimum tables will be crowded, and the $25 tables will have some empty seats. Look carefully before you sit, so as to avoid the embarrassment of parking yourself at a $25 table with $1 chips.

There are generally six or seven betting circles (or squares) on a blackjack layout. When you find an empty space at a table with your chosen minimum, you can join a game in progress between hands. Sometimes you'll have to squeeze in and the other players might not be too anxious to make room for you for one reason or another (almost every one of them superstitious). The dealer should help make room for you. If everybody is particularly unfriendly, feel free to leave at any time, but it's to your advantage to spend as much time as possible playing at a crowded table, especially if your intention is to be rated for comps. The more crowded the table, the fewer hands will be played every hour, which reduces your risk. If everybody makes plenty of room for you to be comfortable and the dealer is friendly, you've got it made for hours.

Once you're settled, it's time to "buy in" (convert your cash to casino chips). Place your money on the layout between the betting circles or in the insurance space. If you lay cash *inside* the betting area, the dealer will say something like, "Money plays," and you might wind up betting your whole buy-in amount on the next hand! The dealer should exchange your cash for chips and deposit the bills in the drop slot, using a small plastic "pusher."

Now you can place your wager in the betting circle. You're dealt your two cards. If they're face down, you can pick them up, with one hand, and hold them. If they're face up, don't touch them. If you have a natural, turn them over and the dealer will pay you immediately and take your cards. Otherwise, everyone plays out his or her hand one at a time, from the right side of the table ("first base") to the left ("third base"). If you opt to stand pat, slide your two cards under your chips, then sit back and relax. If you want to hit, scratch the cards on the layout (seeing this done once will show you how). When you're ready to stand pat, slide the cards under the chips; if you bust, turn the cards over and the dealer will collect them and your bet. When everyone else has played, the dealer will turn over her down (or "hole") card and play out her hand, then pay off all the players according to whether they won, lost, or pushed. Then the whole process will start all over again.

Playing blackjack is not only knowing the rules and etiquette. It's also knowing *how* to play. Many people devote a great deal of time to learning strategies, two of which are discussed in the sections that follow. However, if you don't have the time, energy, or inclination to get seriously involved, the following basic rules, which cover more than half the situations you'll face, should allow you to play the game with a modicum of skill and a paucity of humiliation:

1. When your hand is a stiff (a total of 12, 13, 14, 15, or 16) and the dealer shows a 2, 3, 4, 5, or 6, always stand.
2. When your hand is a stiff and the dealer shows a 7, 8, 9, 10, or ace, always hit.
3. When you hold 17, 18, 19, or 20, always stand.
4. When you hold a 10 or 11 and the dealer shows a 2, 3, 4, 5, 6, 7, 8, or 9, always double down.
5. When you hold a pair of aces or a pair of eights, always split.
6. Never buy insurance.

Basic Strategy Available to anyone with an interest in the game, a system called "basic strategy" consists of a large set of exact decisions for optimum play at blackjack based on a player's hand versus the dealer's up card. These decisions have been developed via computer simulations of hundreds of millions of blackjack hands; they're not open to debate. You must spend several hours memorizing the basic-strategy chart and then spend another several hours practicing basic strategy with playing cards. And then you must make the correct play on every hand, regardless of your "hunches" or what the person sitting next to you might recommend.

The accompanying Basic Strategy Chart (*see below*) lists all the possible combinations of blackjack hands against the dealer's up card. Here's how to read it. Say you're dealt a 7 and a 5 and the dealer is showing a 9. First look at the left-hand column, under YOUR HAND for the total, 12. Then follow the line across to the column under the number 9. The "H" stands for hit. So you would hit this hand. Now, suppose

Your Hand	\multicolumn{10}{c}{Dealer's up card}

Your Hand	2	3	4	5	6	7	8	9	10	A
5	H	H	H	H	H	H	H	H	H	H
6	H	H	H	H	H	H	H	H	H	H
7	H	H	H	H	H	H	H	H	H	H
8	H	H	H	H	H	H	H	H	H	H
9	D	D	D	D	D	H	H	H	H	H
10	D	D	D	D	D	D	D	D	H	H
11	D	D	D	D	D	D	D	D	D	D
12	H	H	S	S	S	H	H	H	H	H
13	S	S	S	S	S	H	H	H	H	H
14	S	S	S	S	S	H	H	H	H	H
15	S	S	S	S	S	H	H	H	H	H
16	S	S	S	S	S	H	H	H	H	H
17	S	S	S	S	S	S	S	S	S	S
18	S	S	S	S	S	S	S	S	S	S
19	S	S	S	S	S	S	S	S	S	S
20	S	S	S	S	S	S	S	S	S	S
21	S	S	S	S	S	S	S	S	S	S
A,2	H	H	D	D	D	H	H	H	H	H
A,3	H	H	D	D	D	H	H	H	H	H
A,4	H	H	D	D	D	H	H	H	H	H
A,5	H	H	D	D	D	H	H	H	H	H
A,6	D	D	D	D	D	H	H	H	H	H
A,7	S	D	D	D	D	S	S	H	H	H
A,8	S	S	S	S	S	S	S	S	S	S
A,9	S	S	S	S	S	S	S	S	S	S
A,A	SP	SP	SP	SP	SP	SP	SP	SP	SP	SP
2,2	H	SP	SP	SP	SP	SP	H	H	H	H
3,3	H	H	SP	SP	SP	SP	H	H	H	H
4,4	H	H	H	D	D	H	H	H	H	H
5,5	D	D	D	D	D	D	D	D	D	H
6,6	SP	SP	SP	SP	SP	H	H	H	H	H
7,7	SP	SP	SP	SP	SP	SP	H	H	H	H
8,8	SP	SP	SP	SP	SP	SP	SP	SP	SP	SP
9,9	SP	SP	SP	SP	SP	S	SP	SP	S	S
10,10	S	S	S	S	S	S	S	S	S	S

you're then dealt a 4. Look back at the left-hand column for the new total, 16. Then follow it across to the number-9 column again. Again you have to hit. (Pray for a 5 or less, your only way out of this worst-case blackjack scenario. Most of the time you'll bust.)

Say you're dealt, on the next hand, an ace and a 4 against the dealer's 3; counting the ace as 11, you have a total of 15. Find the A,4 listing in the YOUR HAND column and follow it across to the dealer's 3. According to basic strategy, you should hit. If you get a 6, you've got 21, not 12. If you get a 5, you've got 20; of course you should stand. (If you're in doubt, look up the A,9 listing.) If you get a 9, however, you'll have to count the ace as a 1, for a total of 14; otherwise you'd bust with 23. Now you look up the proper play for 14 against a dealer's 3; you'd stand.

Finally, suppose you're dealt a pair of 7s against a dealer 7. The chart tells you to split the pair. Here you place both cards face up near your initial bet (don't worry about the exact position; no matter how close you place them, the dealer will *always* rearrange them slightly) and then place a second bet equivalent to the first. Then you play each 7 as its own hand. What if you're dealt a 4 on your first 7 for a total of 11? Some casinos will let you double down after splitting. Ask the dealer if she doesn't volunteer this information. What if you're dealt another 7? Again, some casinos will let you split the new pair and play out three hands.

Rules vary from house to house and city to city. The chart printed here holds for common Las Vegas rules. In Reno, you can only double down on a 10 or 11. In Las Vegas, some places allow you to surrender; some don't. At some places, dealers stand on soft 17; some places they don't. Basic strategy can get fairly advanced, and there are times when certain variations apply. The best place to play high-level basic-strategy blackjack is at the Las Vegas Club downtown. Here you can double down on any 2, 3, or 4 cards; surrender; and split and resplit pairs, including aces. If you're dealt a six-card "charlie," you win automatically. You might alter your strategy for certain low-card plays and double-down or surrender situations at the Las Vegas Club, but even without the fine tuning, this is the best multi-deck game in town.

Card Counting Card counting is an exacting technique for tracking the cards that have been played during a blackjack round and thereby determining whether the cards remaining to be played are favorable or unfavorable to the player. Card counters designate different plus or minus values for cards that are removed from the deck in play; based on the count, players can make better-informed decisions about playing and betting strategies. *Blackjack Count Analyzer*, a new computer program written by the inimitable blackjack guru Stanford Wong, provides a hands-on and interactive training course in card counting for use on IBM or compatible computers. It's available from Huntington Press (5280 S. Valley View Blvd. Suite B-3F, Las Vegas, NV 89118, tel. 702/597–1884).

Roulette

Roulette is a casino game that utilizes a perfectly balanced wheel with 38 numbers (0, 00, and 1 through 36), a small white ball, a large layout with 11 different betting options (*see* the Roulette Table illustration, *below*), and special "wheel chips." The layout organizes 11 different bets into six "inside bets" (the single numbers, or those closest to the dealer) and five "outside bets" (the grouped bets, or those closest to the players).

The dealer stands between the layout and the roulette wheel, and chairs for five or six players are set around the roulette table. At crowded times, players also stand among and behind those seated, reaching over and around to place their bets. *Always* keep a close eye on your chips at these times to guard against "rack thieves," clever sleight-of-hand artists who can steal from your pile of chips right in front of your nose.

To buy in, place your cash on the layout near the wheel. Inform the dealer of the denomination of the individual unit you intend to play (usually 25¢ or $1, but it can go up as high as $500). Know the table limits (displayed on a sign in the dealer area); don't ask for a 25¢ denomination if the minimum is $1. The dealer gives you a stack of wheel chips of a different color from those of all the other players, and places a chip marker atop one of your wheel chips on the rim of the wheel to identify its denomination. Note that you must cash in your wheel chips at the roulette table before you leave the game. Only the dealer can verify how much they're worth.

The dealer spins the wheel clockwise and the ball counterclockwise. When the ball slows, the dealer announces, "No more bets." The ball drops from the "back track" to the "bottom track," caroming off built-in brass barriers and bouncing in and out of the different cups in the wheel before settling into the cup of the winning number. Then the dealer, who knows the winning bettors by the color of their wheel chips, places a marker on the number and scoops all the losing chips into her corner. Depending on how crowded the game is, the casino can count on roughly 50 spins of the wheel per hour.

How to Place Inside Bets You can lay any number of chips (depending on the table limits) on a single number, 1 through 36 or 0 or 00. If the number hits, your payoff is 35 to 1, for a return of $36. You could, conceivably, place a $1 chip on all 38 numbers, but the return of $36 would leave you $2 short, which divides out to 5.26%, the house advantage.

Roulette Table

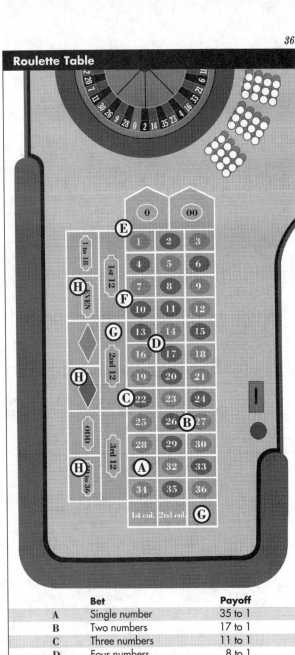

	Bet	Payoff
A	Single number	35 to 1
B	Two numbers	17 to 1
C	Three numbers	11 to 1
D	Four numbers	8 to 1
E	Five numbers	6 to 1
F	Six numbers	5 to 1
G	12 numbers (column)	2 to 1
G	1st 12, 2nd 12, 3rd 12	2 to 1
H	1-18 or 19-36	1 to 1
H	Odd or Even	1 to 1
H	Red or black	1 to 1

If you place a chip on the line between two numbers and one of those numbers hits, you're paid 17 to 1 for a return of $18 (again, $2 short of the true odds).

Betting on three numbers returns 11 to 1, four numbers returns 8 to 1, five numbers pays 6 to 1 (this is the worst bet at roulette, with a 7.89% disadvantage), and six numbers pays 5 to 1.

How to Place Outside Bets Lay a chip on one of three "columns" at the lower end of the layout next to numbers 34, 35, and 36; this pays 2 to 1. A bet placed in the first 12, second 12, or third 12 also pays 2 to 1. A bet on red or black, odd or even, and 1 through 18 or 19 through 36 pays off at even money, 1 to 1. If you think you can bet on red *and* black, or odd *and* even, in order to play roulette and drink for free all night, think again. The green 0 or 00, which fall outside these two basic categories, will come up on average once every 19 spins of the wheel.

The house advantage of 5.26% on every roulette bet (except, as noted, the five-number bet) is five times as much as the best bets at craps and five times less than the average bet at keno. Only one roulette game in Las Vegas features the European-style wheel, which has a single green 0. This slashes the house edge in half to 2.7%. If you like to play roulette and want to double your playing time without adding to your bankroll, play the game on the second floor of Sam's Town. Occasionally, places like the Mirage and Caesars will offer single-0 roulette to high rollers who want to play, usually with a $25 minimum.

Craps

Craps is a dice game played at a large rectangular table with rounded corners. Up to 12 players can crowd around the table, all standing. The layout (*see* the Crap Table illustration) is mounted at the bottom of a surrounding "rail," which prevents the dice from being thrown off the table and provides an opposite wall against which to bounce the dice. It's important, when you're the "shooter," to roll the dice hard enough so that they bounce off the end wall of the table; this ensures a random bounce and shows that you're not trying to control the dice with a "soft roll." The layout grid is duplicated on the right and left side of the table, so players on either end will see exactly the same design. The top of the railing is grooved to hold the bettors' chips; as always, keep a close eye on your stash to prevent victimization by rail thieves.

It can require up to four pit personnel to run an action-packed, fast-paced game of craps. Two dealers handle the bets made on either side of the layout. A "stickman" wields the long wooden "stick," curved at one end, which is used to move the dice around the table; the stickman also calls the number that's rolled and books the proposition bets (*see below*) made in the middle of the layout. The "boxman" sits be-

Craps Table

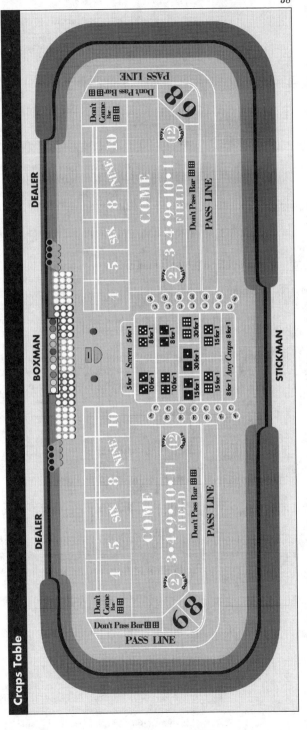

38

tween the two dealers and oversees the game; he settles any disputes about rules, payoffs, mistakes, etc. A slow crap game is often handled by a single employee, who performs stick, box, and dealer functions. A portable end wall can be placed near the middle of the table so that only one side is functional.

To play, just dive in and stand at the table wherever you can find an open space. You can start betting casino chips immediately, but you have to wait your turn to be the shooter. The dice move around the table in a clockwise fashion: The person to your right shoots before you, the one to the left after (the stickman will give you the dice at the appropriate time).

Playing craps is fairly straightforward; it's betting on it that's complicated. The basic concepts are as follows: If, the first time the shooter rolls the dice, he or she turns up a 7 or 11, that's called a "natural"—an automatic win. If a 2, 3, or 12 come up on the first throw (called the "come-out roll"), that's termed "craps"—an automatic lose. Each of the numbers 4, 5, 6, 8, 9, or 10 on a first roll is known as a "point": The shooter has to keep rolling the dice until that number comes up again. If a 7 turns up before the number does, that's another loser. Then, when either the point (the original number thrown) or a 7 is rolled, this is known as a "decision"; one is made on average every 3.3 rolls.

But "winning" and "losing" rolls of the dice are entirely relative in this game, because there are two ways you can bet at craps: "for" the shooter or "against" the shooter. Betting for means that the shooter will "make his point" (win). Betting against means that the shooter will "seven out" (lose). (Either way, you're actually betting against the house, which books all wagers.) If you're betting "for" on the come-out, you'd place your chips on the layout's "pass line." If a 7 or 11 is rolled, you win even money. If a 2, 3, or 12 (craps) is rolled, you lose your bet. If you're betting "against" on the come-out, you place your chips in the "don't pass bar." A 7 or 11 loses, a 2, 3, or 12 wins. A shooter can bet for or against himself or herself, as well as for or against the other players.

At the same time, you can make roughly two dozen wagers on any single roll of the dice. Besides the "for" and "against" (pass and don't pass) bets, you can also make the following wagers at craps.

Come/Don't Come: After a pass-line point is established, the come bet renders every subsequent roll of the dice a come-out roll. When you place your chips in the come box, it's the same as a pass line bet. If a 7 or 11 is rolled, you win even money. If a 2, 3, or 12 is rolled, you've crapped out. If a 4, 5, 6, 8, 9, or 10 is rolled, it becomes another point, and the dealer moves your chips into the corresponding box on the layout. Now if that number comes up before the 7, you win the come bet. The opposite is true for the don't come box: 7 and 11 lose, 2, 3, and 12 win, and if the 7 is rolled before the point, you win.

Odds: The house allows you to take odds on whether or not the shooter will make his or her point, once it's established. Since the house pays off these bets at "true odds," rather than withholding a unit or two to its advantage, these are the best bets in a crap game. Odds on the 6 and 8 pay off at 6 to 5, on the 5 and 9 at 3 to 2, and on the 4 and 10 at 2 to 1. "Back up" your pass line bets with single, double, triple, or up to 10 times odds (depending on the house rules) by placing your chips behind your line bet. For example, if the point is a 10 and your bet is $5, backing up your bet with single odds ($5) returns $25 ($5 + $5 on the line and $5 + $10 single odds); taking triple odds returns $55 ($5 + $5 on the line and $15 + $30). To take the odds on a come bet, toss your chips onto the layout and tell the dealer, "Odds on the come."

Place: Instead of waiting for a point to be rolled on the come, you can simply lay your bet on the point of your choice. Drop your chips on the layout in front of you and tell the dealer to "place" your number. The dealer puts your chips on the point; when it's rolled you win. The 6 and 8 pay 7 to 6, the 5 and 9 pay 7 to 5, and the 4 and 10 pay 9 to 5. In other words, if you place $6 on the 8 and it hits, you win $7. Place bets don't pay off at true odds, which is how the house maintains its edge (1.51% on the 6 and 8, 4% on the 5 and 9, and 6.66% on the 4 and 10). You can "call your place bet down" (take it back) at any time; otherwise the place bet will "stay up" until a 7 is rolled.

Buy: Buy bets are the same as place bets, except that the house pays off at true odds and takes a 5% commission if they win. Since buy bets have an edge of 4.7%, you should only buy the 4 and 10 (rather than place them at a 6.6% disadvantage).

Big 6 and **8:** Place your own chips in these boxes; you win if the 6 or 8 comes up, and lose on the 7. Since they pay off at even money, rather than true odds, the house edge is large—9.09%.

Field: This is a "one-roll" bet (a bet that's decided with each roll). Numbers 3, 4, 9, 10, and 11 pay even money, while 2 and 12 pay 2 to 1 (the 12 or "boxcars" pays 3 to 1 in Reno). The house edge on the field is 5.5%.

Proposition Bets: All the proposition bets are booked in the grid in the middle of the layout by the stickman. "Hardways" means a pair of numbers on the dice (two 3s for a hardways 6, two 4s for a hardways 8, etc.). A hardways 4 or 10 pays 7 to 1 (11.1% edge), and 6 or 8 pays 9 to 1 (9.09%). If a 7 *or* the 4, 6, 8, or 10 is rolled the "easy way," hardways bets lose. "Any seven" is a one-roll wager on the 7, paying 4 to 1 with a whopping 16.6% edge. "Yo'leven" is also a one-roll wonder paying 14 to 1 with a 16.6% edge. "Any craps" is a one-roll bet on the 2, 3, or 12, paying 7 to 1 (11.1%). Other bad proposition bets include the "horn" (one-roll bet on 2, 3, 11, or 12 separately; 16.6%), and "c and e" (craps or 11; 11.1%).

Note: The players place their own pass line, field, Big 6 and 8, and come line bets. Players must drop their chips on the table in front of the dealers and instruct them to make their place and buy bets, and to take or lay the odds on their come bets. Chips are tossed to the stickman, who makes the hardways, any craps, any seven, and c and e bets in the middle of the layout.

Baccarat

The most "glamorous" game in the casino, American baccarat (pronounced BAH-kuh-rah) is a version of *chemin de fer*, popular in European gambling halls. The Italian word *baccara* means "zero"; this refers to the point value of 10s and picture cards. Most Las Vegas casinos like to surround baccarat with an aura of mystique: the game is played in a separate pit, supervised by personnel in tuxedos (including a "ladderman" who sits high up over the table); the game's ritual is somewhat esoteric; and the minimum bet is usually $20 to $25. Mini-baccarat is the same game but played in the main blackjack pit, sans tuxedos, ritual, and $20 minimums.

Up to 15 players can be seated around a baccarat table (six or seven at mini-baccarat). The game is run by four pit personnel. Two dealers sit side by side in the middle of the table; they handle the winning and losing bets and keep track of each player's "commission" (explained below). The "caller" stands in the middle of the other side of the table and dictates the action. The ladderman supervises the game and acts as final judge if any disputes arise.

Baccarat is played with eight decks of cards dealt from a large "shoe" (or card holder). Each player is offered a turn at handling the shoe and dealing the cards. Two two-card hands are dealt, the "player" and the "bank" hands. The player who deals the cards is called the banker, though the house, of course, banks both hands. The players bet on which hand, player or banker, will come closest to adding up to 9 (a "natural"). The cards are totaled as follows: ace through 9 retain face value, while 10s and picture cards are worth zero. If you have a hand adding up to more than 10, the number 10 is subtracted from the total. For example, if one hand contains a 10 and a 4, the hand adds up to 4. If the other holds an ace and 6, it adds up to 7. If a hand has a 7 and 9, it adds up to 6.

Depending on the two hands, the caller either declares a winner and loser (if either hand actually adds up to 8 or 9), or calls for another card for the player hand (if it totals 1, 2,

Baccarat Table

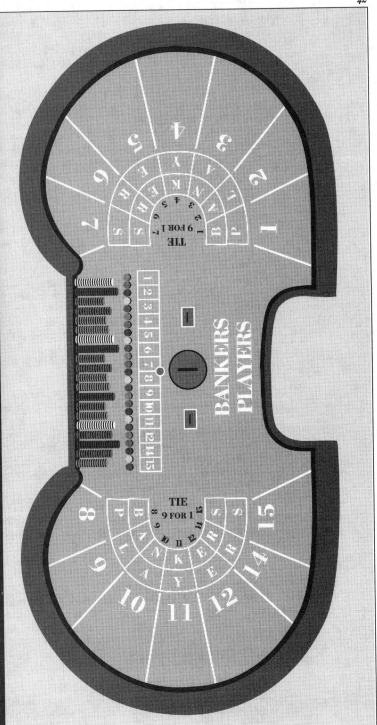

3, 4, 5, or 10). The bank hand then either stands pat or draws a card, determined by a complex series of rules depending on what the player's total is and dictated by the caller. When one or the other hand is declared a winner, the dealers go into action to pay off the winning wagers, collect the losing wagers, and add up the commission (usually 5%) that the house collects on the bank hand. Both bets have a house advantage of slightly more than 1%.

The player-dealer (or banker) continues to hold the shoe as long as the bank hand wins. As soon as the player wins, the shoe moves counterclockwise around the table. Players are not required to deal; they can refuse the shoe and pass it to the next player. Most players bet on the bank hand when they deal, since they "represent" the bank, and to do otherwise would seem as if they were betting "against" themselves. This isn't really true, but it seems that way.

Making a bet at baccarat is very simple. All you have to do is place your money in either the bank, player, or tie box on the layout (*see* the Baccarat Table illustration, *below*), which appears directly in front of where you sit at the table. If you're betting that the bank hand will win, you put your chips in the bank box; bets for the player hand go in the player box. (Only real suckers bet on the tie.)

Because the caller dictates the action, the player responsibilities are minimal. It's not necessary to know any of the card-drawing rules, even if you're the banker. Playing baccarat is a simple matter of guessing whether the player or banker hand will come closest to 9, and deciding how much to bet on the outcome.

Keno

Craps, blackjack, baccarat, and roulette arrived in Nevada casinos from Europe, but an early version of keno was brought over in the mid-1800s from China, where this bingo-type game was popular. It was rapidly Americanized in Reno casinos as soon as gambling was legalized in the 1930s.

Keno games are played once every seven or eight minutes. You participate by using a black crayon (provided) to mark a "ticket," imprinted with 80 boxes numbered 1 through 80, with one to 15 "spots" or numbers of your choice. You decide how many spots you want to mark based on how much money you're willing to bet. Eighty numbered Ping-Pong balls lying in a round plastic or wire bowl (the "goose") are mixed by an electric fan; the forced air blows the balls into two elongated tubes that hold 10 balls each. The numbers on the balls are announced over a public-address system to the players in the keno "lounge," and are displayed on keno "boards" that hang all around the casino—in the coffee shop, restaurants, and bars. If enough of your numbers match the board's numbers, you win an amount enumer-

Keno Payoffs *(for a bet of $1)*

Numbers Marked	Winning Numbers	Pays $	Numbers Marked	Winning Numbers	Pays $
1	1 number	3	11	5 numbers	1
				6 numbers	8
2	2 numbers	12		7 numbers	72
				8 numbers	360
3	2 numbers	1		9 numbers	1,800
	3 numbers	42		10 numbers	12,000
				11 numbers	28,000
4	2 numbers	1	12	6 numbers	5
	3 numbers	4		7 numbers	32
	4 numbers	112		8 numbers	240
				9 numbers	600
5	3 numbers	2		10 numbers	1,480
	4 numbers	20		11 numbers	8,000
	5 numbers	480		12 numbers	36,000
6	3 numbers	1	13	6 numbers	1
	4 numbers	4		7 numbers	16
	5 numbers	88		8 numbers	80
	6 numbers	1,480		9 numbers	720
				10 numbers	4,000
7	4 numbers	2		11 numbers	8,000
	5 numbers	24		12 numbers	20,000
	6 numbers	360		13 numbers	40,000
	7 numbers	5,000	14	6 numbers	1
				7 numbers	10
8	5 numbers	9		8 numbers	40
	6 numbers	92		9 numbers	300
	7 numbers	1,480		10 numbers	1,000
	8 numbers	18,000		11 numbers	3,200
				12 numbers	16,000
9	5 numbers	4		13 numbers	24,000
	6 numbers	44		14 numbers	50,000
	7 numbers	300	15	7 numbers	8
	8 numbers	4,000		8 numbers	28
	9 numbers	20,000		9 numbers	132
10	5 numbers	2		10 numbers	300
	6 numbers	20		11 numbers	2,600
	7 numbers	132		12 numbers	8,000
	8 numbers	960		13 numbers	20,000
	9 numbers	3,800		14 numbers	32,000
	10 numbers	25,000		15 numbers	50,000

ated in the keno payoff booklet (*see* the Keno Payoffs chart, *below*).

You can bring your ticket to the central keno "counter," where a "writer" gives you a duplicate ticket and books your wager, or you can fill out a ticket at one of the casino's bars and restaurants, which are served by keno "runners," who collect tickets and bets and run them to the central counter where they are processed. The runners then deliver the duplicate tickets to the far-flung customers. After the game has been played and the winning numbers are displayed, the runner returns to check if there are any winners. If there are, the runner redeems the winning tickets for her customers—at which point it's customary to tip her.

There are six different types of keno tickets, the most common of which are the "straight," "replay," and "split" tickets. On a straight ticket, you mark off your chosen numbers—say, eight of them (remember, you're allowed to mark as many as 15). Looking at the payout chart, you can see that if four or less of your numbers match the called numbers, you lose. If five out of the eight match, you win $9 (on the $1 bet). If all eight match, you're an $18,000 winner. If you mark 15 spots and all 15 match (fat chance!), you win the big jackpot, usually $50,000.

A replay ticket uses the same numbers that you bet on with a previous ticket. Simply hand your bet (which doesn't have to be for the same amount) and the duplicate from a prior game to the writer. A split ticket means that you're making two straight bets on a single ticket. Mark your numbers for the first straight bet and draw a line to separate them from the numbers for the second straight bet. Be sure to tell the writer that this is a split ticket.

Like the split ticket, "way" and "combination" wagers use one ticket to make what are often large and complex numbers of bets—a method of reducing paperwork. But these bets are really just a fancier and faster way to lose money at keno. If you want to try them out, most keno lounges have a booklet explaining the way and combination bets.

Keno has the highest house advantage in the casino, but this doesn't seem to have much of an effect on its popularity. Even though you can expect to lose 25¢ to 40¢ on every dollar you wager, many people like keno. Why? It's easy to play and slow-paced; you can sit in the lounge, drink, and visit with your fellow suckers. You can also maintain a level of action while eating or drinking in a restaurant or bar. But mostly it's a long-shot game, at which you can win $25,000, $50,000, and, at some places, even $100,000 by risking only a buck.

Video keno is played similarly to "live" keno. You drop your nickel or quarter into the machine, then use the attached "pen" to touch your numbers of choice. When you press the button that says "play" or "start," the machine illuminates the winning numbers, usually accompanied by a beep. If enough of your numbers match the machine's, you're paid off either in coins or credits.

Wheel of Fortune (Big Six)

Prize wheels are some of the oldest games of chance and some of the easiest to play and lose. Nevada-style big six is modeled after the old carnival wheels that attracted suckers on the midway. The standard wheel, usually six feet across, is divided into nine sections and 54 individual slots or stops. Fifty-two of the stops are marked by dollar denominations: 23 $1, 15 $2, eight $5, four $10, and two $20 stops. The other two stops are marked by a joker or the casino logo. A leather "flapper" mounted at the top of the wheel clicks as it hits the wood or metal pegs that separate each slot. When the wheel stops, the flapper falls between two pegs and indicates the winning number.

You lay your bet on a glass-covered table in front of the wheel. The layout display consists of the actual currency which matches the numbers on the wheel (a Washington, Lincoln, Hamilton, Jackson, etc.). To play, you simply place a chip or cash atop the bill you think the flapper will stop at. The payoff is a multiple of the denomination: A $1 bet on the $1 bill pays a buck; a $1 bet on the $2 bill pays $2; a $5 bet on the $20 pays $100. The joker, casino logo, or other nonnumerical symbol on the machine, however, pays 40 to 1: a successful $1 bet on one of these will get you back $40.

The house advantage starts at 11.1% on the $5 bet and rockets to 22.2% on the $20 bet and 24% on the joker. This isn't a game you'll want to play all night, or for more than a few spins. But the big six often draws a crowd. Even hardened gamblers like to stop and watch and listen to the wheel spin, with its hypnotic clicking of flapper against pegs, to see where it stops. They'd probably even lay down a buck or two, but they'd be too embarrassed in front of the dealer! If you want to take a look at the king of all the money wheels, go to Vegas World: The one there is 26 feet in diameter and powered by an electric motor.

Slot Machines

Of all the games in the casino, slot machines are the most American: Around the turn of the century, Charlie Fey built the first mechanical slot in his San Francisco basement. Today, slot machines occupy more casino floor space and account for more gross casino winnings than all the table games combined. In fact, 1992 was the first year in history that machine profits surpassed those of table games on the toney Las Vegas Strip. Slots (along with video poker, keno, and blackjack machines) are the state of Nevada's number-one export product.

Slot-machine technology has exploded in the past 20 years, and now there are hundreds of different models, which accept everything from pennies to specially minted $500 tokens. The old "mechanical" or "electromechanical" slots—all more than 25 years old—can be found at some casinos. They feature small skinny reels with fruit symbols; usually accept only one coin; don't have any lighting or sound effects; have a single pay line; and pay back minor amounts. "Multipliers" are machines that accept more than one coin (usually three to five, maximum) and are mostly electronically operated—with flashing lights, bells, and whistles, and spin, credit, and cash-out buttons. Multipliers frequently have a variety of pay lines: three horizontal for example, or nine horizontal and diagonal.

The major advance in the game, however, is the progressive jackpot. Banks of slots within a particular casino are connected by computer, and the jackpot total is displayed on a digital meter above the machines. Generally, the total increases by 5% of the wager. If you're playing a dollar machine, each time you pull the handle (or press the spin button), a nickel is added to the jackpot. Progressive slots in many casinos are also connected by modem throughout the state, and these jackpots often reach into the millions of dollars. The largest slot jackpot ever paid—roughly $9.3 million, won by a California nurse at Harrah's Reno in 1992—was on a Megabucks progressive, which is competitive with surrounding state lotteries. (One form of gambling that is specifically illegal in Nevada is the lottery.) Nevada Nickels and Quartermania are the lower-denomination versions of the statewide progressive. The largest progressive nickel jackpot in history was won at the Stardust in Las Vegas in 1993: nearly $865,000.

To play, insert your penny, nickel, quarter, silver dollar, or dollar token into the slot at the far right edge of the machine. Pull the handle or press the spin button, then wait for the reels to spin and stop one by one, and for the machine to determine whether you're a winner (occasionally) or a loser (the rest of the time). It's pretty simple—but because there are so many different types of machines nowadays, be sure you know exactly how the one you're playing operates. If it's a progressive machine, you must play the maximum number of coins to qualify for the jackpot. For example, the maximum bet at Megabucks is $3. You *can* play $1; this limits the action to the first-coin "payline" (usually the middle line across the reels). The same goes for $2 and the second-coin payline (the top line). But to win the progressive total, the four Megabucks symbols must be lined up on the third-coin payline (not surprisingly, the bottom line). Can you imagine lining up four Megabucks symbols on the third payline with only a dollar or two played? Instead of winning $3 to $4 million, you wind up with bupkus!

The house advantage on slots varies widely from machine to machine, between 3% and 25%. Casinos that advertise a 97% payback are telling you that at least one of their slot machines has a house advantage of 3%. Which one? There's really no way of knowing. Generally, $1 machines pay back at a higher percentage than quarter or nickel machines. On the other hand, machines with smaller jackpots pay back more money more frequently, meaning that you'll be playing with more of the house's money.

One of the all-time great myths about slot machines is that they're "due" for a jackpot. Slots, like roulette, craps, keno, and the big six, are subject to the Law of Independent Trials, which means the odds are permanently and unalterably fixed. If the odds of lining up three sevens on a 25¢ slot machine have been set by the casino at 1 in 10,000, then those odds remain 1 in 10,000 whether the three 7s have been hit three times in a row or not hit for 90,000 plays. Don't waste a lot of time playing a machine that you suspect is "ready," and don't think if someone hits a jackpot on a particular machine only minutes after you've finished playing on it that it was "yours."

If you have the hots for slots, remember to join as many slot clubs as you can. You're paying a pretty hefty commission for your romance with cherries, lemons, and 7s, so it's more than worth it to be rewarded with comps and perks.

Video Poker

Like blackjack, video poker is a game of strategy and skill, and at select times on select machines, the player actually holds the advantage, however slight, over the house. Unlike slot machines, you can determine the exact edge, of video poker machines. Like slots, however, video poker machines are often tied into a progressive meter; when the jackpot total reaches high enough, you can beat the casino at its own game.

The variety of video poker machines is already large, and it's growing steadily larger. All of the different machines are played in similar fashion, but the strategies are different. This section deals only with straight draw video poker. The best book about joker-poker and deuces-wild machines is *Mastering Joker Wild Video Poker* by Bradley Davis.

You must first ascertain what denomination of coin a straight-draw video poker machine accepts. The only penny video poker machines in Nevada are at the Gold Spike Casino in downtown Las Vegas. Thousands of nickel, quarter, and dollar machines occupy casinos in Las Vegas, Reno, and Tahoe. Five-dollar machines are becoming more popular around the state, and $25 and $100 machines can be played at places like the Mirage, Golden Nugget, and Caesars Palace.

9/6 Video Poker Payout Schedule					
Royal Flush	250	500	750	1000	4000
Straight Flush	50	100	150	200	250
Four of a Kind	25	50	75	100	125
Full House	9	18	27	36	45
Flush	6	12	18	24	30
Three of a Kind	3	6	9	12	15
Two Pair	2	4	6	8	10
Jacks or Better	1	2	3	4	5

The schedule for the payback on winning hands is posted on the machine, usually above the screen. It lists the returns for a high pair (generally jacks or better), two pair, three of a kind, a flush, full house, straight flush, four of a kind, and royal flush, depending on the number of coins played—usually 1, 2, 3, 4, or 5. (The machine assumes you're familiar with poker and its terminology.) Look for machines that pay with a single coin played: one coin for "jacks or better" (meaning a pair of jacks, queens, kings, or aces; any other pair is a stiff), two coins for two pairs, three for three of a kind, six for a flush, nine for a full house, 50 for a straight flush, 100 for four of a kind, and 250 for a royal flush. This is known as a 9/6 machine: one that gives a nine-coin payback for the full house and a six-coin payback for the flush with one coin played (see 9/6 Video Poker Payout Schedule chart, below). Some machines pay a unit for a pair of 10s, but get you back by returning only one unit for two pair. Other machines are known as 8/5 (8 for the full house, 5 for the flush), 7/5, and 6/5.

The return from a standard 9/6 straight draw machine (with a 4,000-coin "flattop" or royal-flush jackpot) is 99.5%; you give up a half percent to the house. An 8/5 machine with a 4,000 flattop returns 97.3%. In 6/5 machines (such as you find in supermarkets, 7-Elevens, and laundromats around the city), the figure drops to 95.1%, slightly less than roulette. The return from a 25¢, 8/5 progressive machine doesn't reach 100% until the meter hits $2,200—a rare sight. (You can figure nickel, dollar, and $5 progressives by the $2,200 figure. A 100% payback on nickels is $440, on $1 is $8,800, and on $5 is $44,000.) Machines with varying paybacks are scattered throughout the casinos. In some you'll see an 8/5 machine right next to a 9/6, and someone will be blithely playing the 8/5 machine! So far only Bob Stupak's Vegas World has broken the 9/6 barrier, and now offers 9/7 and 10/6 machines, which boast a payback of nearly 101%, with perfect play. Any mistakes will drop you right back down to where the house has the edge.

As with slot machines, it's always optimum to play the maximum number of coins in order to qualify for the jackpot.

You insert five coins into the slot and press the "deal" button. Five cards appear on the screen—say, 5, J, Q, 5, 9. To hold the pair of 5s, you press the hold buttons under the first and fourth cards. The word "hold" appears underneath the two 5s. You then press the "draw" button (often the same button as "deal") and three new cards appear on the screen—say, 10, J, 5. You have three 5s; with five coins bet, the machine will give you 15 credits. Now you can press the "max bet" button: five units will be removed from your number of credits, and five new cards will appear on the screen. You repeat the hold and draw process; if you hit a winning hand, the proper payback will be added to your credits. Those who want coins rather than credit can hit the "cash out" button at any time. Some machines don't have credit counters and automatically dispense coins for a winning hand.

Like blackjack, video poker has a basic strategy that's been formulated by the computer simulation of hundreds of millions of hands. The most effective way to learn it is with a video poker computer program that deals the cards on your screen, then tutors you in how to play each hand properly. The best program is *Stanford Wong's Video Poker*, available from Huntington Press (5280 S. Valley View Blvd. Suite B-3F, Las Vegas, NV 89118, tel. 702/597–1884).

If you don't want to devote that much time to the study of video poker, memorizing these six rules at least will help you make the right decision for more than half the hands you'll be dealt:

1. If you're dealt a completely "stiff" hand (no like cards and no picture cards), draw five new cards.

2. If you're dealt a hand with no like cards but with one jack, queen, king, or ace, always hold on to the picture card; if you're dealt two different picture cards, hold both. But if you're dealt three different picture cards, only hold two (the two of the same suit, if that's an option).

3. If you're dealt a pair, always hold it, no matter what the face value.

4. Never hold a picture card with a pair of twos through tens.

5. Never draw two cards to try for a straight or flush.

6. Never draw one card to try for an inside straight.

Bingo

Bingo is one of the world's best known and best loved games. In the United States alone, more than 35,000 bingo halls serve an estimated 30 million players, 20 million of whom are women. Bingo is also responsible for raising more money for charities, service organizations, religious institutions, and Native American tribes than any other fund-raising activity.

One of the least profitable games for casinos, bingo was originally included in the roster of casino games for the same reason that extravaganzas were introduced to the showrooms, cheap steaks and breakfasts appeared in the restaurants, and coupons for free souvenirs are distributed via funbooks: To attract people into the casino. Simply by offering bingo, casinos can fill large halls full of players, who have to pass through the casino on the way in and out, where they'll drop a few bucks on a roulette wheel or in a slot machine.

Bingo is derived from the Italian game lotto, but is similar to the original Chinese game of keno. Both use numbered cards, numbered Ping-Pong balls blown from a cage, a caller, and a master board. There, however, the similarities pretty much dissolve. Bingo is played on paper cards marked with a "dauber" or on two-ply cardboard "boards" marked with little round plastic tabs. The bingo cards contain 25 squares. Five horizontal columns are topped with the letters B-I-N-G-O. Under the B are five boxes, with a number in each box from 1 to 15; under the I five boxes with numbers 16 to 30; under the N four numbered boxes (31 to 45) and a "free" box in the center of the card; under the G numbers 46 to 60; and under the O 61 to 75.

The caller announces the letter and number of each ejected Ping-Pong ball and illuminates them on the master board. For example, if the caller announces "G-58" or "Number 58, under G," the players check their cards under the column topped by the G for the number 58. If it appears, they mark the number with the ink dauber or the plastic tabs. A winning card will have five numbers lined up in a row, either horizontally, vertically, or diagonally. The "free" square is always considered marked, so frequently you'll only need to match four numbers to win a game.

When a player lines up a card with the proper configuration of markings, she yells out "Bingo!" A floor person picks up the card and verifies the player's numbers by those on the big board, then declares her the winner. The caller gives the other players a few moments to determine whether they, too, have won; if there's another winner, the two split the total prize money. Most of the time, however, there's only one winner per game, because great pains are taken to ensure that each card is unique. Prize money can range from $10 on a regular bingo game up to $50,000 for a progressive jackpot.

The variety of patterns for bingo games is vast, from the "no-number" card, where not a single number on the card has been called, to the "coverall" or "black-out," where every number on the card is marked. Configurations such as "inside corner," "outside corner," and shapes such as "diamond," "square," "picture frame" or the letters "L," "X," "T," "H," and "U" are announced by the caller at the start of each game, and the patterns illuminated on secondary boards around the room.

There are almost as many different buy-ins as there are patterns. Cards start at 25¢ and can go up to $500 and higher for special promotions and tournaments. Different-color cards have different buy-in denominations (for example, blue costs $3, green $6, orange $9, etc.); the prize money is determined by the card's worth. "Game packs" or "booklets" consist of a given number of paper cards stapled together and used up in a "session." A quick call to the bingo room can tell you which sessions are played when.

Each game moves fairly quickly. The numbers are called one right after the other, leaving the players just enough time to look for them on their cards. Old bingo hands can play scores of cards simultaneously, but beginners should limit themselves to a dozen at the most. When you buy in, if it's a paper session (i.e., one played on paper cards), make sure you have a dauber on hand when the game starts; they're for sale at the bingo cashier for $1 or so. After the first few games of a session, by watching, asking your neighbors or a floor person a quick question about something you don't quite understand, and playing, you'll be right into the swing of things.

Though the pace of bingo can often be blistering, the games start out fairly relaxed, when the cards are empty and the players are gearing up for the pattern. The tension mounts as more numbers are called, the cards fill up, and the players await the magic number or two that will make them winners. Finally, someone yells, "Binnnnnngooooo!" and for a brief moment the tension remains while the other players catch up on the last number or two. Then, as people realize they're not cowinners, the room deflates like a popped balloon. Quickly, the winner is verified and a new game starts the process all over again.

Sports Betting

In Las Vegas, the word "book" rarely denotes a work of literature. More often than not, book isn't even used as a noun, but when it is, book almost always refers to the large room, generally an annex of a casino, where sports wagers are made and paid, the odds on sporting events are displayed, and sports bettors (often called "wise guys") watch the main events on large TV screens. Bookmakers (or bookies) are people in the business of taking wagers. Book as a verb is the action of accepting and recording a wager, primarily on sporting events, but also on casino games; the house books your blackjack, craps, and slot-machine action.

The first sports book opened in a casino in 1975. Today, nearly every major casino books sports bets. A sports book can be as small as a table with a clerk who quotes the odds and handwrites your receipt for a bet, or as large as the Las

Vegas Hilton's "super book," which boasts 46 video screens and 500 seats.

In Nevada, you can bet on professional football, baseball, basketball, and hockey; college football and basketball; boxing matches; horse racing; and special events. But of all the sports, pro football draws the most action by far.

Football Betting A wager laid on a football game is one of the best gambling (and entertainment) bargains in the business. It costs you all of $1 in commission to the house to place a $10 bet on a team; the return is several hours of heightened excitement while the game is played. As anyone who's made a casual bet with a friend or group of coworkers knows, having a little money riding on a game introduces a whole new level of energy and interest to it.

There are four ways to bet a football game: point spread, money line, parlay, and teaser. A wager based on the "point spread" (or "straight") means that you're not only betting that one team will beat the other, but that it will win by a predetermined number of points. The point spreads are calculated for all pro football games by an outside "handicapper" (or oddsmaker) based on the relative strengths or weaknesses of the teams playing. For example, when a strong team, such as the San Francisco 49ers, plays a weak team, such as the New England Patriots, the spread will favor the 49ers by, say, 17 points. This means that the 49ers have to beat the Patriots by 18 points in order for a wager placed on San Francisco to win. If the 49ers beat the Patriots by 10 points, they didn't "cover" the spread, so a bet on the Patriots would win. If the 49ers win by 17 points exactly, it's a "push" or a tie, and the original bet (minus the commission) is returned.

The "money line" bet on a pro football game uses odds instead of points, and is determined simply by who wins and who loses. The money line for the San Francisco–New England game might be a "minus 240 plus 180." This means you have to bet $24 to win $10 (for a total of $34) on the heavily favored 49ers; conversely, a bet of $10 on the underdog Patriots will win you $18 (for a total of $28).

A "parlay" is a bet on two, three, or four teams (sometimes more), all of which have to cover the point spread for you to win. (*See* Parlay Betting Odds chart, *below*.) If two out of the three teams cover and the third team wins but doesn't cover, you lose the whole bet. The payout on a two-team parlay is generally 13 to 5, on a three-team parlay 6 to 1, and on a four-team parlay 10 to 1.

A "teaser" is similar to a parlay, except that the point spreads are more variable than for a straight or parlay bet. (*See* Teaser Betting Odds chart, *below*.) If you win a three-team teaser after taking an additional 6 points on the spread, you're paid at 9 to 5; with 6½ additional points it's 8 to 5 and with 7 additional points, 3 to 2.

Parlay Betting Odds

Number of Teams	Payout Odds	True Odds
2	13–5	3–1
3	6–1	7–1
4	10–1	15–1
5	20–1	31–1
6	35–1	63–1
7	50–1	127–1
8	100–1	225–1
9	200–1	511–1
10	400–1	1023–1

Teaser Betting Odds

Number of Teams	6 points	6½ points	7 points
2	even	10–11	1–12
3	9–5	8–5	3–2
4	3–1	5–2	2–1
5	9–2	4–1	7–2
6	7–1	6–1	5–1

Football bets are usually made in denominations of $11, which includes the house's $1 commission for booking the bet. Winning bets pay off in denominations of $10. So, for example, you might bet $33 on the 49ers to cover the point spread. If the 49ers cover, you win $30 (for a total payback of $63).

To make a football bet (or a bet on any sporting event), go to the sports book and step up to the counter. Study the board that lists all the games, and pick out the one(s) you want to put your money on. The teams are numbered. Give the team number, amount of the bet, and type of bet (points or money line) to the "writer," who inputs your bet into a computer, and prints out your "ticket" or receipt. (Parlay and teaser cards are filled out and presented to the writer.) Check your ticket carefully to make sure the writer has given you the exact bet that you intended to make.

Then sit back and root for your team. If you lose, wallpaper your bathroom with the ticket. If you win, return to the casino where you made the bet, present the ticket to the sport book cashier, and receive your due.

3 Casinos

Popular wisdom notwithstanding, you *can* win in the casinos and many people do. But, as discussed in the previous chapter, almost all of the odds are riding against you. And that's just for starters. The dazzling lights, the free beer and cocktails, the play money, the lack of windows and clocks, even the oxygen—and, lately, seductive aromas—pumped into the air are all calculated to overwhelm you with a sense of holiday impetuousness that keeps you reaching into your pocket or purse for the green.

Tens of millions of people who *don't* know the odds of, or the strategies for, casino games come to Las Vegas every year, and some of them even win now and then. But let's face it. Kirk Kerkorian didn't invest a billion dollars to build his new MGM Grand on the Strip because he expected to make a lot of money on hotel rooms and bacon-and-egg breakfasts. He knew that millions of people would come to gawk at his new showplace—and deposit their bankrolls in his vault while they were at it.

The casinos make a fortune, more than $5 billion a year, simply by keeping most of the money that comes out of millions of pockets. With table games they keep around 20% of the money; with the slot machines—the number one game in Nevada—they hold around 30%.

If you want to beat the odds, take the time to read up on the games before you go to Nevada. Then, when you have some idea of the basics, plan on attending the free gambling lessons provided at most casinos. Even if you think you know the rules, these lessons will give you an opportunity to play the game at an actual session and learn the etiquette using practice chips instead of your own cash.

Casino Etiquette

Casinos can be confusing places for the first-time visitor. They tend to be large, open rooms full of people who seem to know exactly what they're doing, while you wander around lost. Cameras hung from the ceiling watch your movements, and all the security guards seem to be doing the same. Worst of all, there are no signs, announcements, or tour guides to inform newcomers of the rules of behavior. So we'll do that right here.

All players must be 21 years of age. No exceptions. A pit boss or security guard is likely to ask to see your ID if you look underage. If you're 19 or 20 and can pass for 21, you might get away with gambling—until you hit a jackpot. Any slot, video poker, or keno winnings of more than $1,200 to $1,500 require the casino to fill out IRS form W-2G. When the manager asks to see your identification, if you're under 21, not only will you not be paid, you'll also be summarily evicted. Many court cases over the years have challenged this procedure, every one to no avail. If you're playing a slot with a kid by your side, a security guard will quickly appear (dispatched by central casino surveillance) and ask you to leave. But you can walk through the casino with your youngster in tow; as long as you're on the move, you're okay.

No photographs may be taken in most of the casinos: Management fears that players may feel uncomfortable if captured on film and will get up and leave. (You can take pictures in the Four Queens, Excalibur, and California casinos if you like.)

Always take a few moments to orient yourself to a casino when you first arrive. Allow your senses to become accustomed to the surplus of stimuli. You can check out the slot machines without any problem. But be careful when walking around the pit (main table-game area). Never cut between the tables to get to the other side; the inner sanctum of the tables is an employees-only area.

Before you sit down or step up to a table, be sure to look at the little placard that announces the betting minimum and maximum. For example, blackjack tables have minimums of $1, $2, $3, $5, $10, $25, or $100 and maximums of $500 to $2,000. Minimums of casinos on the Strip are generally higher than those of downtown casinos.

If you're with a friend who chooses not to gamble, he or she will have to stand and watch; the chairs are for players only. (To watch roulette and craps, primarily standing games, your friend should stand behind the row of players.) An old wives' tale holds that dealers aren't allowed to talk to players. Not true. Don't hesitate to ask any question you like. If a dealer doesn't answer, or is rude, walk away to another table—or another casino. The trend among dealers is to be friendlier and more helpful, but there will always be those stony-faced dealers who grumble when spoken to.

At some of the smaller and slower gambling houses, dealers will take time with new players to point out the right ways and wrong ways of the game. If you're a newcomer to the tables, avoid the larger houses, especially at peak hours, because much of the time the personnel will be too busy to give you effective help should you become confused.

Consider also the timing of your casino visit. If you arrive at a busy hour, it may be hard to find room for two at a table or room at a table with the minimum bet that's right for you. Your best move is to arrive early—the earlier the better. The activity of Las Vegas starts to get under way around 11 AM, builds to 5 PM, remains steady until 8 PM, and then grows busier and peaks between 11 PM and midnight. If you can play at 9 AM, do it. If you can play at 6 AM, do it. At those hours the dealers will be more amicable, and less smoke will be blown in your face. Silver City (3001 Las Vegas Blvd. S, tel. 702/732-4152), across the street from Circus Circus, is the only casino in Vegas entirely for nonsmokers, although several houses now have tables for nonsmokers.

Money Management

The trick is to know enough to walk away while you're ahead. Remember, the goal of the casino is to keep you playing as long as possible. Set your own goals, and when you reach one, go out for a breather: Get something to eat or drink or do some sightseeing.

Tipping Dealers are paid near the minimum wage at the casinos, and they expect to be tipped when you are winning. It's a silly custom; after all, they work for the house, not for you, and they have nothing to do with your winning. But if you're new to the game and a dealer is friendly and helpful, slipping him or her a chip is like any other tip: a small gratuity for services rendered. You can also place a bet for the dealer, and not only at blackjack, but at any table. Simply lay down an extra chip or two and announce, "This one's for you." (At craps, the expression is "a two-way bet.") This small generosity usually relaxes the dealer, and thus the game, considerably. At most casinos, dealers pool their tips and then split them evenly. So be aware that no matter how much you toke a good dealer, he or she will receive only a percentage.

Las Vegas Lingo

Before you enter the neon jungle of Las Vegas, you'll want to learn some key words in the local language.

Buy-in. The amount of cash money with which a player enters a game.

Checks. Casino chips; for some reason, dealers and the pit bosses insist on calling them "checks."

Click. The sound a pit boss makes, using a clicker, when a player is spotted winning. It's a signal to a cocktail waitress to deliver a drink to that lucky person.

Comp. A gift from the casino of a complimentary drink, room, dinner, or show; a freebie (*see* Chapter 2, Playing the Games, for details).

Drop. To exchange money for chips at a gaming table: The dealer pushes the currency through a slot in the table, and it "drops" into a box beneath the table.

Grind joint. A gambling house that promotes cheap slot machines. You won't find too many high rollers at one.

Juice. Influence, the ultimate Vegas intoxication. Politicians use juice daily to get what they want. "You scratch my back, and I'll scratch yours" is another way of putting it.

High roller. A person with a good deal of money who looks for action (high-stakes games) and who drops thousands of dollars in a night without blinking.

Pit boss. The person who supervises the action on the gaming tables. The pit boss's domain, the pit, is an area surrounded by tables that is off-limits to the general public.

RFB. The cream of the comps—room, food, and beverage, courtesy of the casino. All you have to do is play (on average) for eight hours at $100 a hand.

Shill. A person employed by the casino to sit at the tables and play games during the less busy hours—with the casino's money. Casino bosses believe that gamblers are more comfortable playing at a table with other people rather than at an empty table.

Stiff. Cheapskate. When you fail to tip your dealer or a cab driver, you might hear him mutter that you're a stiff. Not to worry; a contract has not been put out on you.

Toke. A tip (short for token, or token of your esteem). This may be the word you'll hear most often; many of the folks you encounter will be expecting a toke.

The Casinos

Our review of the casinos begins at Hacienda Road, the southern end of the Strip, and proceeds north on Las Vegas Boulevard for the entire length of the Strip. Then we cover the downtown casinos on and near Fremont Street. The descriptions that follow are intended to help you find the casinos that will most appeal to you. If you'd like to save time by sleeping where you gamble, *see* Chapter 8, Lodging, for details of the hotels in which many of these casinos are found.

The Strip

Thirty casinos line the Strip, 23 major and seven minor— more than two million square feet of gambling fever. Strip casinos run the gamut of size and style, from the overwhelming spectacle of Caesars Olympic wing to the mini-pit at the Boardwalk, and from low-roller heaven at Circus Circus to high-roller tension at the Mirage. In general, however, Strip casinos are big and ritzy, with high-playing minimums; dealers wear bow ties, and you might sense that management would like to see you dressed up. Remember, however, that the casinos really care about only one aspect of your attire: that it include a wallet or purse from which you can easily remove your cash.

Hacienda Hotel and Casino (3950 Las Vegas Blvd. S, tel. 702/739–8911). The large building outstretched parallel to the bottom end of the Strip is a good place to begin a casino tour: It's usually half empty, there's almost always a seat at a $2 blackjack table, the poker room isn't filled with sharks, and there are often parking spaces directly in front of the hotel. Cascading water greets you when you pass through the swinging doors, and slots jangle in the background. The

Las Vegas Strip Casinos

Aladdin Hotel and Casino, **7**

Bally's Casino Resort, **10**

Barbary Coast Hotel and Casino, **12**

Bourbon Street Hotel and Casino, **9**

Caesars Palace, **11**

Circus Circus, **28**

Excalibur, **4**

The Flamingo Hilton and Tower, **13**

Frontier Hotel and Gambling Hall, **21**

Gold Coast Hotel and Casino, **33**

Hacienda Hotel and Casino, **1**

Harrah's Hotel and Casino, **16**

Imperial Palace Hotel and Casino, **15**

ITT Sheraton Desert Inn Hotel and Casino, **20**

Las Vegas Hilton, **25**

Little Caesar's Gambling Casino, **6**

Luxor, **2**

Maxim Hotel and Casino, **8**

MGM Grand Hotel and Theme Park, **5**

The Mirage, **17**

O'Sheas Casino, **14**

Palace Station Hotel and Casino, **29**

Rio Suites and Casino, **32**

Riviera Hotel, **26**

Sahara Las Vegas Hotel, **30**

Sands Hotel and Casino, **19**

Silver City, **24**

Slots-A-Fun, **27**

Stardust Hotel and Casino, **22**

Treasure Island, **18**

Tropicana Resort and Casino, **3**

Vegas World Hotel and Casino, **31**

Westward Ho Motel and Casino, **23**

Sahara Ave.

THE STRIP

Circus Circus La.

Riviera Blvd.

Paradise Rd.

Stardust Rd.

Convention Center Dr.

Desert Inn Rd.

Rancho Dr.

Westwood Ave.

Highland Dr.

Industrial Rd.

Emerson Ave.

Spring Mountain Rd.

Twain Ave.

Sands Ave.

Las Vegas Blvd.

Dauphine Wy.

Audrie St.

Koval Ln.

Flamingo Rd.

Harmon Ave.

Mirage Golf Course

Nick Kelly

Tropicana Ave.

THE STRIP

Reno Ave.

KEY

AE American Express Office

McCarran International Airport

Hacienda Ave.

N

| 0 | | 1 mile |

| 0 | | 1 km |

casino has a special video poker machine on which you can test your speed skills for tournament play.

Luxor (3900 Las Vegas Blvd. S, tel. 702/262–4000). This magnificent bronze pyramid, under development by Circus Enterprises, is scheduled to open in October 1993. The sheer scale of interior space, open nearly to the apex, is eye-popping. A 1,200-seat arena, state-of-the-art special effects, and, of course, thousands of slots and video poker machines, hundreds of table games, and a race and sports book will be contained in this re-creation of ancient Egypt.

Tropicana Resort and Casino (3801 Las Vegas Blvd. S, tel. 702/739–2222). To hear them tell it, the Tropicana is not a hotel-casino, but the "Island of Las Vegas." The Trop's 5-acre water park, set off by the two hotel towers, features the only swim-up blackjack in Las Vegas: Yes, you can actually sit in the pool and play 21. Stuff some cash in your swimsuit pocket and when you reach the table, put it into the Trop's money dryer. If you wind up blowing your soggy bankroll, just return to your breaststroke. Indoors, the casino continues the tropical theme, with palms, parrots, and Polynesiana. An exquisite stained-glass dome extends the length of the main pit. The casino offers excellent perks for points accumulated by members of its Island Winners slot club; card-reading machines around the casino give you your totals. There are nonsmoking crap tables and slots, and the hotel has recently introduced a penny roulette session, though the upscale Tropicana has few $2 blackjack tables. Crap and blackjack lessons are given daily.

Excalibur (3850 Las Vegas Blvd. S, tel. 702/597–7777). This medieval-theme 4,032-room resort, opened by Circus Circus in 1990, has 100,000 square feet of casino space. The castle offers inexpensive and plentiful meals, low minimums on all table games, 2,630 slot machines, a poker room, and race and sports book. The King's Pavilion is a beautiful circular bar in the middle of the casino, with a grand fake oak and bartop video.

MGM Grand Hotel and Theme Park (3805 Las Vegas Blvd. S, 702/891–1111). Construction continues for the third year on this meta-mega-resort, scheduled to open in February 1994. The gargantuan complex will house a 171,500-square-foot casino—the largest in the world by fully 50,000 square feet—with 3,500 slot machines (some with animated characters) and 165 table games, plus keno, a race and sports book, bars and lounges—all with a Wizard of Oz theme.

Little Caesar's Gambling Casino (3665 Las Vegas Blvd. S, tel. 702/734–2827). Whenever the national media carry a story about Nevada sports betting, the managers of Little Caesar's are almost always quoted. That's because this little hole-in-the-wall, located in a minimall, is recognized as the haven of sports bettors. Unlike the grand sports books at the major casinos, with their plush seating and rows of large TV screens, Little Caesar's is a stand-up sort of place with no video at all inhabited by guys who wear hats and smoke stogies. There's free parking directly in front. It was here that Vegas World casino owner Bob Stupak's $1 million 1989 Super Bowl bet was accepted. (Stupak won and walked away with almost $2,000,000). In addition to sports betting, Caesar's has two $1 blackjack tables and 50¢ craps.

Aladdin Hotel and Casino (3667 Las Vegas Blvd. S, tel. 702/ 736–0111). Here's another great Las Vegas image: atop a hotel roof, a neon genie's lamp that glows all night long. If only you could rub it, maybe your wish—and what else would it be but to make a killing?—would come true! Although the Aladdin was extensively remodeled in 1987, the original *Arabian Nights* theme remains, with Islamic arches and the decor of a harem. Gamblers will find low- to upper-range minimums: plenty of $2 tables and 25¢ slots, plenty of $25 tables and $1 slots. Tables for nonsmokers are available.

Maxim Hotel and Casino (160 E. Flamingo Rd., tel. 702/ 731–4300). The near-in location of the Maxim makes it a nice alternative to the Strip's busier casinos and a favorite with local residents. The dark-green casino has some $2 tables and lots of slots. Cab drivers like to steer slot players here; the Maxim doesn't have a slot club per se, but the house rewards jackpot winners (four of a kind at video poker, $100 hits at $1 slots) with coupons for room, food, and gift-shop comps. In addition, card counters swear by the Maxim, not only for its laissez-faire blackjack policy, but also for its consistent deep penetration (dealing the entire deck out).

Bourbon Street Hotel and Casino (120 E. Flamingo Rd., tel. 702/737–7200). New Orleans is the theme here, with Dixieland bands and French Quarter decor. In order to compete with its larger neighbors, Bourbon Street keeps food prices and table-game minimums low, and runs frequent gambling promotions for low rollers. The $1.99 breakfasts are served all day in the French Market Restaurant, and there are plenty of $2 tables. When the crowds at the Flamingo and Bally's get you down, the neighboring Bourbon Street will bring you back up.

Bally's Casino Resort (3645 Las Vegas Blvd. S, tel. 702/ 739–4111). Bally's is often described as a "city within a city." The casino, at 100,000 square feet, is certainly one of the largest in Las Vegas, though the Riviera, Circus Circus, Excalibur, and Las Vegas Hilton casinos are at least as big. What makes Bally's seem so monumental is that, unlike the others, it's a single expanse, front to back and side to side. Also, Bally's is usually packed. It owns a huge chunk of one of the most popular intersections in the world—it's across the street from the Flamingo and Caesars Palace—and it accommodates a perpetually large convention trade. Yet the casino is so roomy that when the crowds become at all oppressive, you can almost always find a more open part of the floor. Bally's tends to attract high rollers, with $5 minimum tables, but at slow times the minimum can go down to $3. Craps, baccarat, blackjack, and roulette lessons are given daily.

Caesars Palace (3570 Las Vegas Blvd. S, tel. 702/731–7110). Caesars is home to the never-ending casino, two sprawling wings in a gentle horseshoe shape that extends from one end of the huge property to the other. The old wing—low-ceiling, many pits, high stakes—is home to *serious* gamblers, people who are probably comped in Caesars exclusive suites, restaurants, and shops. The new Olympic Casino wing, with its high ceiling, soaring marble columns, graceful rooftop arches, and low limits, accommodates the low-stakes gamblers. Since the Mirage opened next door, Caesars has embraced the middle market with a slot club, food court, and nickel slots. The huge, plush race and sports book with its megadisplay must be seen to be believed.

Barbary Coast Hotel and Casino (3595 Las Vegas Blvd. S, tel. 702/737–7111). The Barbary Coast casino is modeled after a San Francisco saloon of the late 19th century, with Victorian chandeliers and lamps, tasteful stained-glass signs (including the largest stained-glass mural in the world), dealers who wear red garters on their sleeves, and Klondike Annie cocktail waitresses who wear garters on their thighs. Want to send a message from the Coast? A Western Union office here will wire it. The casino is usually pretty crowded, though not on the same scale as its neighbors—Bally's, the Flamingo Hilton, and Caesars. A pleasant brick plaza with wooden benches fronts the casino. Photo fans should remember that they can capture a bit of the interior action by placing a subject on the platform that leads into the casino and taking a few quick shots through the doorless entryway.

The Flamingo Hilton and Tower (3555 Las Vegas Blvd. S, tel. 702/733–3111). History lovers: This is where modern Las Vegas began. Prior to 1946, when Benjamin (Bugsy) Siegel imported Miami luxury to the desert, Las Vegas was still trying to keep alive the last little sliver of the Wild West. But Bugsy was intent on introducing a class joint to the new casino town, a place where his Hollywood buddies and Manhattan partners could gamble legally, where the lure of big-time entertainment would bring the beautiful people to play, and where the ordinary Joe would show up because he wanted to feel like a big shot. Bugsy, of course, wasn't able to hang around long enough to enjoy the fruits of his labor or to observe the impact of his vision, but the Fabulous Flamingo has had one hell of a 50-year run. The Flamingo hasn't officially been "Fabulous" since the Hilton organization took over in 1970, but the most massive expansion project in town has rendered it unofficially fantastic.

There are now a magnificent casino, a casino annex—the two-story **O'Sheas,** with an Irish theme, opened in a portion of what had been the parking lot—a poker parlor and sports book, and some of the most intense action in town. Table minimums at the Flamingo are on the high side. The neon rainbows above the slot machines point out the Hilton Pot of Gold slots, which pay off a million bucks (at a cost of $3 per arm pull), and the Hilton has had a parade of million-dollar winners.

Imperial Palace Hotel and Casino (3535 Las Vegas Blvd. S, tel. 702/731-3311). A blue pagoda-style building with an Oriental theme, this house of dragons does a booming business with tour groups. The casino is large, crowded, and confusing; of all the hotel-casino mazes in Las Vegas, the Imperial Palace is probably the most intricate. Plan on spending a few minutes confronting the splendid Zen challenge of finding your way around (the fact that there are no signs adds to the sport). Escalators behind the hotel's front desk carry you up to the third floor (showroom and sports book) and beyond to the fifth floor (five restaurants); escalators in the middle of the casino go to the coffee shop and buffet. The gaming school, one of the first and best in town, offers free blackjack and crap lessons Monday through Friday. The tables minimums are more in the $5 than the $3 range.

Harrah's Hotel and Casino (3475 Las Vegas Blvd. S, tel. 702/369-5000). You can't miss Harrah's, the 450-foot-long "Ship on the Strip," with its 80-foot neon paddlewheel and 85-foot-tall smokestacks; it even toots at intervals—perhaps so those who can no longer see straight after staring at slots for hours can *hear* their way back here. Strips of red neon hang above the slots, red wallpaper covers the walls, and the dealers adorn their white shirts with red string ties and garters. Harrah's is a good place for beginning gamblers and players on a budget. In keeping with the "good old days" theme, dealers here tend to be friendly and table limits are low (some $2 tables). The best deal may be the computerized, video bingo parlor on the third floor. If you don't relish the hassle of adding up the cards in blackjack or figuring out the odds at craps, but you want to play a live game, then bingo is its name. Cards can cost as little as 20¢, drinks are free, and winners get cash prizes in the $200 to $500 range, with progressive jackpots of $12,500.

The Mirage (3400 Las Vegas Blvd. S, tel. 702/791-7111). On its November 1989 opening day, this premier gambling showplace of Steve Wynn—known then primarily as the owner of the Golden Nugget—was the site of a $4.6 million Megabucks jackpot payoff, the largest in Las Vegas history. The Mirage is the ultimate carpet joint, with high limits, intense security, $500 slots, and a plush private room where the minimum bet is $1,000. Games in the Polynesian Village–style casino (where pits are distinguished by separate thatched roofs) include slots, video poker, craps, blackjack, and baccarat, plus an elaborate race and sports book. The Mirage has acres of open parking, but they're so far from the casino you might want to turn your car over to the valet instead.

Treasure Island (3300 Las Vegas Blvd. S, 89109, no tel. at press time). Scheduled to open in October 1993, Treasure Island will have a 3,000-room hotel and casino, complete with swashbuckling pirates engaging in battle in the lagoon outside.

Sands Hotel and Casino (3355 Las Vegas Blvd. S, tel. 702/733–5000). You can still live the 1950s and 1960s Sands experience in the hotel's gardens and pool area, which haven't changed much since the day the Las Vegas News Bureau shot a classic publicity photo of the "floating" crap game in the Sands pool. Indoors, however, the casino has changed a lot: Now comprising 30,000 square feet, it offers a race and sports book, keno, craps, blackjack, roulette, baccarat, nickel slots, and Megabucks. Yellow, red, blue, green, and pink neon overhangs various sections of the casino, which has more neon than any other in town (yellow for the quarter slots, red for the dollar slots, etc.). The Sands has a few blackjack tables for nonsmokers and more $2 blackjack tables than most casinos of its size.

ITT Sheraton Desert Inn Hotel and Casino (3145 Las Vegas Blvd. S, tel. 702/733–4444). The Desert Inn is one of the few hotels in Las Vegas that has not undergone a series of expansions in recent years. Opened in 1950 as Wilbur Clark's Desert Inn and once owned by Howard Hughes, the hotel has just 800 rooms—small compared to the other Las Vegas monoliths. The DI has always gone for an upscale clientele who like to golf (the hotel has the best golf course in the city) and gamble; the casino is more refined, smaller, and less noisy than most others on the Strip; over the years, renovations have given a fresh, bright look to the once dark and clubby casino. Because of its freewheeling clientele, its casino betting limits start higher than at the other hotels; some of its 400 slot machines cost $100 to play.

Frontier Hotel and Gambling Hall (3120 Las Vegas Blvd. S, tel. 702/794–8200). Across the street from the Desert Inn, the Frontier is the last remnant of the beginnings of the Las Vegas Strip. Those who like places with a "good old days" feeling, and that make no pretense of serving the upper crust of society, will love the Frontier. When Margaret Elardi bought the property in 1988, she took it drastically downscale. Rather than glitzy shows, the star is now single-deck blackjack. Diamond Jim's Gourmet Room steakhouse was replaced with a Mexican restaurant where tortillas are made in an open area overlooking the slots. The casino has nickel to $1 slots and lots of $2 and $3 tables, and the crowds are larger than they used to be. Beginning poker lessons are given every day but Sunday.

Stardust Hotel and Casino (3000 Las Vegas Blvd. S, tel. 702/
732–6111). The Stardust has one of the best neon shows on
the Strip: Pink and blue neon tubing runs down the front of
the hotel, leading to a 183-foot multiprogrammed sign that
erupts in bursts of neon stars; on its debut in 1958, the sign
was the largest and brightest in Las Vegas, its glow visible
for miles. Because of its size and sprawling layout, the Stardust never feels overly crowded or claustrophobic. In fact,
some people complain that the Stardust is *too* large, that it's
a long walk from the sports book up front to the video poker
room out back. A nice touch is the collection of overstuffed
red chairs in the slot area that allow you to take a comfortable break from the play (an unusual courtesy in Vegas).
The Stardust attracts gamblers who don't intend to spend a
lot of money. It has plenty of $2 blackjack tables, nickel
slots, and roulette with 50¢ chips (minimum bet $2). Black-
jack, craps, and roulette lessons are given daily.

Westward Ho Motel and Casino (2900 Las Vegas Blvd. S, tel.
702/731–2900). The Ho has something few Strip casinos can
offer: parking *right out front!* It also has plenty of $2 black-
jack tables and chances to play slots for new cars or boats.
One more thing makes the Ho interesting: Male dealers
wear four-in-hand ties rather than the bow or string ties
you'll see in virtually every other gaming house. The bias
against the four-in-hand lies in the fact that dealers can
stick money in them; with a bow tie there's little room for
shenanigans.

Las Vegas Hilton (3000 W. Paradise Rd., tel. 702/732–
5111). What began in 1969 as Kirk Kerkorian's International Hotel became, just a few years later, the Hilton organization's first foray into gambling. Today the Hilton hotel-
casinos in Las Vegas, Laughlin, and Reno account for 75%
of the corporation's annual profits. Unlike other large Las
Vegas casinos, which tend to be placed in a separate side or
back area, the one in the Hilton is in the middle of the floor,
surrounded by slot areas, a keno lounge, and a race and
sports book, all laid out so you can stand in the lobby and see
where everything is. Each week, the Nation's Oddsmaker,
Las Vegas's largest and most elegant sports book (with 46
video screens), issues the first nationally recognized betting lines on NFL and college football games. The Hilton's
clientele is high rollers and $1 slot players, and the casino
tends to have high minimums. You may find a few $3 black-
jack tables, but most begin at $5, especially during a busy
convention. Because the Hilton is next door to the Las
Vegas Convention Center, many delegates stay here, and
they pack the casino at all hours. Crap, blackjack, and roulette lessons are given daily.

Silver City (3001 Las Vegas Blvd. S, tel. 702/732–4152). Another gambling house in the style of the Wild West, with
free popcorn, 50¢ hot dogs, $1 blackjack, and pictures of
cowboys on the walls, Silver City has a much more relaxed

atmosphere than that of its next-door neighbor, the large Riviera. You can park in the lot directly in front of the casino, and, best of all, Silver City is the only casino south of Reno that has a strict no-smoking policy. It's worth stopping in here just to clear your lungs for a while.

Riviera Hotel (2901 Las Vegas Blvd. S, tel. 702/734– 5110). When the Riviera was built in 1955, it was the tallest hotel in town, a nine-story, T-shape structure; in an almost continual state of expansion for the last 40 years, it now boasts an enormous casino—125,000 square feet, the largest in the world until the 171,000-square-feet MGM Grand (*see* above) opens. The Riviera appealed primarily to the nabobs and high rollers until it changed its image in the 1980s and went after a less extravagant clientele. The casino has a new race and sports book, two new keno parlors, and a convenient fast-food court. With nearly 90 table games, the casino has betting minimums ranging from $3 to $5; there are more than 1,500 slot and video poker machines.

Circus Circus (2880 Las Vegas Blvd. S, tel. 702/734– 0410). Only in Las Vegas would you find a 125-foot neon sign of a clown sucking a lollipop next to a statue of a nude dancer. And only in Las Vegas could you find Circus Circus, the tent-shape casino with live circus acts performing over the gamblers' heads. (Under the Circus Circus tent, the clowns, trapeze stars, high-wire artists, unicyclists, and aerial dancers perform daily every 20 minutes from 11 AM to midnight.) Jay Sarno, who built Caesars Palace, believed he could follow it up with a casino that had a totally different philosophy. He was certain that a low-roller haven could prosper on the Strip, and was he ever right! In addition to the circus acts, a midway features such games as dime toss, milk can, bushel basket, and Fascination, along with clown-face painting, a video arcade, funhouse mirrors, corn dogs, and pizza. Many parents park their kids on the midway while they go off to pull handles and press buttons downstairs. On the casino floor, almost always packed solid, you'll walk and walk and walk, passing dealers in pink shirts and cocktail waitresses wearing yellow toga outfits that look like rejects from Caesars Palace. The two must-see attractions here are the slot merry-go-round—20 slots sit on a revolving stage, and players ride in circles as they operate the machines—and the merry-go-round bar on the midway, with actual carousel horses. Don't look for $100 blackjack games here; bets of more than $10 will raise eyebrows. Because the slots pay the bills, you'll see lots more slot machines than table games. Blackjack, crap, and roulette lessons are given every morning.

As you leave Circus Circus, you'll be handed a sheet of coupons for free popcorn, 50¢ hot dogs, 99¢ shrimp cocktails, free pulls of a slot machine, and a free gift (usually a key chain) at **Slots-A-Fun,** another noisy, smoky casino with lots of slots and $1 and $2 blackjack tables.

Sahara Las Vegas Hotel (2535 Las Vegas Blvd. S, tel. 702/737–2111). Fronted by the tallest freestanding neon sign in Las Vegas—222 feet by 18 feet—the Sahara retains the oasis theme it established when it opened in 1952, with statues of camels in the parking lot. It's one of the roomiest casinos in town, with slots on one side and table games on the other. A second section of table games on the north side of the casino takes on the overflow when the principal pit becomes too crowded. A middle-market hotel, the Sahara appeals to weekend slot and table game players, and minimums are in the middle range, with a few $2 tables. The slot club and frequent gambling promotions make the Sahara a popular place to play. Baccarat lessons are offered daily, and the baccarat commission is only 4%. The strains emanating from the open Casbar lounge, which hosted Shecky Green, Keely Smith, and Don Rickles in the 1950s, create a musical presence that surpasses the sounds of coins dropping from slots and pit bosses clicking for drinks.

Beyond the Strip

Vegas World Hotel and Casino (2000 Las Vegas Blvd. S, tel. 702/382–2000). This is without a doubt the most unique casino in town. A mannequin of an astronaut is suspended from the star-twinkling ceiling, floating alongside a Skylab replica and meteors that adorn the walls. Vegas World is Bob Stupak's place, and he won't let you forget it: His name and his picture are everywhere. A gambler who regularly shows up at poker tournaments, the author of a fascinating book on winning at craps from the point of view of a casino owner (autographed copies for sale in the gift shop), and the biggest sports-book winner in Las Vegas history ($1 million on the Super Bowl in 1989), Stupak is now in the process of building a tower more than 1,000 feet tall with a revolving restaurant on top. The casino's Big Six wheel is the largest in the world, nearly 25 feet across, so heavy that it takes a motor to spin it. One million dollars in cash is lined up in a large Plexiglas display in the casino; a million-dollar slot jackpot is offered to the player who lines up four 7s on the center line of a special million-dollar slot ($3 investment). Vegas World's location—beyond the Strip and short of downtown—is less than desirable, sort of in the middle of wedding chapel and motel row. As a result, Stupak goes to great lengths to attract customers. The casino has low table minimums and lots of slots, and coupons available around town (check the visitors centers) offer $50 in playing money free—$20 for keno, blackjack, and craps, $30 for slots. You must have out-of-state identification and pay a $2 registration fee to get the tokens, which are doled out in 45-minute increments over a two-and-a-half-hour period. While you're waiting for the funny money, feed the 9/7 and 10/6 video poker machines near the rear entrance; with perfect play, you're even with the house (*see* Chapter 2, Playing the Games).

Palace Station Hotel and Casino (2411 W. Sahara Ave., tel. 702/367–2411). Palace Station was originally the Bingo Palace, and it still has one of the most popular bingo rooms in town, but the theme has been updated (or backdated): railroads. Palace Station looks and feels like a big, smoky railroad station, with Pullman cars for restaurants and a depot for the lobby. This is a friendly, low-minimum casino whose only fault is that it's so popular with local gamblers that it can become too crowded for comfort's sake.

Rio Suites Hotel and Casino (3200 W. Flamingo Rd., tel. 702/252–7777). Rio Rita symbolizes the Brazilian theme of this popular off-Strip hotel, opened in 1990. Known for its vibrant Latin atmosphere and its remarkable buffet, the Rio is a favorite place for locals, as well as knowledgeable visitors, to gamble, eat, and party. The big neon sign out front wins the Best Sign honors annually, as do the cocktail waitress uniforms. The table minimums are affordable and the dealers are friendly. An interesting feature is TV monitors above video poker screens—if you get tired of dealing and drawing, simply look up to see "America's Funniest Home Videos" or "Mr. Ed."

Gold Coast Hotel and Casino (4000 W. Flamingo Rd., tel. 702/367–7111). Whenever you're at the airport and you see people losing money in the slots, think of the Gold Coast: This casino west of the Strip and west of Interstate 15 was built on airport slot losses. Popular with local gamblers, the Gold Coast shows up regularly in the *Las Vegas Review-Journal*'s reader polls for having some of the loosest slots in town. There's also a poker room, bingo parlor, race and sports book, 72-lane bowling center, and a movie theater. Like Palace Station (*see* above), the Gold Coast has low minimums, a friendly atmosphere, and considerable local crowds at times.

Downtown

Fremont Street is the place to come for low table minimums, food bargains, a motley streetlife, and the brightest and most colorful concentration of neon lights in the world. The downtown casinos have enough quarter craps, 50¢ roulette, $1 blackjack, and even penny video poker to accommodate Las Vegas's hordes of beginning and low-stakes players, tinhorns, and slummers. In keeping with downtown's original Old West motif, which prevailed from Las Vegas's founding in 1905 through the early 1960s, a pair of neon cowpokes, Vegas Vic and Sassy Sally, preside over Glitter Gulch (the core four blocks between Main and 4th on Fremont).

Plaza Hotel and Casino (1 Main St., tel. 702/386– 2110). Back in the 1920s, when cowboys rode their horses on Fremont Street and miners came to town to gamble and buy grub, the corner of Main and Fremont was anchored by the

Binion's Horseshoe
Hotel and Casino, **4**

California Hotel and
Casino, **2**

El Cortez Hotel, **11**

Fitzgerald Hotel and
Casino, **8**

Four Queens Hotel
and Casino, **6**

Fremont Hotel and
Casino, **7**

Gold Spike Hotel and
Casino, **10**

Golden Nugget Hotel
and Casino, **5**

Lady Luck Casino and
Hotel, **9**

Las Vegas Club Hotel
and Casino, **3**

Plaza Hotel and
Casino, **1**

Sam's Town Hotel and
Casino, **12**

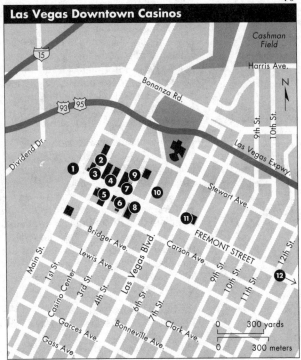

Las Vegas Downtown Casinos

railroad depot. It still is, but today that station has a 1,000-room hotel and giant casino around it. As a result, Amtrak passengers have it over those who fly into Las Vegas: The airport has only 25¢ to $1 slots, but the Plaza has low-minimum ($1 and $2) tables as well as a bank of eight 1¢ slots where the jackpots can reach $30,000.

California Hotel and Casino (12 E. Ogden Ave., tel. 702/385–1222). The California is a hotel that doesn't quite have its geography together. Given the name, you might expect a Gold Rush or sunny southern California theme, but instead you'll find that the motif is Hawaiian: All the dealers wear Hawaiian shirts, the carpet features tropical flowers, the snack bars serve Hawaiian dishes, and the customers are distinctly islanders: Aggressive marketing on the part of tour operators in the 50th state brings many Hawaiian tourists to this hotel. The casino has lots of $2 tables, 5¢ slots, and room in which to move around.

Las Vegas Club Hotel and Casino (18 E. Fremont St., tel. 702/385–1664). A lobby wall devoted to hall-of-fame memorabilia and dealers wearing baseball shirts announces the sports theme of the Las Vegas Club. The house rules for 21 purport to be the most liberal in town. You can double down on two, three, or four cards at any time; you can split and resplit aces and split and resplit any pair as often as you want; six cards totaling 21 or less wins automatically; and you may surrender your original hand (first two cards) for half the amount of your bet. All the blackjack games are four-deckers, making the Las Vegas Club the best multideck game in town. You'll need to be proficient in basic strategy, however, to take advantage of all these good rules. (*See* Chapter 2, Playing the Games.)

Binion's Horseshoe Hotel and Casino (128 E. Fremont St., tel. 702/382–1600). The Horseshoe is where serious gamblers come to play, the only house in town where you'll see a line of people waiting to get to a 21 table; it's also the only place with a pit that holds 10 crap tables, all crowded. Behind the hotel, by the parking garage, is a 15-foot statue of Horseshoe founder Benny Binion, wearing a Stetson and sitting on a horse. A former bootlegger, Binion came to Vegas from Texas in the 1950s, set up a respectable shop (though he served time on a tax-evasion charge in the 1950s), and built a joint boasting the highest table limits in the world. No entertainment, no fancy hotel rooms—just good cheap food and gambling. Benny never did come around to calling it "gaming," as most everybody else now does: "That's like calling a whorehouse a brothel." Binion died in 1989, and the Horseshoe is run by his son, Jack, and his daughter, Becky. In 1988 they bought their neighbor, the Mint, knocked a wall down, and the Horseshoe became an entire city block long and wide. It's still like two different establishments. On one side is the rustic, smoky, Wild West atmosphere of the original Horseshoe; on the other side, now the West Horseshoe, is a modern red casino. This is the home of the annual World Series of Poker in April, which has a $10,000 buy-in and a million dollar first prize. It is also the only place in Las Vegas where you can have your picture taken with $1 million in cash—a hundred gorgeous $10,000 bills. The Horseshoe will provide a complimentary photograph of you standing in front of all that money.

Golden Nugget Hotel and Casino (129 E. Fremont St., tel. 702/385–7111). This is the only major casino in Las Vegas that has no neon and the only one downtown that can truly be called elegant. The enormous Golden Nugget sign, a common subject of Las Vegas postcards and photographs for 30 years, was torn down as part of the upgrading done by Steve Wynn, who acquired the hotel in the 1970s. But there's enough glitter inside to compensate: gold-plated elevators, pay phones, slot machines—and the world's largest gold nugget. Weighing 63 pounds and valued at $1 million, it was discovered in Australia and now resides behind plate glass in the lobby. No longer the exclusive province of the well-heeled that it was when Wynn took it over, the Nugget today has become a luxurious grind joint: The 5¢ slots and $1 tables wouldn't have been found here in the days before the Mirage forced even its sister hotel to lower its sights. The high-roller blackjack tables in the baccarat pit have a minimum of a mere $10, even on a busy weekend night.

Four Queens Hotel and Casino (202 E. Fremont St., tel. 702/ 385–4011). You'll know you've found this casino when you walk along Fremont Street and come upon four painted playing cards in the pavement—four queens, in fact. The Queens Machine has been certified by Guinness as the world's largest slot: It's the size of a motor home, 18 feet long and seven feet high, and six people can play at one time. The players sit in chairs and invest dollar tokens from their consoles; then a slot attendant pulls the machine's handle. The goal is to get at least three of the eight reels (queen faces, cherries, lemons, etc.) to line up consecutively either from the right or left on the three pay lines. If all 24 symbols come up queens, it's a $300,000 jackpot. Free poker and slot classes are given daily.

Fremont Hotel and Casino (200 E. Fremont St., tel. 702/ 385–3232). Located in the heart of Glitter Gulch and adding immeasurably to the light show with its block-long neon facade, the Fremont has been a popular landmark since it opened in 1956. Now owned by the Boyd Group, the resort has undergone an extensive modernization over the past five years. The hotel also has one of the oldest and most respected race and sports books, which attracts a lot of gamblers, especially during football season. Wayne Newton made his debut in the lounge of this casino.

Fitzgerald Hotel and Casino (301 E. Fremont St., tel. 702/ 388–2400). This was the Sundance Hotel & Casino until a group of Reno businessmen who run a Fitzgerald up north bought it, painted it green, and renamed it. The Fitz calls itself the Luck Capital of Las Vegas: Its theme is the luck of the Irish, and leprechauns and four-leaf clovers are rampant. A lucky horseshoe from the Triple Crown winner, Secretariat, is in the Blarney Castle, and there's a wishing fountain, as well as "lucky" wishing steps. The Fitzgerald funbook always features a good free souvenir and $3 to $4 worth of gambling coupons. And the Fitz has an entire area of the second floor reserved for nonsmoking slot players. Twenty-one, craps, roulette, and Red Dog instruction is available daily.

Lady Luck Casino and Hotel (206 N. 3rd St., tel. 702/ 477– 3000). The Lady Luck, at 3rd and Ogden streets across from the Gold Spike, is a bit off the beaten track, but folks are drawn here by good dollar video poker machines: 9/6 with a 4,700-coin royal jackpot. Many professional tournament players come to the Lady's popular minitournaments—with $25 entry fees and $500 first prizes—to hone their skills for the major tournaments at places like the Riviera, Stardust, and Imperial Palace. The casino has a few $1 blackjack tables and areas for nonsmokers.

Gold Spike Hotel and Casino (400 E. Ogden Ave., tel. 702/ 384–8444). This small gambling hall, one block north of Fremont Street, is the sort of place you'd imagine might have lurked in the room behind a cigar or candy store in the old days. The blackjack table limits are the opposite of usual—$1 and $2 mostly, with a $5 here and there. The Spike features 5¢ video keno and poker machines, live 40¢ keno, and 10¢ roulette. But the casino's unique feature, in terms of both the game and the gamers, is the bank of penny video poker machines, jammed day and night with the hard core, the desperate, the addicted—in short, the downtown fringe. For a fistful of penny rolls you can join, if only for a few minutes, Las Vegas's looniest subculture.

El Cortez Hotel (600 E. Fremont St., tel. 702/385–5200). The oldest standing casino in Las Vegas, El Cortez opened for business on Fremont Street in 1941, when cowboys still rode up and down the street on horses. While the venerable sign out front proclaims GAMBLING/COFFEE SHOP/FLOOR SHOW, there are no more floor shows at El Cortez. (The last bona fide floor show in Las Vegas is believed to have been Donn Arden's dancers, at the Desert Inn in 1951.) The casino makes up in history what it lacks in charm. A newer wing (built in the mid-1980s) provides a grand contrast. The gambling-table minimums are low; food is as inexpensive as the portions are large.

Beyond Downtown

Sam's Town Hotel and Casino (5111 W. Boulder Hwy., tel. 702/456–7777). About five miles from downtown, on the route to the Hoover Dam, stands this monument to Las Vegas past. Sam's Town isn't a casino, it's a gambling hall; it doesn't have bars, it has saloons. Everything is larger than life here, the food is cheap, and the emphasis is on having a good-ol' down-home time, same as when the ranch hands came into town on a payday. Sam's Town is nickel slots, $1 tables, and crowds of locals. The California Hotel (*see* Downtown, *above*) offers free shuttle service to Sam's Town. Or you might stop in on your way out to Hoover Dam; Boulder Highway is much more picturesque than the freeway. If you're driving, just head out East Fremont Street, which turns into Boulder Highway; you'll be at Sam's Town, on the left-hand side of the road, in 10 minutes.

4 Exploring Las Vegas

The heart of Las Vegas is the Strip, the 3½-mile stretch of Las Vegas Boulevard South between Hacienda and Sahara avenues. The soul of Las Vegas is the downtown area north of the Strip, whose core is Fremont Street. By exploring these two areas, you'll experience both the commercial life-blood and pioneer spirit of this most flamboyant of American cities.

Tour 1 proceeds the length of the Strip, starting just south of Hacienda Avenue and taking in all the major hotels and casinos, two shopping malls, a museum, a water park, and other attractions. You can start from the beginning of this tour, or jump in at any point, at any hour of the day. But the earlier you set out, the fewer crowds and the less heat you'll have to contend with. The best time would be around 10 AM, after morning rush hour.

Tour 2 takes you to Fremont Street and honky-tonk downtown, with its hawkers and grinds, rock-bottom prices, and overwhelming neon facade. The best time to see Glitter Gulch is after dark; a few of the nearby attractions are better experienced in the daytime, perhaps in an afternoon.

It's easy to get around Las Vegas by car, even for those who are terrible with directions. Las Vegas Boulevard is the major thoroughfare. Most of the major east–west streets that cross the Strip portion of it are named for major hotels: Tropicana Avenue, Flamingo Road, Desert Inn Road, Sahara Avenue.

Although the 3½ miles from one end of the Strip to the other may not seem such a great stretch, when you add walking from the street to and around the hotels, especially the large ones, you can easily double that distance. Even a stroll "next door" from one enormous property to another may take 15 minutes. And if you're from a place with high humidity, you might not realize just how hot Las Vegas is and get dehydrated rather quickly. The Strip Trolley, which runs every 30 minutes, is the most convenient means of hotel-hopping, since it picks up and drops off passengers at the hotel front door. The local buses are more frequent, though less handy.

Driving the length of the Strip might take only five minutes on a Tuesday morning, but it could take 35 minutes at mid-afternoon or on a Friday or a Saturday night. The best way to use a car on these tours is to park and see the sights in sections. Caesars' garage is accessible to Mirage, Barbary Coast, Flamingo, Imperial Palace, Harrah's, and Sands, as well as to Caesars. You can leave your car in the Frontier parking lot to tour the Stardust, Silver City, Riviera, Circus Circus, Slots A Fun, and Westward Ho. Parking downtown is a snap in the lots or structures; it's also free if you validate your ticket at the casino cashier.

Highlights for First-time Visitors

Caesars Palace casino and shops (Tour 1: The Strip)
Circus Circus (Tour 1: The Strip)
The Mirage volcano, tigers, dolphins (Tour 1: The Strip)
Liberace Museum (*see* Museums and Galleries in Sight see-
ing Checklists, *below)*
Downtown Las Vegas at night (Tour 2: Downtown)
At least one Las Vegas show (*see* Chapter 9)

Tour 1: The Strip

*Numbers in the margin correspond with points of interest
on the Las Vegas Strip map. More details on the casinos
and hotels noted below are provided in Chapters 3 and 8,
respectively.*

At the southern end of Las Vegas Boulevard, two blocks
south of Hacienda Avenue, the WELCOME TO LAS VEGAS
sign, a familiar part of the landscape since the early 1950s,
makes a fitting start for a Las Vegas tour and a great photo
backdrop, especially at the beginning of a home-video record of your trip. Wait for an ebb in traffic: The sign is on an
island in the middle of the street.

Across the street are the big blue gates of the **Las Vegas Air
Charter Terminal** at the southwest corner of McCarran International Airport. The traffic here is that of charter
flights and fixed base operators, those who fly their own
planes into town.

Heading north on the boulevard, you'll see the Las Vegas
Tourist Bureau on your right. This is a good place to pick up
brochures, casino coupon promotions, and funbooks (good
for free souvenirs and shrimp cocktails, lucky bucks, 3-
for-2 coupons, etc.); you can also book hotel rooms here. Be
aware, however, that if you stop in, you're likely to be pres-
sured to sign up for a tour, and that a hefty service charge is
added to any show tickets you buy here; you're better off
dealing directly with the hotel that offers the entertainment. *5191 Las Vegas Blvd. S, tel. 702/739–1482. Open daily 8 AM–midnight.*

If you continue up the Strip about a mile to Reno Avenue,
you'll see the brand-new (opened October 1993) **Luxor Hotel,** a perfect pyramid with 2,500 rooms and a breathtaking
29-million cubic feet of enclosed space; right next door is
Luxor's sister hotel—both are owned by the Circus Circus
corporation—the pink-and-blue, turreted-and-towered,
4,032-room **Excalibur,** about to be deposed of its title of
largest resort hotel in the world when the MGM Grand (*see
below*) opens.

Across the Strip from Excalibur, sprawling at the southeast corner of Tropicana Avenue and Las Vegas Boulevard,
is the **Tropicana Resort and Casino,** featuring the "Island of

77

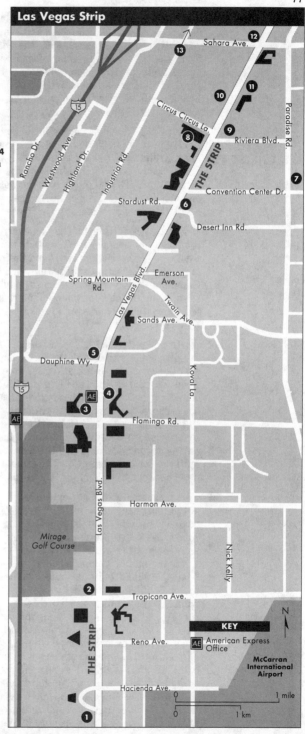

Bonanza, **12**
Caesars Palace, **3**
Candlelight Wedding Chapel, **9**
Circus Circus, **8**
FREE ASPIRIN AND TENDER SYMPATHY sign, **2**
Guardian Angel Cathedral, **6**
Guinness World of Records Museum, **10**
Imperial Palace Automobile Museum, **4**
Las Vegas Convention Center, **7**
The Mirage, **5**
Paul-Son Dice & Card Inc., **13**
WELCOME TO LAS VEGAS sign, **1**
Wet 'N Wild water park, **11**

Las Vegas," an oversize swimming pool within a simulated lagoon that has rock waterfalls and exotic fish, birds, and vegetation. In February 1994, the **MGM Grand**—with 5,009 rooms, a 171,000-square-foot casino, and a 33-acre movie-backlot theme amusement park—is due to open across Tropicana Avenue. When both the Luxor and the Grand are in service, this may well be the most magnetic tourist intersection in the country.

A photo that frequently accompanied magazine articles on Las Vegas in the 1950s showed a Strip gas station with a ❷ FREE ASPIRIN AND TENDER SYMPATHY sign. The sign still stands today, with an invitation on the other side: ASK US ANYTHING. You'll find the sign on the west side of the Strip, one block north of Tropicana Avenue, at the front of the Kenneth L. Lehman Strip Union 76 gas station.

About a block farther up the boulevard, on the east side, the large gold hotel with a magic lamp shining atop is—what else?—the **Aladdin Hotel and Casino.** In a small shopping center that adjoins the hotel, you'll find **Little Caesar's Gambling Casino,** one of the most popular sports books in town, an old-fashioned, smoke-filled room with no TV projection system or deli sandwiches, just wise guys (sports bettors, not gangsters) and hot dogs.

North of Little Caesar's is the Four Corners area of the Strip, named for the four large casino hotels that once ruled over the intersection of Las Vegas Boulevard and Flamingo Road. The **Dunes Hotel and Country Club,** closed since January 1993, held sway on the southwest corner; **Caesars Palace** occupies the northwest corner (plus more than half of the long block); **Bally's Casino Resort** stretches from the southeast corner its own city block to the east; and the **Flamingo Hilton and Tower** had the northeast corner covered until the small **Barbary Coast Hotel and Casino** interposed itself between the Flamingo Hilton and Flamingo Road.

❸ **Caesars Palace** (3570 Las Vegas Blvd. S, tel. 702/731–7110) is the must-see casino of Las Vegas. Caesars's designers have done the best job of transforming Bugsy Siegel's vision of Las Vegas into a reality: Walking into Caesars is like entering another world. The best way to approach the hotel is via the middle people mover, where a muscular guard bearing a shield and wearing ancient garb invites you into the $2.5 million domed World of Caesar. The moving sidewalk carries you on into a darkened rotunda with a miniature re-creation of ancient Rome that employs holography, fiber optics, and laser-powered audio effects; it then proceeds on into the monumental Olympic Casino. Now you're on your own. If you go right, you enter the Forum Shops, one of the most imaginative and upmarket malls in the country (*see* Chapter 5, Shopping, for details). Head to the left and you'll pass the old high-roller casino, the sumptuous buffet, the huge race and sports book, and the shopping area, overseen by a giant replica of Michelangelo's *David*.

Continue in this general direction and you'll run into Cleopatra, smiling down at you from the bow of her vessel, Cleopatra's Barge, where lounge musicians—and the dancing they inspire—get the boat rocking, literally.

East of the corner of Flamingo and the Strip, beyond the Barbary Coast, are two off-Strip casinos popular with local residents. **Bourbon Street Hotel and Casino** and **Maxim Hotel and Casino** offer lower table minimums, smaller crowds, and better gambling promotions than you'll find in the Strip casinos. The Flamingo Hilton's solution to the crowd-control problem in 1989 was to build another casino next door—**O'Sheas Casino,** with a Luck of the Irish theme.

The next stop north on the Strip, the Oriental-style **Imperial Palace Hotel and Casino** hosts the **Imperial Palace Automobile Museum,** a collection of more than 200 antique, classic, and special-interest vehicles displayed on an upper level of the hotel's parking garage. Among the cars, trucks, and motorcycles on view is a 1939 Mercedes touring sedan once owned by Adolf Hitler, said to be worth more than $600,000. In 1992, the museum opened the world's largest Deusenberg collection, comprising 25 vehicles built between 1925 and 1937. *3535 Las Vegas Blvd. S, tel. 702/731–3311. Admission: $6.95 adults, $3 children under 12 and senior citizens (Note: coupons for free admission are usually handed out in front of the hotel). Open daily 9:30 AM–11:30 PM.*

Harrah's showboat, adjoined by a small outdoor shopping arcade, is north of the Imperial Palace. One of Las Vegas's most popular spectacles, the gleaming, golden **Mirage** stands opposite the showboat on the west side of the boulevard. A towering, man-made waterfall, cascading over several levels into a giant pool, marks your entrance. Crowning the waterfall and stopping nighttime traffic along the Strip, a computer-driven volcano erupts every 30 minutes in a tower of flames. And the rare white tigers used in the Siegfried and Roy show guard the south entrance behind a Plexiglas enclosure.

Back on the east side of the Strip, beyond Harrah's Casino, the **Sands Hotel and Casino** was the locale in 1960 for the film *Ocean's 11*, with Frank Sinatra, Dean Martin, Sammy Davis Jr., Peter Lawford, and Joey Bishop.

The large building at the northwest corner of Spring Mountain Road and Las Vegas Boulevard is the **Fashion Show Mall,** a Strip shopping attraction that has more than 140 specialty shops and boutiques (*see* Chapter 5, Shopping, for details). The **Frontier Hotel and Gambling Hall,** north of the mall, was the second resort to open on the Strip (as the Last Frontier); these days, its lure is low minimums. Opposite the Frontier, on the east side of the boulevard, the **Desert Inn Hotel and Casino** is where the reclusive millionaire

Howard Hughes resided on the ninth floor; from Thanks-giving 1966 until December 1970, he never left his room.

❻ The busiest church in town, **Guardian Angel Cathedral** (302 E. Desert Inn Rd., tel. 702/735–5241), just east of the Strip, has standing room only on Saturday, as visitors pray for luck and drop casino chips in the collection cups during a special tourist mass. Once a week a priest takes the chips to Caesars Palace to cash them in. The 4 PM mass on Saturday is so crowded, usually with 300 standees, that visitors are asked to attend the 5:15 mass or one of the five Sunday masses instead.

Back on the west side of Las Vegas Boulevard, the **Stardust Hotel and Casino,** with one of the most impressive neon signs in Las Vegas, and, to the north, the **Westward Ho Motel and Casino,** a large motel with a small casino, are separated by the only McDonald's in America with a flashing neon sign. The window seats inside the restaurant provide a good view of the lights and the traffic on the Strip.

Opposite the Stardust, Convention Center Drive leads east from Las Vegas Boulevard to Paradise Road, where you'll see the now-closed **Landmark Hotel and Casino,** a large building in the shape of a spaceship. Just to the north, on the east side of Paradise Road, stands what was for many years the country's largest hotel, the **Las Vegas Hilton,** with 3,147 rooms. While other hotels have succeeded to the title, the Hilton is still immense by any standards. Go see for yourself by checking out the casino and the race and sports book, which has 46 video screens.

One of the most important aspects of Las Vegas's commer-cial life is its conventions, which account for about 15% of the visitor volume. More than 600 conventions of varying **❼** sizes are held here every year, most of them in the **Las Vegas Convention Center** (3150 Paradise Rd., tel. 702/892–0711). One of the most attractive aspects of the convention center is its proximity to all of the hotels and the airport.

If you head back to the Strip and continue up on the west side of Las Vegas Boulevard north of Convention Center **❽** Drive, you'll come to **Circus Circus,** the busiest casino in town. It's almost always a madhouse beneath this pink-and-white big top, and it may require an effort to deal with the traffic in getting here, but if you have kids, you will proba-bly want to visit. On the main floor are a mammoth casino, gift shops, a buffet, and a wedding chapel. The mezzanine boasts a midway with carnival games, funhouse mirrors, and free circus acts daily, 11 AM–midnight. Kids seem to prefer Circus Circus to any other Las Vegas casino experi-ence. The smaller casino out front, **Slots A Fun,** has the least expensive snack-bar food on the Strip, some of the lowest minimums, and—what else?—lotsa slots.

Back on the east side of the Strip, you'll find the smoke-free **Silver City,** a Circus Circus enterprise with lower minimum betting and smaller crowds than either the parent casino (or sister, Slots A Fun) across the street. Beyond it, the **Riviera Hotel** has an indoor fast-food court, along with three production shows and a comedy club, and the world's largest casino (until, of course, the MGM Grand opens).

❾ Just north of the Riviera, the **Candlelight Wedding Chapel** (2855 Las Vegas Blvd. S, tel. 702/735–4179) is the busiest place to get married in town. Especially on Saturday, you'll see couples lined up here, waiting to tie the knot. This is a convenient place to watch a Las Vegas wedding ceremony; just walk in and take a seat. Some ceremonies take place in the gazebo outside the chapel.

Adjacent to the chapel are another shopping minimall and **Trader Ann's Trading Post,** a good spot to buy tacky Las Vegas souvenirs at night; it's open until 1 AM.

Back on the west side of Las Vegas Boulevard and a short distance to the north, you'll find the **Guinness World of Records** ❿ **Museum,** with colorful displays, video footage, and computer data banks of the best, biggest, and most bizarre in sports, science, nature, entertainment, and more. *2780 Las Vegas Blvd. S, tel. 702/792–3766. Admission: $4.95 adults, $3.95 senior citizens and military, $2.95 children under 12. Open 9 AM–midnight.*

If you cross the Strip again, you'll come to the entrance of ⓫ the 26-acre **Wet 'N Wild water park,** which provides family-oriented recreation in a 500,000-gallon wave pool, three water flumes, a water roller coaster, slides, cascading fountains, and lagoons. Showers, changing rooms, and lockers are available, and inner tubes and rafts are for rent. Shops and concession stands sell souvenirs and food. *2601 Las Vegas Blvd. S, tel. 702/737–3819. Admission: $16.95 adults, $13.95 children 3–12. Open May–Oct., daily 10–8.*

Just to the north is the **Sahara Hotel,** where most people think the Strip ends; however, Vegas World (*see below*) is the final casino you'll encounter along Las Vegas Boulevard.

Those who are determined to visit only one gift shop in Las ⓬ Vegas will want to make it **Bonanza,** World's Largest Gift Shop, on the west side of the Strip opposite the Sahara. If it's not really the world's largest, it is the biggest and best in town, with an impressive collection of Las Vegas knick-knacks, gimcracks, and gewgaws (this is where you'll find your life-size Wayne Newton blow-up doll), the most extensive selection of Las Vegas T-shirts and postcards, along with jewelry, gambling supplies, western memorabilia, film, fudge, and aspirin. *2460 Las Vegas Blvd. S, tel. 702/ 385–7359. Open daily 8 AM–midnight.*

At Sahara Avenue, you've come to the end of the Strip and the last casino you'll want to see: **Vegas World Hotel and Casino,** on the west side of Las Vegas Boulevard, about a half

mile north of the avenue, has a Lost in Space theme—
strange planets float in the casino airspace, the space shuttle hangs in the buffet, and the interior light show is otherworldly in the extreme.

If by now you're beginning to think about chucking your
present job, moving to Las Vegas, and going to work as a
13 dealer, **Paul-Son Dice & Card Inc.** (2121 Industrial Rd.,tel.
702/598–1669) will teach you the ins and outs of the profes-
sion. Run by Geno Munari, a former executive at the Imperial Palace and Bourbon Street casinos who writes a
syndicated column on gambling, the school has four-week
and five-week courses on dealing blackjack, baccarat, roulette, and craps. Courses cost from $200 to $500, and there's
a job placement program for graduates. To find Paul-Son,
drive a few blocks north of Sahara Avenue on Industrial
Road, which runs parallel to Las Vegas Boulevard and is
about ½ mile west of it.

Tour 2: Downtown

*Numbers in the margin correspond with points of interest
on the Las Vegas Downtown map. More details on the casinos and hotels described below are provided in Chapters 3
and 8, respectively.*

Two miles from the northern end of the Strip at Sahara Avenue, Las Vegas Boulevard meets Fremont Street in downtown Las Vegas. One of the world's great collections of neon
signs is here, but it can only be appreciated after the sun
has gone down. Because the downtown hotels are almost on
top of each other, you're hit with a blast of bright lights
when you first turn the corner left from Las Vegas Boulevard onto Fremont Street at night. Las Vegas gambling began on Fremont in the 1930s, and the original honky-tonk
atmosphere remains. The 50-foot-tall neon cowboy (Vegas
Vic) and cowgirl (Sassy Sally), the street barkers and loud-
speakers, and the crowds of wide-eyed international tourists all lend a carnival atmosphere to the street.

To enter fully into the swing of downtown, don't be afraid to
get sucked in by the aggressive sidewalk solicitors. The
come-ons vary (spin the wheel, crack the safe, take the tokens), but the object is always the same: to hustle you inside and get you to feed the hungry slots. As long as you
don't succumb to the hard sell, start pulling out big bills,
and making sucker bets, you can enjoy whatever outra-
geousness is going on in the vicinity, take as much advantage as you can of the free or extremely inexpensive food
and drink, and bring home a special memory of the wacky
world of downtown Las Vegas.

Fremont Street runs east from Main Street, which is five
blocks west of, and runs parallel to, Las Vegas Boulevard.
At the corner of Main and Fremont, the **Plaza Hotel** houses
the Amtrak station and a casino. The heart of downtown

Las Vegas, called Glitter Gulch, is the four-block stretch of Fremont Street that begins at the Plaza. Up the block from the Plaza, on the north side of Fremont Street, is the neon cowgirl with sexy blue legs, **Sassy Sally,** one of the two famous neon images of downtown Las Vegas. Below Sally is the **Las Vegas Club Hotel and Casino,** with its sports theme and, like many downtown casinos, relatively low table minimums; unlike most other Fremont Street joints, it has a nice high ceiling. Across the street, atop the venerable Pioneer Club, is **Vegas Vic,** who's been waving to and welcoming visitors to downtown Las Vegas since 1951.

At 1st Street, you might walk a block north to Ogden Avenue to inspect the **California Hotel and Casino** (that's the one with the Hawaiian decor). The 100 block on Fremont Street finds the block-long **Binion's Horseshoe Hotel and Casino** on the north facing the **Golden Nugget Hotel and Casino** on the south. Binion's hosts the annual World Series of Poker, and people often wait in line for a place at a blackjack table; its old-time ambience—hardwood walls and dealers wearing string ties—is so convincing that you get the feeling Binion's has been here forever. The white-marble walls, gold-plated slots, and display of the world's largest gold nuggets of the upscale Golden Nugget put this casino in a radically different class from that of all the other downtown gambling halls.

In the next block east on Fremont Street, the **Fremont Hotel and Casino** on the north, with a photogenic neon sign outside and a bingo room inside, faces the **Four Queens Hotel and Casino** on the south; stop into the Queens to see the largest slot machine in the world.

A turn to the north on 3rd Street and a one-block walk to Ogden Avenue will take you to the crowded **Lady Luck Casino and Hotel,** which, with its big picture windows, is the brightest and airiest casino downtown. In the next block east on Ogden Avenue, the **Gold Spike Hotel and Casino** offers Las Vegas's lowest limits on everything—blackjack, keno, craps, and video poker.

In the 300 block of Fremont Street, across 3rd Street from the Four Queens, the 34-story **Fitzgerald's Hotel and Casino**—formerly the Sundance—is the tallest and greenest building in Nevada.

For a look at the other convention center in Las Vegas, which doubles as a sports facility, drive one mile north from Fremont Street on Las Vegas Boulevard. **Cashman Field** (850 Las Vegas Blvd. N, tel. 702/386–7100) has a 100,000-square-foot exhibit hall, 17,000 square feet of meeting space, and the 2,000-seat auditorium that was used as the courtroom for the trial of Wayne Newton's libel suit against NBC News.

Our last casino stop on Fremont Street, one block east of Las Vegas Boulevard between 6th and 7th streets, is the

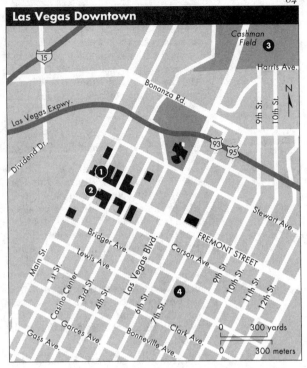

Las Vegas Downtown

city's oldest standing casino, **El Cortez Hotel,** which opened for business in 1941. Contrary to what it says on the sign out front, there are no more floor shows here.

4 A two-block stroll south on 7th Street to Bridger Avenue will take you miles from the honky-tonk of downtown and bring you to the everyday life of **Las Vegas High School** (315 S. 7th St.), the oldest permanent school building in Las Vegas. Built in 1930 for $350,000, the structure is a state historical landmark, the only example of 1930s Art Deco architecture in the city. Many Nevada officials are Las Vegas High graduates.

Las Vegas for Free

Circus acts at Circus Circus (Tour 1: The Strip).

Ethel M. Chocolates Factory and Cactus Garden. Self-guided tours introduce you to candy-making and a large variety of desert plants (*see* Chapter 5, Shopping, *below*). *2 Cactus Garden Dr., tel. 702/458–8864. Open daily 8:30AM–6PM. Closed major holidays.*

The **Festival Fountain** performance at the Forum Shops at Caesars.

Funbook souvenirs: Sands's mug, Circus Circus fanny pack, Fitzgerald wristwatch, Lady Luck key chain.

James R. Dickinson Library. The special-collections department of this library of the University of Nevada, Las Vegas, has the best gathering of materials about Las Vegas and gambling that you'll find anywhere. *4505 Maryland Pkwy., tel. 702/739-3285. Open Mon.-Thurs. 8 AM-midnight, Fri.-Sat. 9-6, Sun. 9-7.*

Popcorn at the Slots A Fun Casino (Tour 1: The Strip).

White tigers and the **volcano** at the Mirage (Tour 1: The Strip).

What to See and Do With Children

Las Vegas is focusing more and more on family entertainment. Amusement parks, dramatic spectacles, and G-rated theme hotels are sprouting up on the Strip faster than you can say, "Look out, Disney!" Grand Slam Canyon, Luxor, Treasure Island, MGM Grand, the Stratosphere Tower— for the first time ever in Las Vegas, all the new projects are targeting the growing family market. More and more production shows are offering performances suitable for youngsters. Bowling, midways, even ice-skating are growing in popularity. Arcades are expanding and feature the latest in video technology. And new museums now provide both educational and entertaining diversions for children.

Bonnie Springs Ranch. (Old Nevada, tel. 702/875-4191) is terrific for children (*see* Excursion 4, *below*).

Circus Circus's performances, midway, and video game room (Tour 1: The Strip).

Excalibur Hotel/Casino (3850 Las Vegas Blvd. S, tel. 702/597-7700). Excalibur's Medieval Village has shops, an open stage where jugglers, puppeteers, and magicians perform, and themed restaurants. Fantasy Faire is a carnival of games, Magic Motion Machine rides, and international gifts. Families enjoy live shows, King Arthur's Tournament.

Imperial Palace Automobile Museum (Tour 1: The Strip).

Las Vegas Museum of Natural History displays mammals from Alaska to Africa and has rooms full of sharks (including a 300-gallon aquarium), birds, dinosaur fossils, and hands-on exhibits. It also houses a big gift shop full of games, puzzles, books, clothes, and animals. *900 Las Vegas Blvd. N, tel. 702/384-3466. Admission: $5 adults; $4 senior citizens, military personnel, and students; $2.50 children 4-12; children under 4 free. Open daily 9-5.*

Lied Discovery Children's Museum. One of the largest children's museums in the nation, the Lied contains more than 100 hands-on exhibits geared toward kids in the sciences, arts, and humanities. Children can pilot a space shuttle, perform on stage, or stand in a giant bubble. *833 Las Vegas Blvd. N, tel. 702/382-5437. Admission: $5* *adults, $4 senior citizens and children 12–17, $3 children 3–11, children under 3 free. Open Tues. and Thurs.–Sat. 10–5, Wed. 10–7, Sun. noon–5.*

Omnimax Theater. The large-screen, 70mm movies shown in the round at the Caesars Palace cinema are the kind you'll see at major expositions and at the Smithsonian in Washington, D.C. Their subjects include such topics as rafting the Grand Canyon, surfing in Hawaii, and space exploration. *Caesars Palace, 3570 Las Vegas Blvd. S, tel. 702/731–7900. Admission: $4.50 adults, $3 children under 13. Shows daily, on the hour, Tues.– Thurs. 2–10 PM, weekends 1–11 PM.*

Scandia Family Fun Center. The center has three 18-hole miniature-golf courses, a video arcade, baseball batting, and the Li'l Indy Raceway for miniature-car racing. *2900 Sirius Ave., tel. 702/364–0070. Admission free; fee to play each game. Open Sun.–Thurs. 10 AM–11 PM, Fri.–Sat. 10 AM–midnight.*

Silver Safari takes kids under 12 on daylong excursions to points of interest including Wet 'N Wild, Old Nevada, Scandia Family Fun Center, Guinness World of Records Museum, and Omnimax Theater. Tours are fully supervised and include lunch and transportation. *Reserve through World Travel Center, 3661 S. Maryland Pkwy, Las Vegas, tel. 702/737–6680 or 800/245–0028. Cost: $43.50–$57.50, depending on length of tour and admission charged for attraction.*

At **Southern Nevada Zoological Park,** five minutes from downtown, the hot desert air helps keep a Bengal tiger, an Asian spotted leopard, and African green monkeys happy. Among other attractions are a large collection of exotic birds, a rare- and endangered-species breeding program, and a petting zoo with smaller animals. *1775 N. Rancho Dr., tel. 702/648–5955. Admission: $5 adults, $3 children 2–12. Open daily 9–5.*

The best **video arcades** are found at Bally's, Circus Circus, the Riviera, and downstairs at the Forum Shops at Caesars Palace (Tour 1: The Strip).

Wet 'N Wild water park (Tour 1: The Strip).

Youth Hotel (*see* "Traveling with Children" in Chapter 1).

Off the Beaten Track

Young Electric Sign Company (YESCO; 5119 Cameron St., tel. 702/876–8080). The headquarters of the company that has been taking advantage of Nevada's liberal sign regulations for 60 years is less than 2 miles west of the Strip. Its backyard is a bizarre yet picturesque "graveyard" of old neon signs. You probably won't get permission to rummage through them, but you can drive by and around the parking lot to get a good glimpse of a unique neon history. YESCO is on Cameron St., near the corner of Tropicana Avenue.

Sightseeing Checklists

These lists of Las Vegas's principal attractions include those that were covered in the preceding tours and others that are described here for the first time.

Historical Buildings and Sites

Golden Gate Hotel. Recently stripped of a facade that was installed over the original adobe in the mid-1950s, the building is now restored to its appearance in the early days of Las Vegas. The **Victory Hotel,** a block south on Main Street, was built in 1910 and retains the original balcony and veranda.

El Cortez casino wing (Tour 2: Downtown).

Las Vegas High School (Tour 2: Downtown).

Old Las Vegas Mormon Fort. Southern Nevada's oldest historical site was built by the Mormons in 1855 as an agricultural mission to give refuge to travelers along the Salt Lake–Los Angeles trail, many of whom were bound for the California gold fields. Left to the Indians after the gold rush, the adobe fort was later revitalized by a miner and his partners. In 1895 it was turned into a resort, and the city's first swimming pool was constructed by damming Las Vegas Creek. Today the restored fort contains more than half the original bricks; antiques and relics help re-create a turn-of-the-century Mormon living room. *Corner of Washington Ave. and Las Vegas Blvd. N, at Cashman Field (enter through parking lot B), tel. 702/486–3511. Admission: Free. Open Sat. and Sun. 8–4.*

Wedding Chapels

At the same time that "wide-open" gambling was legalized in 1931, Nevada also adopted liberal divorce and marriage laws as part of the strategy to attract tourists. A divorce could be obtained after six weeks of residency. A wedding could be arranged without a blood test or a waiting period; once you had a license, a justice of the peace could unite you in marital bliss in five minutes. The rules haven't changed for more than 60 years, and today weddings are big business in Las Vegas, to the tune of nearly $3 million in marriage licenses alone. New Year's Eve and Valentine's Day are the most popular wedding dates.

Celebrities (Bruce Willis, Bette Midler, Joan Collins, Michael Jordan, Richard Gere) have found it handy to pop into a chapel and have a quick ceremony. It's also a popular formula for nearly 80,000 couples a year from around the country. Critics complain that the 15-minute weddings have all the charm of an assembly line; proponents argue that, at a time when families can drive a couple crazy with expensive preparations and guilt-producing obligations, the bride- and groom-to-be can hop in a car and enjoy the experience by themselves.

Candlelight Wedding Chapel (2855 Las Vegas Blvd. S, tel. 702/735–4179), **Little Church of the West** (3960 Las Vegas Blvd. S, tel. 702/739–7971), and **Little White Chapel** (1301 Las Vegas Blvd. S, tel. 702/382–5943 or 800/545–8111) are the three most popular wedding chapels. All operate in ba- sically the same way: You make an appointment, show up, pay a fee for the ceremony (usually $50), and everything else (photos, music, flowers, videos) is extra. So is the sug- gested "donation" of $25 for the minister. Most chapels ac- cept credit cards but ask that the donation be paid in cash. Wedding ceremonies can also be performed in your hotel room, your car at the drive-up wedding window of L'Amour Chapel, in a hot-air balloon, or wherever your heart, your wallet, and your fiancé, desire.

Marriage **Clark County Marriage License Bureau** is the place to ob-
Licenses tain a marriage license, which costs $35. Both applicants must apply in person; those ages 16 to 18 need the consent of their parents or legal guardians. Blood tests are not re- quired, and there is no waiting period. *200 S. 3rd St., tel. 702/455–3156 or 702/455–4415 (after 5 PM, weekends, and holidays). Open Mon.–Thurs. 8 AM–midnight and from Fri. at 8 AM to Sun. at midnight.*

Throughout Vegas you'll see signs offering "free wedding information" services; what you'll get from them is what you've just read here—plus a sales pitch for whatever chap- el is paying that service a commission. If you have questions about Las Vegas weddings, call the chapels.

Museums and Galleries

Clark County Heritage Museum. Exhibits on settler life, early gambling, and nuclear testing are displayed in a chro- nological history of southern Nevada. Other attractions in- clude a fully restored bungalow home from the 1920s, built by a pioneer Las Vegas merchant; a replica of a 19th-centu- ry frontier print shop; and buildings, structures, and ma- chinery dating from the turn of the century. The gift shop sells Native American artifacts. *1830 S. Boulder Hwy., Henderson, tel. 702/455–7955. Admission: $1 adults, 50¢ children 6–15 and senior citizens. Open 9–4:30.*

Guinness World of Records Museum. Various Guinness world records (the most married man, the smallest woman, the largest snowplow, etc.) are brought to life in graphic exhibits, video and audio, and computer data banks. The Las Vegas display alone is worth the price of admission. *2780 Las Vegas Blvd. S, tel. 702/792–0640. Admission:*

$4.95 adults; $3.95 senior citizens, students, and military personnel. Open Fri.–Sun. 9 AM–11 PM, Mon.–Thurs. 9–9.

Imperial Palace Automobile Museum (Tour 1: The Strip).

Las Vegas Art Museum. Constructed in 1935 from railroad ties, the art museum has both a permanent collection and changing exhibitions of the work of local and national artists. *3333 W. Washington Blvd., tel. 702/647–4300. Admission free. Open Tues.–Sat. 10–3, Sun. noon–3.*

Las Vegas Museum of Natural History (*see* What to See and Do With Children, *above*).

Liberace Museum. Costumes, cars, photographs, even mannequins of the late entertainer make this museum the kitschiest place in town. In addition to Lee's collection of pianos (one of them was played by Chopin; another, a concert grand, was owned by George Gershwin), you can see his Czar Nicholas uniform and a blue-velvet cape styled after the coronation robes of King George V. Be sure to check out the gift shop—where else can you find Liberace soap, ashtrays, and other novelties? *1775 E. Tropicana Ave., tel. 702/798–5595. Admission: $6.50 adults, $4.50 senior citizens, $2 children under 12. Open Mon.–Sat. 10–5, Sun. 1–5.*

Nevada State Museum and Historical Society. Regional history from the time of the Spanish exploration and the building of Las Vegas after World War II are the big subjects in this museum of the history, archaeology, and anthropology of southern Nevada. Outdoors, the park and ponds that surround the lakeside museum in Lorenzi Park show plants and animals native to the region. *700 E. Twin Lakes Dr., tel. 702/486–5205. Admission: $1 adults. Open Mon.–Tues. 11:30–4:30, Wed.–Sun. 8:30–4:30.*

Photographing Las Vegas

Among the top 10 tourist destinations in the United States, Las Vegas is the only one whose major attractions discourage photography. At Disney World, the Grand Canyon, Washington D.C., or anywhere in California, your camera is as welcome as your kids. But walk into a Vegas casino with a camera hanging from your neck, and the security guard will give you stares. Start to pull off the lens cap, and the guard will tell you sternly, "No pictures in the casino."

"But I'm just taking a photo of my wife."

"No pictures in the casino. No exceptions."

The Nevada Gaming Control Board has issued hundreds of rules for Nevada casinos to follow, but picture taking isn't mentioned in any of them. (You can, in fact, take pictures in the Excalibur, California, and Four Queens casinos, but these are the only exceptions.)

The practice goes back to the 1940s and 1950s, when men who had been criminals outside Nevada for most of their lives were making the rules in Las Vegas. In New York, Miami, Chicago, most of them had always gone to great lengths to avoid being photographed, especially while gambling, which was illegal in every other state in the country. And even though it was legal in Nevada, their old habits and phobias died hard. Remember the scene at Don Corleone's daughter's wedding in *The Godfather,* when a photo is taken of one of the dons and he orders that the film be exposed and the camera broken?

Although gambling in Las Vegas no longer has a stigma attached to it, the current no-photo policy might be rationalized as follows: If a guy is sitting at a 21 table with a woman at his side who is not his wife, and a photograph is taken, the guy might get angry and leave. Or certain people who handle other peoples' funds—a banker, say, or politician—might feel that a photo could be (or at least look) incriminating. And others may simply not want folks to think they were dropping thousands of dollars in a casino.

There are consolations, however: Outside the casinos, Las Vegas is a great city to photograph, and for the most part, all you have to do is point and shoot. During the day, the desert light is sharp; at sunrise and sunset it's magical. At night Las Vegas is brighter than any other city in America. Subjects abound: the big picture, the small details, the people, the signs, the statues. And if you're a little crafty, you can always whip out a camera and shoot a casino. The worst that'll happen is you'll be 86ed.

Cameras and Film

An ordinary point-and-shoot camera will do fine, but if you have 35mm equipment and a wide-angle lens, your pictures will look even better. With so much to take in when shooting Las Vegas, the wide-angle (28mm or 35mm) really pays off by fitting as much as possible into the picture. When you're shooting video, you'll probably want to leave your lens set at the widest point of view and zoom in only for the occasional close-up.

If you're shooting color-print film (as most of us do), get the 100 ISO film; it's cheaper, and it offers the best color reproduction. I recommend Fuji film, which has sharper and more vibrant colors than Kodak's print film. In Las Vegas you won't have much need for high-speed film (400 or 1000 ISO) because most of your subjects will be outdoors, under the bright desert sun.

Those who want the best possible color will go for slide film. Fuji 50 produces hues so rich you won't believe it; the bright colors of Las Vegas will look surreal.

When you shoot neon signs at night, and when you shoot slides, the low-ISO films are a must. High-speed films dilute the colors and give you a bland photo. Signs will photograph best when you mount your camera on a tripod and make exposures of up to half a second. You can still get decent color prints of signs by using 100 ISO print film; the important thing to remember is not to shoot them at night. The best time is immediately after the sun has gone down, when the sky is still blue and a desert haze has fallen, leaving strands of reds and yellows in the sky. At that time, the neon signs have been turned on, giving you full-strength "signage" against a blue sky, which will be far more photogenic than a black sky. Take a look at any hotel's promotional brochures, and you'll notice that every one of the marquee pictures has been shot this way.

Shooting immediately after sunset is the best time for people pictures, too, because the light adds a nice warm tone to the skin. If you're shooting with a flash, you can easily light the person posed in front of the sign and not have to worry about the sign being overexposed.

All of the above applies to video as well. Just after sunset, you'll get the flickering of the signs against a blue rather than a black sky—and a much more pleasing picture. But keep in mind that these signs are very large; it'll take steady camera work to get everything into the frame. Rest the camcorder on your shoulder, not on your hand, take a deep breath, and move your body up and down to pan across the sign.

Subjects

Go downtown for the best neon photos; there's simply more neon here than anywhere else. At the corner of Fremont and Third, place your subject on the street during a red light, and you've got either the Fremont and the Horseshoe, or the Vegas Vic and Sassy Sally signs as backdrops.

Many of the neon signs on the Strip (Dunes, Circus Circus, Sahara) are so large that they are quite difficult to photograph. The manageable ones are those of the Stardust and the Flamingo Hilton.

Overhead shots of the Strip are pretty easy to get. Most hotels have hallways with picture windows overlooking the Strip; all you need to do is to take an elevator to the floor of your choice, aim your camera out the window, and shoot.

How about a photo of your subject out in the desert with all the big hotels of Vegas in the background? It's easy: Drive south on the Strip toward the Hacienda. About a block before you get there, on your right, you'll see a dirt road with no sign. Turn down it, heading west. At the end of the road, pull over, and you'll have a perfect view of the middle of nowhere—and a big city rising out of the sand. This photo should also be taken just after sundown, with the light still on the sand and the colorful signs in the background. It's a good location for both still and video photography.

Excursions from Las Vegas

If the city of Las Vegas lacks in variety, the number of man-made and natural scenic wonders a short drive away more than makes up for it. The price categories of hotels and restaurants mentioned in the excursion tours are those used in the Reno section of Chapter 10.

Excursion 1: Hoover Dam and Lake Mead

Numbers in the margin correspond with points of interest on the Excursions from Las Vegas map.

Boulder City, the enormous Hoover Dam, and Lake Mead to the north of it are where most day-trippers head first.

On leaving Las Vegas, follow Boulder Highway (U.S. 93/95) through the Las Vegas suburbs, city of Henderson, and desert terrain for 23 miles to reach **Boulder City.** In the early 1930s, this town was built by the federal government to house 5,000 construction workers on the Hoover Dam project. A strict moral code was enforced, and to this day, the 60-year-old model city is the only community in Nevada where gambling is illegal. After the dam was completed, the town shrunk by more than half, kept alive by the management and maintenance crews of the dam and Lake Mead. But Boulder City slowly recovered, and is now a vibrant little Southwest town with a movie theater, numerous gift shops, and a historic hotel. The **Boulder City Chamber of Commerce** (tel. 702/293–2034) is a good source of information.

Continue east on U.S. 93 about 11 miles to reach the site of **Hoover Dam.** Congress authorized the funding of the $175 million dam in 1928 for two purposes: flood control and the generation of electricity. One of the seven man-made wonders of the world, the dam is 727 feet high (the equivalent of a 70-story building) and 660 feet thick (greater in width than two football fields). Construction of the dam required 4.4 million cubic yards of concrete—enough to build a two-lane highway from San Francisco to New York. Originally called Boulder Dam, the structure was renamed for Herbert Hoover, Secretary of Commerce during the critical planning stages of the dam. More than 700,000 people a year (29 million since the tours began in 1937) take the Bureau of Reclamation's one-hour guided tour, which leads visitors deep inside the structure for a look at its inner workings. Tours leave every few minutes from the exhibit building at the top of the dam. *Hwy. 93 east of Boulder City, tel. 702/293–8367. Admission: $2 adults, $1 senior citizens. Tours daily 8–6:30.*

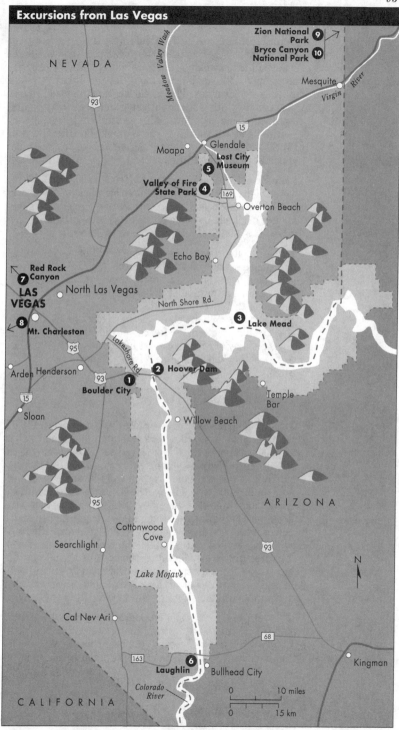

❸ For the approach to **Lake Mead,** return west on U.S. 93 about 6 miles to the intersection with Lakeshore Drive. Here the **Alan Bible Visitor Center** (tel. 702/293–8906) can provide information on the history of the lake and on the accommodations available along its shore. Lake Mead's surface covers 229 square miles and its irregular shoreline extends for 550 miles. This is the largest man-made lake in the country, with Colorado River water backed up behind the dam. Come here for fishing, waterskiing, swimming, boating, and sailboarding. The **National Park Service** (tel. 702/293–8906) can give you details on the lake's recreational opportunities and facilities.

Lake Mead Cruises (Lake Mead Marina, tel. 702/293–6180) has a 250-passenger stern-wheeler that plies the lower portion of the lake; breakfast, cocktails, and dinner with dancing are available on some of the cruises. *Cost: $12–$32.50 adults, $5–$10.50 children 3–12, under 3 free.*

A five-minute drive along the shore will bring you to the first marina, **Lake Mead Marina** (tel. 702/293–3484). Here you'll find boat rentals, a beach, camping facilities, a gift shop, and a restaurant. A drive of about an hour will take you along the north side of the lake, where you'll find five more marinas. When you reach the upper arm of the lake, about a mile past Overton Beach, look for the sign announcing the Valley of Fire. Turn left here, and go about 6 miles to reach the **Valley of Fire Visitor Center** (tel. 702/397–2088).

Excursion 2: Valley of Fire

❹ The 56,000-acre **Valley of Fire State Park,** dedicated in 1935, was Nevada's first state park, situated less than 2 miles west of the upper arm of Lake Mead and 55 miles northeast of Las Vegas. The Valley of Fire takes its name from its distinctive coloration, which ranges from lavender to tangerine to bright red, giving the valley an otherworldly appearance. Here the incredible rock formations that have been weathered into unusual shapes suggest elephants, domes, beehives. Mysterious signs and symbols, called petroglyphs (carvings etched into the rock) and pictographs (pictures drawn or painted on the rock's surface), are believed to be the work of the Basketmaker and Anasazi Pueblo people, who lived along the nearby Muddy River between 300 BC and AD 1150.

The visitor center has exhibits, films, lectures, slide shows, and information about the 50 campsites within the park. The park is open year-round; the best times to visit, especially during the heat of the summer, are sunrise and sunset, when the light is especially spectacular. *Hwy. 169, Overton, 89040, tel. 702/397–2088. Visitor center open daily 8:30–4:30.*

⑤ To visit the **Lost City Museum,** head east from the Valley of Fire on South Highway 169 for about 8 miles. Turn left at the "T" and continue for another 8 miles to the museum. Here you'll find on display early Pueblo Indian artifacts, Paiute basketry, weapons, and a restored Basketmaker pit house. *721 S. Hwy. 169, tel. 702/397–2193. Admission: $1 adults. Open daily 8:30–4:30.*

Excursion 3: Laughlin, Nevada

For those who'd like to see a chunk of southern Nevada and the Mojave Desert and still have a major gambling center as **⑥** a destination—on a river no less—**Laughlin,** Nevada, is the place. From Las Vegas, take Boulder Highway (U.S. 95/93) east, and follow U.S. 95 south almost to the California border. There, a left turn onto Highway 163 will take you east into Laughlin. It's 90 miles away and should take no more than an hour and a half to reach.

Laughlin is a classic state-line city, separated from Arizona by the Colorado River. Nevada's newest community, Laughlin has become the state's third major resort area, with 10,500 rooms added in the past 10 years. The city generally attracts older, mostly retired travelers who spend at least part of the winter in Arizona. Like Las Vegas, Laughlin draws folks who like to gamble—especially those who prefer low-pressure, low-minimum tables, cheap food, low-cost rooms, and slots galore.

If you've been shuttered in Las Vegas casinos for a few days, you'll be amazed by the big picture windows overlooking the Colorado River and the bright, airy, and open feeling that they lend to the Laughlin joints. The dealers are generally friendlier and the bettors more relaxed than in Las Vegas.

A turn to the south off Highway 163 onto Casino Drive will take you to the gambling halls: **Riverside Resort** (1650 S. Casino Dr., tel. 702/298–2535 or 800/227–3849), **Regency Casino** (1950 S. Casino Dr., tel. 702/298–2439), **Edgewater** (2020 S. Casino Dr., tel. 702/298–2453), **Colorado Belle** (2100 S. Casino Dr., tel. 702/298–4000), **Golden Nugget** (2300 S. Casino Dr., tel. 702/298–7111 or 800/ 237–1739), **Pioneer Hotel** (2200 S. Casino Dr., tel. 702/ 298–2442 or 800/634–3469), **Ramada Express** (2121 S. Casino Dr., tel. 702/298–4200 or 800/2–RAMADA), **Gold River** (2700 S. Casino Dr., tel. 702/ 298– 2242 or 800/835–7903), and **Flamingo Hilton** (1900 S. Casino Dr., tel. 702/298–5111 or 800/HILTONS).

The **Laughlin Chamber of Commerce** (tel. 702/298–2214 or 800/227–5245) can provide further information on the area.

Excursion 4: Red Rock Canyon and Old Nevada

For a 13-mile drive through the red rock formations and unusual high-desert scenery of southern Nevada, head west

(about 16 miles) from Las Vegas on Charleston Boulevard to
Red Rock Canyon and its scenic loop. The BLM Visitor Center here has exhibits of plant, animal, and desert life. *Charleston Blvd., tel. 702/363–1921. Open daily 9–4. Loop open daily during daylight hours.*

Leave the loop by exiting south onto Highway 159 (Charleston Blvd.), and go 3 miles to **Spring Mountain Ranch State Park.** This prime piece of property became a ranch in the 1860s; it was designated a state park in 1971. The red ranch house, white picket fences, long green lawns, and beautiful mountain backdrop make this a perfect place for a picnic. *Hwy. 159, tel. 702/875–4141. Admission: $3 per car. Open daily 8–7. Ranch house open Fri. and Mon. 12–4, Sat. and Sun. 10–4.*

Continue another mile on Highway 59 until you come to **Old Nevada,** a western theme park. Here the Wild West comes to life with gunfights and hangings staged in the street, silent movies, an opera house, museums, a cemetery, and a mini-train that runs around the grounds. *Hwy. 160, tel. 702/875–4191. Admission: $6.50 adults, $5.50 senior citizens, $4 children 5–11, under 5 free. Open daily 10:30–6.*

After shopping for gifts or souvenirs at Old Nevada, most folks mosey next door to the **Bonnie Springs Ranch,** which offers a duck pond, petting zoo where kids can feed baby lambs or stroke a buffalo, and small railroad that runs on weekends. Equestrians can rent horses from the ranch's large stable; guided trail rides go through the desert past cacti, yucca, and Joshua trees. The **Bonnie Springs Motel** here has rooms for overnight stays. *1 Gun Fighter La., tel. 702/875–4400. 50 rooms. Facilities: swimming pool, some rooms with Jacuzzi, theme rooms. AE, MC, V. Moderate*

Excursion 5: Mt. Charleston, Kyle and Lee Canyons

For a mountain retreat, head northwest from Las Vegas on Highway 95 about 45 miles to **Mt. Charleston,** the fifth-highest mountain in the state. At Highway 157, turn off to Kyle Canyon. In winter this area is a local skiing haven; in summer it's a welcome respite from the 115°F desert heat, as well as a place to hike, picnic, and camp. For camping information, contact the **U.S. Forest Service** (tel. 702/873–8800).

For overnight accommodations, try the **Mount Charleston Hotel.** *2 Kyle Canyon Rd., tel. 702/872–5500. 60 rooms, 3 suites. Facilities: restaurant, lounge, gift shop. AE, DC, MC, V. Expensive–Very Expensive.*

About 4 miles away, the **Mount Charleston Restaurant and Lounge** offers hot food in typical mountainside fashion, with a wood fireplace and picture windows looking onto the mountains. The restaurant also has a full assortment of video slots, and Bummkopps, a German polka band, performs in the lounge on weekends and holidays. *1 Old Park Rd., tel. 702/386–6899 or 800/955–1314. Dress: Informal. Reservations not necessary. AE, D, DC, MC, V. Expensive.*

On leaving Mount Charleston, return to Highway 157, and drive about ½ mile to exit 156. Turn left to Lee Canyon (tel. 702/872–5462 information; 702/646–3805 snow conditions), where the wintertime skiing lasts from November to early March and the 9,000-foot elevation offers a peaceful view all year round.

Excursion 6: St. George, Zion National Park, Bryce Canyon

From the neon jungle of Las Vegas, it's a journey of 116 miles north on Interstate 15 to the small, picturesque town of St. George, Utah. In getting here, you'll pass through Mesquite, one of Nevada's newest and smallest cities, whose 720-room Peppermill resort has a golf course just across the state line in Arizona.

In **St. George** you'll find an assortment of low-priced motels, bed-and-breakfast inns, an old movie theater and a new Twinplex, souvenir shops, a variety of restaurants, Mormon historical sites, and red rocks. On a wintertime visit, you might encounter snow, and in summer you can expect to find temperatures cooler than those in Las Vegas. An evening in St. George can be spent exploring the Victorian-style streets, climbing the red-rock cliffs, or looking out over the town.

Yet the red rocks of St. George are only a preview of the ❾ miles of rich redness to be seen at **Zion National Park,** about 30 miles to the northeast. Follow I–15 to the first Hurricane exit, which will take you through the small town of that name. Driving up the mountain, you'll see signs directing you into the 6-mile park drive among mammoth red rocks. The Mormons believed they had found God's country when they discovered the area now called Zion National Park in 1863. In addition to giving the area its name, they christened the park's major rock formations: *Great White Throne, Angel's Landing, Cathedral Mount, Three Patriarchs,* and *Pulpit.* The elevation ranges from 3,600 feet to 8,700 feet—higher than the North Rim of the Grand Canyon. Many of the park trails are wheelchair accessible; others are narrow climbs with sheer drops that would be difficult treks for small children. *Superintendent, Zion National Park, Rte. 9, Springdale 84767, tel. 801/772–3256. Admission: $5 per vehicle for a 7-day pass. Visitor centers open 8–5 in winter, as late as 9 in summer.*

Two hundred rooms (in both rustic cottages and motel units) in the park are available year-round through the **Zion Canyon Lodge TW Services Inc.** (Box 400, Cedar City, UT 84721, tel. 801/586–7686). You might also try the nearby,

47-room **Best Western Driftwood Lodge** (Rte. 9, Utah Hwy.
9, Springdale, UT 84767, tel. 801/ 772–3262 or 800/528–
1234).

⑩ To reach **Bryce Canyon National Park** and what may seem
like the prehistoric world of the Flintstones, continue east
on Highway 9 to Highway 89, and turn north. Drive about
40 miles to Route 12, turn east, and another 17 miles will
bring you into the park. As at Zion, red is a dominant color
here, but brilliant, iridescent hues of buff and tan also appear on the fantastically shaped rocks—resembling spires,
cathedrals, goblins—sculpted by the waters and weather of
several million years. Most of the activity at Bryce occurs
below the trail entrances, at the foot of the canyons. The
park's hiking trails can be explored in wintertime on snow-
shoes or cross-country skis. *Bryce Canyon National Park,
Bryce Canyon, UT 84717, tel. 801/834–5322. Admission:
$5 per vehicle for a 7-day pass.*

Although there is a 110-room lodge at Bryce (make reservations through Zion Canyon Lodge TW Services Inc.,
above), open from mid-May to October, many visitors like
to stay at **Best Western Ruby's Inn,** 2 miles from the main
entrance. Ruby's, open all year, has basic motel rooms and
rates that drop significantly beginning in October. *Hwy.
63, Bryce, UT 84764, tel. 801/834–5341 or 800/528–1234.
216 rooms. Facilities: restaurant, indoor pool, general
store, campground. AE, DC, MC, V. Inexpensive–Moderate.*

Other accommodations near Bryce are few. Some motel
rooms can be found in Panguitch, 25 miles to the north on
Highway 89, and in Tropic, 7 miles to the east on Route 12.

5 Shopping

Where you shop in Las Vegas will depend more on how much you want to spend—and how far you want to drive—than on what you're looking for. If you don't mind dispensing lots of money in high-rent districts, simply shop in your hotel promenade or at the Strip gift shops and shopping malls. Those not averse to doing a bit of driving might find some of the same high-ticket items at lower prices at one of the town's new factory outlet malls. And those looking for more practical items or for an excuse to drive around the greater metro area can head for the neighborhood malls, supermarkets, shopping centers, and specialty stores.

Major Shopping Districts and Malls

The Strip The Strip is a giant shopping mall in and of itself. Here you will find two large indoor malls, as well as rows and rows of gift shops that sell Las Vegas souvenirs and sundries. Many of the hotels on the Strip have exclusive shops that sell expensive dresses, swimsuits, jewelry, and men's wear. For example, Bally's has a 40-store promenade where you can buy men's and women's high fashions, jewelry, art, and gifts. And, in addition to the adjoining Forum Shops, Caesars has the Appian Way shopping area, which features such toney retailers as Cartier, Ungaro, Ted Lapidus, and Ciro.

Las Vegas's only major shopping mall in a casino resort, the **Forum Shops at Caesars** (3570 Las Vegas Blvd. S, tel. 702/893–4800), opened in 1992, has elevated the mall to high art—or kitsch, depending on how you see it. The 70-store complex resembles an ancient Roman streetscape, replete with immense columns and arches, two central piazzas with fountains, and a cloud-filled, domed ceiling displaying a sky that changes from sunrise to sunset in the course of three hours (perhaps inspiring shoppers to step up their pace of acquisition when it looks as if time is running out). The Festival Fountain (in the west wing of the mall) puts on its own show: A robotic, pie-eyed Bacchus hosts a party for friends Apollo, Venus, and Mars, complete with lasers, music, and sound effects; at the end, the god of wine and merriment gives a sales pitch for the mall. If you can tear yourself away from the electronic wizardry, you'll find both familiar and unusual shops: Ann Taylor, Victoria's Secret, Louis Vuitton, Guess, and Gucci, along with a Warner Bros. Studio Store, where Daffy Duck and others are decked out in gladiator outlets, and a Caesars outlet selling everything from perfume to leather jackets that may bear a Caesars logo. This is also one of the city's best dining destinations: There's a branch of Wolfgang Puck's Spago (every bit as good as the original), an attractive Italian eatery, Lombardi's (*see* Chapter 7, Dining), with great gelato, and the Apsen-based Boogie's Diner (purveying casual clothes and overpriced soda fountain fare), as well as Swensen's, Carnegie Deli, and The Palm. Visitors can glide into the Fo-

Las Vegas Shopping

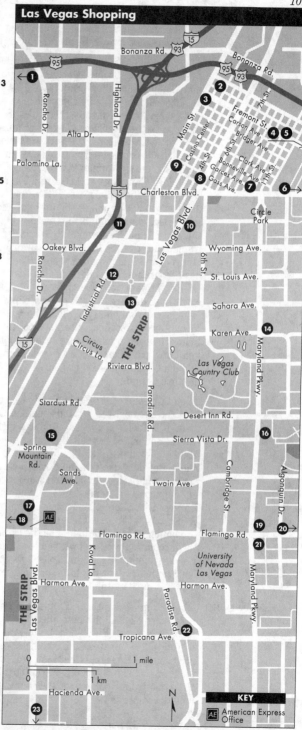

KEY

AE American Express Office

rum from the Strip on a moving sidewalk, but must exit through the Caesars Palace casino. If you try to defeat the one-way people mover, flesh-and-blood guards will quickly change your mind.

Even though it's twice as large as Caesars retail fantasyland, The **Fashion Show Mall** (3200 Las Vegas Blvd. S, tel. 702/369–8382) is tame by comparison. Centrally located on Las Vegas Boulevard across the street from the Desert Inn and next to the Frontier, it's hard to miss, and thus always crowded with visitors. It's very well kept, and not all the stores are overpriced. The two-story building contains 140 shops, including Neiman Marcus, Saks Fifth Avenue, Bullock's, May Company, and Dillards. There are also designer boutiques, Abercrombie & Fitch, and Lillie Rubin (she's the designer who makes clothes for Mary Hart of TV's "Entertainment Tonight"). One unusual mall inhabitant, the American Museum of Historical Documents, offers framed autographed letters of Abraham Lincoln, Marilyn Monroe, and other famous people. The mall's fun food court has everything from hot dogs on a stick to Herbie Burgers; Chin's Chinese restaurant (*see* Chapter 7, Dining) offers more upscale fare. If you're in a panic about last-minute gifts, you'll find plenty of places here to buy expensive Las Vegas souvenirs; this is also the place for those who want to bring the casino experience into their homes to buy such gambling paraphernalia as gaming tables, playing cards, and dice. Waldenbooks, the only bookstore on the Strip, is also in this mall.

The other side of the Strip couldn't be more different. Inside the casinos, the gifts are elegant and expensive; outside, it's Tacky City. The endless gift shops along Las Vegas Boulevard all sell the same dice clocks, inflatable Wayne Newton dolls, jack and queen playing-card earrings, decks of used casino cards, Vegas belt buckles, key chains, and bath towels. Some stores are so schlocky you'll be embarrassed you stepped inside. **Bonanza "World's Largest Gift Shop"** (2460 Las Vegas Blvd. S, tel. 702/385–7359), across the street from the Sahara Hotel, is the best of the bunch. It may not in fact be the *world's* largest, but it is the largest in town, and while it has some of the usual junk, it sells some unusual junk, too. It's so huge that you won't feel trapped, as you might in some of the smaller shops. And it's open until midnight.

Factory Outlet Stores About 5 miles south of Tropicana Avenue on Las Vegas Boulevard South, the half-filled **Las Vegas Factory Stores** (9155 Las Vegas Blvd. S, tel. 702/897–9090) have already begun to lure inveterate bargain seekers to such stores as Mikasa, Van Heusen, Nine West, No Nonsense, and Aldolfo II. Signs on the way to these outlets also promise more of the same from Belz, one of the country's largest discount-mall developers.

Maryland One mile east of the Strip and parallel to Las Vegas Boule-
Parkway vard, Maryland Parkway is the major shopping district for
Las Vegas locals, with scores of fast-food outlets and stores
catering to mall goers. You'll see places to shop all along
this thoroughfare, but **Boulevard Mall** (3528 Maryland
Pkwy., tel. 702/735–8268) has the greatest single concentration of retailers. Less expensive than its counterparts on
the Strip, Boulevard Mall boasts 140 stores, anchored by
the Broadway, Sears, Dillards, and J.C. Penney department stores; smaller shops include Wet Seal, Express, Nature Company, Casual Corner, Harris & Frank, the Disney
Store, and Sweet Factory.

The Meadows The other major Vegas mall, **The Meadows** (4300 Meadows
Ln., tel. 702/878–4849), is located in a residential district
west of downtown. The Meadows has more than 140 specialty stores in addition to the Broadway, Dillards, Sears, and
J. C. Penney department stores.

Specialty Stores

Books **Traveling Books and Maps** (4001 S. Decatur, tel. 702/871–
8082) is a new and attractive store that stocks Las Vegas's
largest selection of guidebooks and maps, along with
globes, traveling jackets, travel accessories, and more. The
Southwest section is particularly comprehensive. Owner
Jerry Netzky is an enthusiastic world traveler (his staff has
been around, too), and can recommend the right book for
the right destination.

Casino Clothes If you've caught the gambling spirit and want to go home in
a white shirt, black pants, and a big red bow tie, two stores
will be happy to sell you dealer's duds: **Dealers Room Casino
Clothiers** (3661 Maryland Pkwy. S, tel. 702/732–3932) and
Casino Clothiers of Nevada (2560 Maryland Pkwy. S, tel.
702/732–0449).

Chocolates **Ethel M. Chocolates Factory and Cactus Garden** (2 Cactus
Garden Dr., Henderson, about 20 minutes southeast of Las
Vegas, tel. 702/458–8864; branches in most hotels). The
Mars family runs an operation in Nevada that isn't allowed
elsewhere in the country: They're permitted to make chocolates containing liqueurs. This is the family—headed by
Ethel in the early days—that brought us Snickers, Milky
Way, Mars bars, Three Musketeers, and M&Ms. More than
1,000 people come each day to watch the candy-making at
this fancy chocolate factory; free samples inspire almost all
to make purchases in the adjoining shop. An adjacent cactus garden contains 2.5 acres planted with more than 350
species of succulents and desert plants that are particularly
colorful when they flower in spring. The factory is closed
New Year's Day, Easter, Thanksgiving, and Christmas.

Film Don't buy your film on the Strip or at the gift shops if you
can help it; their prices are markups of the retail prices at
Union Premiums (1325 E. Flamingo Rd., tel. 702/737–

1717). This is also a good place to shop for camera, video, and audio equipment.

Food **Lucky** (1300 E. Flamingo Rd., in the Mission Shopping Center, tel. 702/733–2947). You might laugh, but just try finding an apple, an orange, a banana, or a box of Special K on the Strip. Lucky is the closest food store, and it's open 24 hours.

Gambling You won't find a better place than Las Vegas to stock up on
Memorabilia gambling books, cards, dice, green felt, and anything else of a gaming nature you might require.

Gambler's Book Club (630 S. 11th St., tel. 702/382–7555 or 800/634–6243) has the best collection of current and out-of-print books about twenty-one, craps, poker, roulette, and all the other games, as well as novels about gambling and crime figures and anything else that relates to gambling and Las Vegas.

Gamblers General Store (800 S. Main St., tel. 702/382–9903) sells all the gambling books, and also offers poker chips, green-felt layouts, slot and video poker machines—just about every item of gambling paraphernalia that you could imagine. It's eight blocks south of the Plaza Hotel on Main Street.

House of Antique Slots (1243 Las Vegas Blvd. S, tel. 702/382–1520). If taking home a classic slot machine would make your trip to Las Vegas complete, you might want to stop in this shop, down the street from the Little White Chapel. But be warned: Old slots can be very expensive, with prices in the $2,000–$5,000 range, and in-home slots are legal in only 40 states. The proprietors will let you know if they are legal where you live.

Paul-Son Dice & Card Inc. (2121 Industrial Rd., tel. 702/384–2425). Want to take home some authentic casino dice and chips? This downtown store, affiliated with a school for aspiring casino professionals (*see* Chapter 4, Tour 1), is a major supplier to the casinos.

Lucky Charms **Bell, Book and Candle** (1725 E. Charleston St., tel. 702/384–6807) is one of the most unusual shops in town, featuring a large selection of intriguing spiritual and metaphysical symbols of luck, from fast-money potions for quick casino kills to quartz crystals for power, prosperity, and romantic success. A trip to BB&C will increase your appreciation for the myriad ways that are available to propitiate the great goddess of luck—a widespread activity in this town.

Pawn Shops Las Vegas is a great place to pick up cheap guitars, watches, and cameras pawned by local residents who couldn't pay their gambling debts—or who got the urge to drop more money at the casinos and needed a little extra cash. All are located in the heart of downtown: **Ace Loan Company** (26 E. Fremont St., tel. 702/384–5771), **Stoney's Loan and Jewelry** (126 S. 1st St., tel. 702/384–2686), and **The Hock Shop Ltd.** (808 Las Vegas Blvd. S, tel. 702/384–3042).

Sporting Goods **Las Vegas Discount Golf** (4813 Paradise Rd., tel. 702/798–6300) has a large selection of golf equipment and clothing.

Video Las Vegas may very well be the VCR capital of the world, largely because so many residents work nights and don't want to miss prime-time television. The video stores, most of which are open 24 hours, are large and well stocked.
Video Park (3230 E. Flamingo Rd., tel. 702/451–4518) bills itself as "the world's largest video store!" and whether it is or not, it's not to be missed. When the Video Software Dealers Association meets here every year, most delegates make a trip to Video Park just for the experience. Each video genre is displayed in its own theatrical setting. To reach the horror section, for example, you have to step around a coffin complete with mannequin and sound effects. The music-video titles are placed within a 40-foot-long, 15-foot-high yellow submarine that you must climb into in order to look around.

Western Goods Las Vegas loves its Western roots, and the city has some of the best Western shops around. The finest one of all is **Sam's Town Western Emporium** (5111 Boulder Hwy., tel. 702/454–8017), a large shopping village with boots,hats, clothing, jewelry, belt buckles, string ties, a bakery, and a barber shop. It's adjacent to Sam's Town Hotel and Casino.
Miller Stockman (3200 Las Vegas Blvd. S, tel. 702/737–7236, and 4300 Meadows Ln., tel. 702/870–2951), a higher-priced Western shop that lacks the atmosphere and old-time feel of Sam's Town, is located in both the Fashion Show Mall and The Meadows Mall.
Adams Western Store (1415 Western Ave., tel. 702/384–6077) is the sort of traditional Western shop you might expect to find in Montana or Wyoming; the emphasis is on equestrian supplies and "wearing apparel." It's also the oldest Western shop in town, circa 1951, and it'll probably be the toughest for you to get to. It's off Sahara Avenue, near the freeway, appropriately enough on a back street named Western.

6 Sports and the Outdoors

The playful spirit of Las Vegas, epitomized in its casinos, is also very much alive in its sports. Vegas's 13 championship golf courses host several prestigious tournaments that include a $1 million stop on the PGA tour. Many boxing superstars—Muhammad Ali, Larry Holmes, Sugar Ray Leonard, Thomas Hearns, Marvin Hagler, and Mike Tyson—have faced each other in a Las Vegas ring.

Participant Sports and Fitness

Biking You can rent bikes at **City Spokes** (4089 S. Industrial Rd., tel. 702/596–2489) and **Bikes USA** (1539 N. Eastern Ave., tel. 702/642–2453). Because of the intense summer heat, you won't find many cycling trails in Las Vegas, but there is one good, long jaunt: Go west on Charleston Boulevard, which will take you out of the city about 16 miles to the beautiful Red Rock Canyon, where you will find a 13-mile, one-way scenic loop.

Boating Boats may be rented at **Jet Skee Fun** (639 N. Pueblo Blvd., Henderson, tel. 702/564–8346) and **Lake Mead Resort and Marina** (322 Lakeshore Rd., Boulder City, tel. 702/293–3484). Both are on the shores of Lake Mead, 30 miles from town, where the fishing is excellent.

Bowling Many casinos offer 24-hour bowling facilities. The 106-lane **Showboat** (2800 Fremont St., tel. 702/385–9153) is the world's largest bowling alley. Several other good bowling spots are the 56-lane **Sam's Town** (5111 Boulder Hwy., tel. 702/456–7777) and the 72-lane **Gold Coast** (4000 W. Flamingo Rd., tel. 702/367–4700).

Golf With an average of 315 days of sunshine a year, Las Vegas's top sports recreation is golf. The two 18-hole courses on the Strip are at the **Desert Inn** (3145 Las Vegas Blvd. S, tel. 702/733–4290) and **The Mirage** (3400 Las Vegas Blvd. S, tel. 702/369–7111); they're both open to the public, but resort guests get top priority and lower rates. **Los Prados** (Jones and Lone Mountain Rds., tel. 702/645–5696) and the **Las Vegas Golf Course** (4349 Vegas Dr., tel. 702/646–3003) are two other public options. Watch out for the hustlers who hang around the resort courses looking for an easy mark.

Health Clubs The **Las Vegas Sporting House** (3025 Industrial Rd., tel. 702/733–8999), behind the Stardust Hotel, has 10 racquetball courts, two tennis courts, a basketball court, a volleyball court, exercise equipment, outdoor jogging tracks, swimming pools, steam and sauna, and aerobics classes; the fee is $15 a visit for guests of any hotel. The three facilities of the **Las Vegas Athletic Club** (1070 E. Sahara Ave., tel. 702/733–1919; 3315 E. Spring Mountain Rd., tel. 702/362–3720; and 5090 S. Maryland Pkwy., tel. 702/795–2582) offer racquetball courts, saunas, Jacuzzis, Nautilus and free weights, indoor and outdoor swimming pools, and aerobics classes; the fee is $10. Most hotels have health-club facilities; those at Bally's, Caesars, Desert Inn, Flamingo, Riviera, and Tropicana are open to the public for a fee.

Hiking Hiking enthusiasts should explore the trails of Mt. Charleston, which are much cooler than the desert trails (*see* Excursions from Las Vegas in Chapter 4).

Horseback **Bonnie Springs Ranch in Old Nevada** (1 Gun Fighter La.,
Riding tel. 702/875–4191), 18 miles from the Strip, offers a one-hour guided ride for $15. **Mt. Charleston Stables** (Kyle Canyon Rd., tel. 702/872–7009), 25 miles from Las Vegas and next door to the Mt. Charleston Hotel, has horses for hire at prices that range from $18 to $22 for one hour (2- to 3-hour rentals are available at a lower rate).

Jogging There are jogging trails behind the **Desert Inn** and **Caesars Palace,** and the **University of Nevada–Las Vegas** (4505 S. Maryland Pkwy., tel. 702/739–3011) has a regulation track (Bill Cosby's favorite hangout when in town) from which you can see the Strip in the distance as you run. The most pleasant times to hit the streets of Las Vegas, especially in the hot months are early morning or late afternoon.

Racquetball **Caesars Palace** (3570 Las Vegas Blvd. S, tel. 702/731–7110), the **Las Vegas Athletic Club** (1070 E. Sahara Ave., tel. 702/733–1919, and 3315 E. Spring Mountain Rd., tel. 702/362–3720), and the **Las Vegas Sporting House** (3025 Industrial Rd., tel. 702/733–8999) have racquetball courts that are open to the public for a fee.

Skiing **Lee Canyon** (Mt. Charleston, tel. 702/646–0008), southern Nevada's skiing headquarters, is equipped with a 3,000-foot double chair lift and chalet. Take Highway 95 north to the Lee Canyon Exit (Hwy 156), and head up the mountain. You'll know you're only 47 miles from Las Vegas when you see the slope names: Blackjack, High Roller, Keno, The Strip, Bimbo 1 and 2, Slot Alley.

Swimming Every hotel and most motels have large outdoor pools that are open from April to October—but only until 6 PM even when it stays light late. Hotel managements maintain that they can't afford to hire lifeguards to work through the night; in fact, they can't afford to have you lounging in the water when you could be spending your time and your money in the casino. Two **public pools** (430 E. Bonanza Rd., tel. 702/386–6309, and 1100 E. St. Louis Ave., tel. 702/386–6395) are open Memorial Day through Labor Day. For lake swimming, take the 30-mile drive to Lake Mead.

Tennis Las Vegas has an abundance of tennis courts, many of them lighted for evening play. The 10 courts at **Bally's Casino Resort** (3645 Las Vegas Blvd. S, tel. 702/739–4111) are open only to hotel guests, but nonguests may book one of the 10 courts at **The Desert Inn** (3145 Las Vegas Blvd. S, tel. 702/733–4444) if they pay a $10 court fee per person (good for the entire day). The **University of Nevada–Las Vegas** (4505 S. Maryland Pkwy., tel. 702/739–3150) has a dozen lighted tennis courts available on a first-come, first-served (as it were) basis.

Spectator Sports

Baseball   The **Las Vegas Stars** of the triple-A Pacific Coast League play at Cashman Field (850 Las Vegas Blvd. N, tel. 702/386–7200), north of downtown, where professional baseball made its Las Vegas debut in 1983. Winners of the league championship in 1986 and 1988, the Stars have become a successful baseball franchise and a thriving farm club for the San Diego Padres.

Basketball   The hottest tickets in town during the school year are the basketball games of the NCAA champions, the **Runnin' Rebels** at the University of Nevada–Las Vegas (4505 S. Maryland Pkwy., tel. 702/739–3267).

Bowling   Las Vegas is home to the **Showboat Invitational Bowling Tournament** (Showboat Hotel, 2800 Fremont St., tel. 702/385–9123), the Professional Bowling Association's oldest competition, which airs on ABC–TV.

Boxing   Championship boxing came to Las Vegas in 1960, when Benny Paret took the welterweight title from Don Jordan at the Las Vegas Convention Center. Since then most of boxing's superstars have fought in Las Vegas. A title match draws the well-heeled and the well-known from all fields— and brings out the high roller in everyone. Spectators willingly fork over $200–$1,500 a seat to watch two guys pummel each other, then hang around the casinos laying down chips for the rest of the evening, sometimes for the rest of the week. Major fights are usually held at the Mirage or Caesars Palace. To learn about upcoming boxing events, look for the fight odds posted on the wall in the race and sports book of any casino. For the most comprehensive fight listings, check **Caesars Palace** (3570 Las Vegas Blvd. S, tel. 702/731–7110), **Little Caesars Gambling Casino** (3665 Las Vegas Blvd. S, tel. 702/734–2827), or the **Stardust Hotel and Casino** (3000 Las Vegas Blvd. S, tel. 702/732–6111).

Golf   October brings the annual **Las Vegas Invitational golf tournament,** with top PGA golfers competing for high stakes at the Desert Inn, Las Vegas Country Club, and Spanish Trails. For more information, contact **Las Vegas Invitational** (tel. 702/382–6616).

Rodeo   When the **National Finals of Rodeo** (tel. 702/731–2115) comes to town in December, the casinos showcase country stars and the fans sport Western gear. The NFR, said to be the Super Bowl of professional rodeo, offers more than $2 million in prize money.

7 Dining

Elliot Krane, the former restaurant editor of the Las Vegas Review-Journal, *made the selection of highly recommended restaurants.*

The restaurants of Las Vegas number more than 750. The major hotel-casinos all have four or five eating places (the Las Vegas Hilton has 13), and the hotel marquees that used to announce revues and celebrity performers now proclaim food bargains: PRIME RIB $4.95! SHRIMP COCKTAIL 49¢! Dining bargains abound at the hotels, which keep the prices of meals, liquor, and rooms low in order to draw you inside and steer you toward the casino—where revenues lost by the hotels in such deals are more than made up.

Hotel restaurants serve every pocketbook, offering a variety that extends from $3 buffets to $50 "gourmet" meals to 49¢ breakfasts in the wee hours. The buffets at breakfast (around $4), lunch ($5), and dinner ($7) are cafeteria-style, all-you-can-eat affairs where the food is plain and generally filling. And who can resist such old favorites as chipped beef, macaroni and cheese, stewed prunes, and canned fruit? Some hotels try harder; many items at the Palace Station buffet, for example, are prepared to order.

Gourmet dining has its place in Las Vegas because hotels recognize that the high roller, the player who may drop $40,000 or $50,000 in a weekend without blinking, expects treatment to match that largesse. No coffee shop or bargain buffet for that person, who looks for the exclusivity of the intimate, dimly lit restaurant where the diners wear a jacket and tie, the chef has been trained in Europe, and the service is attentive and professional. High rollers, of course, enjoy these meals on the house, so the paying customers also help subsidize their cost. Still, as a result, the price of a first-class dinner in Las Vegas is much lower than it is in New York or San Francisco.

Those who want to spend as little money as possible on food should eat at the cheapest buffets (Circus Circus), and snack bars (Slots A Fun, Golden Gate), take advantage of the bargain breakfasts (Rio, Plaza), and stay up to try the famous $2 steak dinners (served between 11 PM and 6 AM at Binion's and California). In addition, there are some excellent meal deals at regular hours: a 16-ounce Porterhouse at the Boardwalk (5–10 PM, $5.95); prime rib at the Four Queens (6 PM–2 AM, $8.95 with a $5 slot rebate); and a pound of Alaskan king crab legs at the El Cortez (5-10 PM, $8.95); and Palace Station (4–11 PM daily, $10.95). What's more, coupons in the major hotel funbooks often provide further discounts on meals. The Sands, for example, features a $1-off coupon good at any hotel dining room.

The recently opened Forum Shops at Caesars has given the city its first branches of familiar big-city names. Tucked among the fancy boutiques and talking statues are Wolfgang Puck's Spago from Los Angeles, Palm from New York and Los Angeles, Lombardi's of Dallas–Fort Worth, and Carnegie Deli of Manhattan.

Outside the hotels, the many other restaurants of the city offer a variety of cuisines and the opportunity to get away from

games of chance for a while. Simply arriving at a restaurant
without having to walk through a noisy casino, fight off
hordes of people, and wait in long lines is an attractive option
for many. The prices at these places are eminently competi-
tive with comparable hotel dining rooms and, in order to lure
patrons away from the casinos, the food is often of much better quality. Generally, the waits are shorter, the service is
finer, and you'll have a greater sense of "dining out."

Restaurants, both in and out of hotels, are reviewed below according to cuisine. A tip of 15% is common practice in Las
Vegas restaurants, and in some circumstances you might
want to slip the maître d' $5 or $10 for a special table. Except
where noted, reservations are unnecessary, and casual dress
is the norm.

Highly recommended restaurants in each price category are
indicated by a star ★.

Category	Cost*
Very Expensive	over $50
Expensive	$20–$50
Moderate	$10–$20
Inexpensive	under $10

*Average cost of a three-course dinner, per person, excluding
drinks, service, and (7%) sales tax.*

The following credit card abbreviations are used: AE,
American Express; D, Discover Card; DC, Diners Club;
MC, MasterCard; and V, Visa.

American

★ **The Flamingo Room.** If you like pink surroundings, ice
sculptures, and a view of pretty swimming pools, the Flamingo Room may be just the place for you. Specialties include the mixed grill (lamb chops, beef medallion, pork
tenderloin, bacon, broiled tomato, potato, and vegetable)
and the medley (sautéed beef medallion with béarnaise
sauce, pork tenderloin with *peccant* sauce, chicken scalop-
pine with mushrooms, potato, and vegetable). The Flamingo Room also boasts the best salad bar in town: smoked fish,
chicken breast, chopped liver, hearts of artichoke and
palm, peel-and-eat shrimp, and tropical fruit in yogurt. At
lunch, the salad bar costs a dollar less, and sandwiches and
burgers are available. *The Flamingo Hilton and Tower,
3555 Las Vegas Blvd. S, tel. 702/733–3111. Reservations
advised. AE, D, DC, MC, V. Moderate–Expensive.*
Center Stage. The Stage's second-story view of downtown
Fremont Street is incomparable, especially from the front-
facing tables. The restaurant is set in a dark-green oval
glass bubble with large windows that let in lots of red and
yellow from the big neon light show outside. Steak, chick-

Alpine Village Inn, **10**

Antonio's, **28**

The Bacchanal, **22**

Baja Restaurant, **29**

Bally's Big Kitchen, **25**

Bamboo Garden, **26**

Battista's Hole in the Wall Italian Restaurant, **23**

Binion's Coffee Shop, **3**

The Bistro, **21**

Café Michelle, **30**

Cafe Roma, **22**

Capozzoli's, **17**

The Carnival World Buffet, **27**

Center Stage, **1**

Chin's, **18**

Circus Circus, **12**

El Sombrero, **2**

Empress Court, **22**

The Feast Buffet, **8**

The Flame, **15**

The Flamingo Room, **24**

Food Fantasy, **24**

The Golden Nugget Hotel, **4**

The Golden Steer, **7**

HoWan, **16**

Joe's Bayou, **20**

Le Montrachet, **11**

Lombardi's, **22**

Manfredi's Limelight, **31**

Margarita's Mexican Cantina, **14**

Mary's Diner, **6**

Mikado, **21**

Oyster Bar, **19**

Palace Court, **22**

Palatium Buffet, **22**

Paradise Buffet, **5**

Pamplemousse Restaurant, **9**

Primavera, **22**

Ralph's Diner, **13**

Ricardo's, **34**

The Silver Dragon, **33**

The Skye Room, **1**

The Steak House, **12**

The Tillerman, **32**

Uptown Buffet, **6**

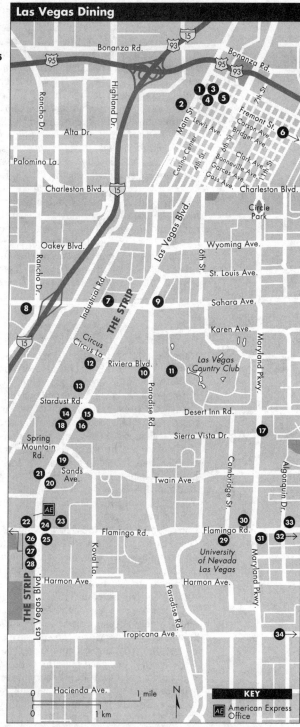

Las Vegas Dining

KEY

AE American Express Office

en, and veal are the principal entrées; all dinners come with soup or salad, potato, vegetable, and beverage. *Plaza Hotel, 1 Main St., tel. 702/386–2513. Reservations advised. AE, D, DC, MC, V. Dinner only. Moderate.*

The Skye Room. Traditional American fare and the best view of Las Vegas—from the 24th floor of the Horseshoe Hotel—are reason enough for being whisked in an outside glass elevator to this vantage point for dinner. The menu offers prime rib, steak, chops, and chicken, all served with potato and salad. *Binion's Horseshoe Hotel and Casino, 128 Fremont St., tel. 702/382–1600. Reservations advised. AE, D, DC, MC, V. Dinner only. Moderate.*

Café Michelle. Here's a café with a European flair that makes a welcome change of pace when the casino experience has gotten to you. Situated in a small strip shopping mall, the café has red-and-white-checked tablecloths indoors and the traditional Cinzano umbrellas above the tables in the plaza outdoors. Omelets, crêpes, seafood, and salads are the fare, with sandwiches and salads at lunchtime. *1350 E. Flamingo Rd., in the Mission Shopping Center, tel. 702/735–8686. AE, MC, V. Inexpensive–Moderate.*

Buffets

All buffets listed below fall in the Inexpensive category.

Bally's Big Kitchen (Bally's Casino Resort, 3645 Las Vegas Blvd. S, tel. 702/739–4111) has been nominated as the best buffet in town for variety and value. True to its name, the buffet is set up in what resembles a big, stainless steel, institutional kitchen; the fare is varied and ample, including roast duck, steak, prime rib, a separate serving line for Chinese food, a baked-potato bar, salads, and a large variety of desserts. The dining room itself is bright and airy.

Circus Circus. (2880 Las Vegas Blvd. S, tel. 702/734–0410) has the busiest buffet on the Strip, serving more than 10,000 people every day at rock-bottom prices, even for Las Vegas. If you're looking for a buffet with an emphasis on volume and economy, as opposed to preparation and taste (most of the dishes are virtually indistinguishable), this is the place for you. Since it's Circus Circus, the food is served on pink plates in a pink-and-white room with circus tents, giraffes, and elephants painted on the wallpaper. There's usually a long line to get in.

The Golden Nugget Hotel (129 E. Fremont St., tel. 702/385–7111) has the most expensive buffet in town; you won't find the Velveeta cheese, chipped beef, or other staples of the less pricey places. Here, the eggs are cooked to order, the cheese and cold cuts are appealing, and the salad bar is always fresh. The bread pudding is renowned far and wide. The Sunday night buffet is best: you get the best of Sunday brunch (eggs, lox and bagels, herring, etc.), plus the dinner entrées. The Nugget buffet costs half again as much as any of the others, but it's worth it.

The Carnival World Buffet (Rio Suites Hotel and Casino, 3200 W. Flamingo Rd., tel. 702/252–7777) ushered in a new age in Las Vegas buffets when it opened in January 1993. The room is colorful, curvy, and always crowded; the variety and volume of food are mind-blowing; the hours are long and continuous; and the prices are a dollar below the average. But the pièce de résistance is the "Amazon Grill," two large Mongolian barbecues where your veggies, spices, and meat are stir-fried to order—and to perfection.

The Feast Buffet (Palace Station Hotel and Casino, 2411 W. Sahara Ave., tel. 702/367–2411) introduced the "action" concept—where your eggs, burgers, fish, etc. are prepared by short-order cooks behind the serving line—to Las Vegas buffets in 1988. Though Bally's Big Kitchen and the Rio's Carnival World buffets have taken the concept a step or two further, The Feast is still among the tops in town.

The **Uptown Buffet** (Sam's Town Hotel and Casino, 5111 W. Boulder Hwy., tel. 702/456–7777), the **Palatium Buffet** (Caesars Palace, 3570 Las Vegas Blvd. S, tel. 702/733–3111), and the **Paradise Buffet** (Fremont Hotel and Casino, 200 E. Fremont St., tel. 702/385–3232) are other good buffet options.

Cajun

Joe's Bayou. Among the Cajun, Creole, and other Southern dishes at Joe's are Louisiana chicken gumbo, Natchez prime rib, shrimp Creole, St. Louis steak, and Memphis barbecue (with slow preparation over mesquite). All dinners include plantation greens, cornbread, and salad. The quiet, dark room has a nautical theme; the statue of a sea captain greets diners up front, and a collection of oars, ships' clocks, and nets hangs from the ceiling. *Harrah's Hotel and Casino, 3475 Las Vegas Blvd. S, tel. 702/369–5000. Reservations advised. AE, D, DC, MC, V. Dinner only. Moderate.*

Chinese

★ **Empress Court.** "We don't serve chop suey here," the tuxedoed maître d' exclaims, "no moo shu pork or cashew chicken either, just traditional Hong Kong–style cuisine." Welcome to the newest addition to the Caesars Palace family of restaurants, a $4 million rest stop for the wealthy Asian gamblers who drop megabucks in the Caesars casinos. The theme is water and the animal life that inhabits it. A two-story staircase has a koi pond at its center; etchings of fish decorate the glass panels in the main dining room; patterns of blue fish swim in the carpeting; and a large aquarium of exotic fish occupies the middle of the room. The food is exotic: braised shark's fin with crabmeat, imperial Peking duck, and double-broiled bird's nest. The Emperor, a set menu for two, includes Cantonese roast duck salad in sesame sauce, velvet chicken soup with mushrooms, prime sirloin strips with rainbow vegetables, braised abalone with sea cucumber, and ginger ice cream and cookies. *Caesars Palace, 3570 Las Vegas Blvd. S, tel. 702/731–7731. Reservations advised. Jacket and tie required. AE, D, DC, MC, V. Dinner only. Very Expensive.*

HoWan. Those who are hungry for familiar Chinese food— cashew chicken, moo shu, and chop suey—will find it in an elegant setting at HoWan. It's a dark room off the Desert Inn casino, decorated in a luxurious mix of modern and antique Oriental decor. The booths are red, the lights turned low, and white-gloved waiters serve meals on oversize plates. The food is warmed at your table. Among the house specialties are HoWan prawns (prawns, steamed mushrooms, snow peas, carrots, baby corn, bamboo shoots, water chestnuts) and sautéed almond chicken. *Howan* is Chinese for "good fortune." *Desert Inn, 3145 Las Vegas Blvd. S, tel. 702/733–4547. Reservations advised. AE, D, DC, MC, V. Dinner only. Very Expensive.*

★ **Chin's.** An upscale Chinese restaurant with a bright, contemporary decor, Chin's specializes in Hong Kong–style cuisine. The specialties here are the likes of deep-fried chicken in strawberry sauce and pepper orange roughy; try the dim sum plate for lunch. Service is somewhat formal. The restaurant is on the Strip, in front of the Fashion Show shopping mall. *3200 Las Vegas Blvd. S, tel. 702/733–8899. Reservations advised. AE, D, DC, MC, V. Expensive.*

Bamboo Garden. Don't let the modest setting in a Flamingo Road shopping center and the reasonable prices fool you: Bamboo Garden has some of the most unusual Oriental cuisine around. Dishes include cream of seafood soup, crab Rangoon, firecracker beef, clams Dou Chi, Hunan eggplant, and more. The room is elegant, with a bamboo motif, and the service is superb. *4850 Flamingo Rd., tel. 702/871–3262. Reservations advised. AE, D, DC, MC, V. Moderate.*

The Silver Dragon. On Flamingo Road, 2 miles east of the Strip (and two blocks east of the Maryland Parkway), stands this Las Vegas landmark, a replica of a Peking palace. If you seek a less crowded restaurant than many of those on the Strip, or if you have a yen for sweet-and- sour at an unlikely hour, the Silver Dragon, open until 5 AM, has traditional Chinese fare and moderate prices as well. *1510 E. Flamingo Rd., tel. 702/737–1234. AE, MC, V. Moderate.*

Coffee Shops

★ **Cafe Roma.** Less expensive than the other restaurants of Caesars Palace, Cafe Roma continues the hotel's Roman theme in a two-tiered dining room with large columns and gold walls. An American menu is available 24 hours, a Chinese menu after 5 PM. Portions are large, the atmosphere pleasant, and you can gaze out on the bustling casino while you eat. Cafe Roma serves one of the best grilled-cheese sandwiches in town, extra large, cut into thirds, with a hefty side of fries. A large basket of crackers and bread sticks comes with every meal. *Caesars Palace, 3570 Las Vegas Blvd. S, tel. 702/731–7731. AE, D, DC, MC, V. Inexpensive–Moderate.*

Binion's Coffee Shop. There's always a line of people to get into this coffee shop, which serves low-priced "just good food" in large portions. The specialties include the misleadingly named Benny Binion's Natural (two eggs; ham, bacon, or sausage; home fries; toast; jelly; and coffee), and Binion's Delight (hamburger, cheese, lettuce, tomato, dressing, and fries). Chili, steaks, and soups fill out the menu. Westernabilia and keno boards cover the walls. *Binion's Horseshoe Hotel and Casino, 128 Fremont St., tel. 702/382–1600. AE, D, DC, MC, V. Inexpensive.*

Food Fantasy. Food Fantasy lets you serve yourself, cafeteria-style, while your eggs or hamburgers or roast-beef sandwiches are prepared to your specifications. This is one of the rare hotel restaurants that has a salad bar, and it is well stocked. Waffle fans take note: Extra-large, piping-hot waffles are made right before your eyes—a terrific evening treat when topped with vanilla ice cream. *The Flamingo Hilton and Tower, 3555 Las Vegas Blvd. S, tel. 702/733–3507. AE, D, DC, MC, V. Open 6 AM–11 PM. Inexpensive.*

Diners

Mary's Diner. Another venture of the Boyd Group, Mary's Diner at Sam's Town follows the same formula as Ralph's Diner at the Stardust (*see* below). *Sam's Town Hotel and Casino, 5111 W. Boulder Hwy., tel. 702/454–8073. AE,D, DC, MC, V. Inexpensive.*

Ralph's Diner. The folks who run the Boyd Group of hotels (California, Fremont, Sam's Town, and the Stardust) can spot a good American trend as well as anyone, and they responded quickly when the diner craze arrived. At Ralph's, jukes are on the tables; the music is 1950s; and an old-fashioned soda fountain serves up milk shakes, sodas, banana splits, and ice-cream sundaes. Daily Blue Plate Specials start at $3.95. *Stardust Hotel and Casino, 3000 Las Vegas Blvd. S, tel. 702/732–6111. AE, D, DC, MC, V. Inexpensive.*

Dinner Shows

At one time nearly all of the major Las Vegas hotel-casinos offered dinner with their shows. These days, only a few hotels accompany their entertainment with food—most likely because few patrons seem to want it. But for those who do, dinner shows are still a great bargain. The hotels accompanying their glitter with grub are: **Tropicana** ("Folies Bergere"), **Flamingo Hilton** ("City Lites"), and **Excalibur** ("King Arthur's Tournament," where eating with your hands is part of the medieval fun). The **Riviera** doesn't serve dinner at the show itself, but offers a dinner-show tandem that combines the World's Fare Buffet with your choice of

"La Cage, Improv," or "Crazy Girls" for one of the cheapest nights out in town. **Bally's** and the **Stardust** also frequently have special dinner/show deals going.

French/Continental

★ **Palace Court.** Popularly regarded as the best white-glove restaurant in town, the Palace offers excellent food served on fine china to the accompaniment of gently tinkling crystal. At lunchtime, a stained-glass skylight illuminates the rotunda-style dining room, hung with portraits of the 12 Caesars by 17th-century painter Camillo Procaccini. Recent menu selections have included sautéed veal chops with roasted leeks and mustard sauce, breast of duck with a pink peppercorn sauce, fresh Maine lobster, and rack of lamb. The wine list is extensive. Dinner seatings at 6–6:30 PM and 9–9:30 PM. *Caesars Palace, 3570 Las Vegas Blvd. S, tel. 702/ 731–7731. Reservations required. Jacket required. AE,D, DC, MC, V. Very Expensive.*

Pamplemousse Restaurant. A small, quiet room that seats just 70, the Pamplemousse is popular with the convention trade—in fact, management suggests you make your reservations even before you start out for Las Vegas. The dominant color is red, orchestral music can be heard on the stereo system, and the food is classic French cuisine. Because the entrées change from day to day, there is no printed menu and the waiter recites the bill of fare. Recent offerings have included veal medallions in cream sauce with Dijon mustard; and roast duckling in red wine and banana rum sauce. All dinners include salad, a basket of breads, steamed vegetables, and crudités. *400 E. Sahara Ave., tel. 702/ 733–2066. Reservations required. AE, D, DC, MC, V. Dinner only. Closed Mon. Expensive–Very Expensive.*

The Bistro. All of the restaurants at the Mirage are imaginative set pieces with superb food and ultra high prices, but the Bistro is possibly the best of the bunch. The many-windowed room is appointed with wood, brass, flowers, statues, murals and peaked by a stained-glass dome. The menu features escargot, duck pâté, lobster with truffles, duck in peach sauce, rack of lamb with a honey-mustard crust, venison, pheasant, and more. *The Mirage, 3400 Las Vegas Blvd. S., tel. 702/791–7111. Reservations advised. AE, D, DC, MC,V. Dinner only. Closed Tues. and Wed. Expensive.*

★ **Le Montrachet.** An elegant room with soft peach lighting, paintings of pastoral scenes, elaborate table settings, and fine linen, Le Montrachet gives you no indication that you're in Las Vegas. The menu changes with the season, approximately every three months. A recent bill of fare offered poached Dover sole stuffed with mousse of lobster, accompanied by lobster sauce on one side, a champagne caviar sauce on the other; broiled veal chops with mussel puree; and rack of lamb. You won't find cigarette girls or gambling paraphernalia here, but you will find fresh flowers at every table and a wine list with 400 selections. *Las*

Vegas Hilton, 3000 W. Paradise Rd., tel.702/732–5111.
Reservations advised. Jacket and tie advised. AE, D, DC,
MC, V. Dinner only. Expensive.

German

★ **Alpine Village Inn.** If you don't have a reservation, the wait
can be up to one hour for this Las Vegas favorite, across the
street from the convention center. The upstairs full-service
restaurant is decked out as a Swiss chalet: there's "snow"
atop the "huts" that serve as booths, a giant replica of a gin-
gerbread house in the middle of the room, and the servers
wear lederhosen or dirndls. In addition to the substantial
German entrées such as *Schweinebraten* (pork roast), *sau-
erbraten* (marinated beef), *Wienerschnitzel* (veal cutlet), or
Bratpfanne (roast chicken), dinners include a relish bowl,
hors d'oeuvres, soup, salad, cabbage, potatoes, a bread
basket, cinnamon rolls, dessert, and a beverage. The downstairs collegiate rathskeller features an organist who sings
while a miniature ski trolley travels back and forth before
her. The food is similar to that served upstairs, but with
smaller portions and lower prices. There's a gift shop if you
want a memento of your dining experience. *3003 W. Paradise Rd., opposite the Las Vegas Hilton, tel. 702/734–6888.
Reservations advised. AE, D, DC, MC, V. Moderate.*

Italian

★ **Primavera.** Homemade pasta and the Primavera hamburger are perfect for an afternoon in this pleasant, bright setting overlooking the enormous Garden of the Gods
swimming pool at Caesars Palace. At dinnertime the mood
is more restrained, the lights low, and, with seating for
only 75, the tables hard to come by. The specialty of the
house is fettuccine Primavera, tossed with sautéed vegetables, sweet butter, fresh cream, and Parmesan cheese. The
dessert tray is outstanding, but if you don't have room, you
might try one of the fine after-dinner grappas, bottled ex-
clusively for this restaurant. *Caesars Palace, 3570 Las
Vegas Blvd. S, tel. 702/731–7731. Reservations advised. No
shorts. AE, D, DC, MC, V. Expensive.*

Antonio's. This quiet restaurant is popular with locals as
well as tourists. Small, with marble walls and murals
depicting Italian scenes and crystal chandeliers, Antonio's
has an open kitchen at one end. The long menu offers well-
prepared Northern Italian cuisine, as well as such old favor-
ites as *cioppino* (seafood cooked with tomatoes, wine, and
herbs and spices) and eggplant Parmesan. If it's available,
order the five-onion soup—and you can ask the waiter for
the recipe. *Rio Suites Hotel and Casino, I–15 and Flamingo, tel. 702/252–7777. Reservations advised. AE, DC, MC,
V. Dinner only. Moderate–Expensive.*

Battista's Hole in the Wall Italian Restaurant. A local insti-
tution that was featured often on TV's "Vegas," Battista's

is a *Hollywood* Las Vegas restaurant, one with celebrity photographs on the walls, alongside the wine bottles, garlic, and peppers. The fare is your basic Italian—pizza, ravioli, lasagna, and other pastas. All dinners include minestrone, garlic bread, salad, a pasta side dish, wine, and cappuccino. You'll hear opera on the stereo, and sometimes Battista Locatelli himself roams the restaurant, singing. His house rules prohibit tank tops and children under 4. *4041 Audrie St. at Flamingo Rd., tel. 702/732-1424. AE, D, DC, MC, V. Dinner only. Moderate.*

★ **Lombardi's.** Tables at this sidewalk café inside the Forum Shops at Caesars are set up in the piazza surrounding the Fountain of the Gods. The sidewalk section is very noisy; if you want to talk, take a table in the dark and clubby interior, where booths line the black-and-yellow antiqued walls and an open kitchen stands at the back, turning out pasta and rice dishes, single-portion pizzas, soups and salads, and chicken, sausage, and fish. Save room for dessert: A gelato bar offers some of the most mouth-watering ice cream and sorbet around. *Forum Shops at Caesars, tel. 702/735-4663. Reservations advised. AE, MC, V. Moderate.*

Manfredi's Limelight. This family-run storefront restaurant about 2 miles east of the Strip serves up light pastas and innovative fish and chicken entrées, plus four "heart healthy" selections including broiled chicken. Popular dishes include stuffed shells Florentine, *agnolotti* (round ravioli filled with ricotta cheese, spinach, and ham, in an Alfredo sauce), and salmon with caper sauce. *2340 E. Tropicana, tel. 702/739-1410. Reservations advised. AE, MC, V. Dinner only. Moderate.*

Capozzoli's. A lighthouse stands at the entrance to this small yet comfortable Italian restaurant in a minimall a little more than a mile east of the Strip. Capozzoli's, which stays open until 5 AM, is popular with local residents. The decor consists of red-and-white tablecloths and wine bottles on the ceiling; the menu offers veal Parmesan, chicken, and tripe, with soups, salads, and breads made fresh daily. Sandwiches, subs, and pizzas are the lunchtime fare. The place tends to be jammed on weekends and during conventions. *3333 S. Maryland Pkwy., tel. 702/731-5311. Reservations advised. AE, DC, MC, V. Inexpensive-Moderate.*

Japanese

Mikado. Just a few steps from the Mirage's noisy casino, this restaurant provides as much of an oasis as is possible amid the city's madness; it's relatively soothing if you're seated far from the door, near the placid streams, gardens, and murals. The menu consists of standard Japanese fare: steak, chicken, and shrimp prepared *teppan-yaki* (chopped, diced, and barbecued on a hot grill) or tempura (deep-fried) style; *yaki-tori* (grilled beef in a thick-noodle soup); plus sushi and sashimi from the sushi bar in the cor-

ner. *Mirage Hotel and Casino, 3400 Las Vegas Blvd. S, tel.
702/791–7111. Reservations advised. AE, DC, MC, V. Dinner only. Expensive.*

Mexican

Ricardo's. Ricardo's, at three spacious Las Vegas locations, has consistently been voted "the best Mexican restaurant in the city" by the local population. Mariachis stroll the rooms, where a varied fare of burritos, fajitas, chimichangas, and other Mexican delights are served, along with the best margaritas in town. *2389 E. Tropicana Ave., tel. 702/798–4515; 4930 W. Flamingo Rd., tel. 702/ 871–7119; 4300 Meadows La., tel. 702/870–1088. AE, D, DC, MC, V. Moderate.*

★ **Margarita's Mexican Cantina.** This was a steak house until Margaret Elardi bought the Frontier and turned it into a grind joint. What do slot players like best? she asked. Not chops but tacos and margaritas. The decor is classic Southwest, with turquoise and pink tiles, hardwood chairs, and pink and purple neon shading the ceiling—authentic except for the keno boards on the wall and the keno tickets and crayons at every table. The cuisine is good Tex-Mex: tacos, enchiladas, chimichangas, burritos. At the *tortilleria* up front, the chef prepares fresh tortillas that you can smell throughout the casino; they're served with salsa, guacamole, and bean dip in lieu of chips. For dessert try the Burrito Tropical, a deep-fried tortilla stuffed with fresh fruit, ice cream on the side, and a rich sauce topping. *Frontier Hotel, 3120 Las Vegas Blvd. S, tel. 702/794–8200. AE, D, DC, MC, V. Inexpensive–Moderate.*

El Sombrero. One of the oldest restaurants in Las Vegas, this tiny Mexican eatery has been run by the same family since 1952. It's in a somewhat depressed section of the city (south of downtown, across from the St. Vincent de Paul thrift shop), but sombrero and serape decorations make it cheerful inside. Offerings include such typical Mexican dishes as burritos and tacos, enchiladas, and tamale combinations, plus seafood specials. *807 S. Main St., tel. 702/382–9234. AE, MC, V. No lunch Sun. Inexpensive.*

Only in Las Vegas

The Bacchanal. Caesars Palace's most elaborate restaurant turns food service into showbiz. To re-create a Roman feast in the atmosphere of a private villa, male guests are served wine by toga-clad "wine goddesses," who also deliver a massage before dessert (a toke is expected). Two stone lions guard the room, and a lighted pool occupies the center. Spectacle and gluttony are the operating principles here: the $65 prix-fixe dinner includes two types of appetizers; soup; salad; a pasta course; a main dish, such as filet mignon, rack of lamb, or prime rib; dessert; coffee; and all the wine you can drink. Don't expect refined dining; it's best to share the three-hour Bacchanalian food orgy experience with a large group. What with the rowdy conversation and the wine goddesses refilling your cup every minute, you'll hardly notice that the food is fairly mundane. *Caesars Palace, 3570 Las Vegas Blvd. S, tel. 702/731-7731. Reservations advised. Dinner seatings at 6–6:30 PM and 9–9:30 PM. AE, D, DC, MC, V. Closed Sun. and Mon. Very Expensive.*

Seafood

Oyster Bar. In the rear of the Sands casino, opposite the entrance to the Copa Room, is one of the only hotel seafood bars in Las Vegas. The 14-seat horseshoe-shape counter serves oysters, clams, and crab claws; Manhattan and New England chowders; seafood louies (salads); and combo platters. It overlooks the theater pit but it's tucked away in a corner, so the oyster bar is noisy only when the theater is seating or emptying. Use your $1-off coupon from the Sands funbook to lower these already low prices even further. *Sands Hotel and Casino, 3355 Las Vegas Blvd. S, tel. 702/ 733-5000. AE, D, DC, MC, V. Inexpensive.*

★ **The Tillerman.** Its location on Flamingo Road, almost 3 miles east of the Strip, makes the Tillerman a quiet refuge from the casinos and a favorite with convention delegates. The garden setting—the restaurant is built around a huge ficus growing in the center of the room—places you under an open skylight on hot desert nights. A dozen different, well-prepared seafood selections are offered each night, and the steaks are always done just right. *2245 E. Flamingo Rd., tel. 702/731-4036. AE, D, DC, MC, V. Dinner only. Moderate.*

Southwestern

Baja Restaurant. This dressed-up diner (strings of red chilis frame an open kitchen, and a cactus sits on each table) in a shopping mall is one of the few places in southern Nevada where you can get piquant New Mexican cuisine. The menu features blue-corn enchiladas, fajita chicken salad, excellent chili relleno, and rice and beans. If you don't like your food spicy, ask for it toned. *3331 E. Tropicana Ave., tel. 702/458-7300. AE, DC, MC, V. Inexpensive.*

Steak Houses

★ **The Golden Steer.** In a town where restaurants come and go almost as quickly as visitors' cash, the longevity of this steak house, opened in 1962, is itself a high recommendation. Over the years, folks have been coming here for the relaxed atmosphere and, especially, for the huge slabs of well-prepared meat: Steak, ribs, and roast beef are particularly popular. Although you wouldn't know it from the outside, the Steer is cavernous; however, lots of small, intimate rooms—done in San Francisco Barbary Coast–style, with red leather chairs, polished dark wood, and stained-glass windows—break up the space. The namesake's image, a big fat yellow cow, beckons from a sign out front. *308 W. Sahara Ave., tel. 702/384-4470. Reservations advised. AE, D, DC, MC, V. Dinner only. Expensive.*

★ **The Steak House.** Believe it or not, the steak house set within the craziness of Circus Circus is one that many local residents contend is the best in town. The atmosphere here is totally unlike that of the rest of Circus Circus; the wood paneling and antique brass furnishings adorn a dark, quiet room reminiscent of 1890s San Francisco. The beef—aged 21 days—is displayed in a glassed-in area at the side; the cooking takes place over an open-hearth charcoal grill in the middle of the room. Steaks, chops, and roast beef make up the menu, and all entrées are accompanied by soup or salad, fresh bread, and a baked potato. *Circus Circus, 2880 Las Vegas Blvd. S, tel. 702/734-0410. Reservations advised. AE, D, DC, MC, V. Dinner only. Expensive.*

The Flame. One of the few restaurants on the Strip that's not set in a hotel, The Flame is a favorite of convention delegates, who crowd the restaurant's closely packed tables. The decor hasn't changed since the 1960s, when this place opened—it's one of the 10 oldest restaurants in town. You can get chicken or seafood here, but go for the steak, cooked on an open grill in the back. The various cuts—T-bone, New York, and Porterhouse—are brought out, rare, for you to choose from; you can go over and chat with the cook and tell him when you think your meat is done. Unlike many of the overly pompous steak houses in town, this is a relaxed place with a sense of humor—and it serves dinner 24 hours a day. *1 Desert Inn Rd., tel. 702/735-4431. AE, D, DC, MC, V. Moderate.*

8   Lodging

For many years, the guiding principle in Las Vegas hotel construction was to make the rooms as loud but minimalist as possible, with no modern amenities such as a TV sets or a clocks. The goal was to keep the guest out of the room and in the casino. While some hotels still subscribe to that theory, most Las Vegas lodging houses have entered the modern age and now offer TVs and pay-TV movies, AM/FM radio, direct-dial telephones, and soft color schemes. High-roller suites, provided by the casino-hotels for those who agree to spend a minimum specified amount of money at the tables are the ultimate in luxury accommodations. Non-smoking floors or rooms are generally available these days, too.

Rooms, especially at the older properties, are often distinguished by the appellations "garden," in older, low-rise wings, and "tower," in newer, high-rise buildings. Many hotels, such as the Alexis Park, Rio, Howard Johnsons, and Frontier, have "minisuites," which are larger and more comfortable than routine hotel rooms. Others, like the Westwood Ho and Residence Inn, have two-bedroom apartments for families or larger parties. A number of motels, such as Sun Harbor Budget Suites, feature complete kitchenettes and weekly rates.

Las Vegas is now home to nine of the 10 largest hotels in the world. The largest hotels, in order (including those in progress), are: the MGM Grand, Excalibur, Flamingo Hilton, Las Vegas Hilton, Mirage, Treasure Island, Bally's, Circus Circus, and Imperial Palace. By early 1994, there will be nearly 90,000 hotel and motel rooms in Las Vegas. If that seems like a lot, consider that the 1994 visitor volume is projected to reach 24 million, which divides into a little less than a half-million visitors a week—the equivalent of every man, woman, and child in Honolulu, Hawaii, being suddenly transported to Las Vegas. In short, accommodations fill up fast around here, even when no major conventions or events are scheduled.

When it's time for a major convention, it's not unusual for Las Vegas to sell out completely. Nearly two dozen conventions a year each attract more than 25,000 participants. Combine those with three-day weekends, holidays, large sporting events, and normally crowded weekends, and it's wise to make your lodging arrangements as far ahead of your visit as possible. On the other hand, things change quickly in Las Vegas. If you arrive at the last minute without accommodations, you'll almost always be able to find a room somewhere in town. And if your original room is not to your liking, you can usually upgrade it around checkout time the next day.

In general, rates for Las Vegas accommodations are far lower than those in most other American resort and vacation cities. In addition, there are often further discounts and package deals. When business is slow, many hotels offer reduced rates on rooms in their least desirable sections, sometimes with a buffet breakfast and a late-night show included. Most "sales" occur from December through February and July through August, the coldest and hottest times of the year. Imperial Palace, for example, often advertises rooms at $10 a night for Sunday through Thursday stays in December.

One useful guide to bargain rates is the Sunday "Calendar" section of the *Los Angeles Times*, where most Las Vegas hotels advertise. Another way to learn about specials is to call a hotel's toll-free number and ask what package deals it has for your vacation dates. When the hotel reservations clerks continually tell you they're sold out, try the **Las Vegas Tourist Bureau** (tel. 702/739–1482) or the **Las Vegas Hotel Reservation Center** (tel. 702/736–1666 or 800/458–6161). One of them may be able to place you in the hotel of your choice.

Highly recommended lodgings in each price category are indicated by a star ★.

Category	Cost*
Very Expensive	over $100
Expensive	$70–$100
Moderate	$40–$70
Inexpensive	under $40

All prices are for a standard double room, excluding service charge and 8% tax.

The following credit card abbreviations are used: AE, American Express; D, Discover Card; DC, Diners Club; MC, MasterCard; and V, Visa.

Hotels

Very Expensive
★

Caesars Palace. If the opulent entrance, fountains, Roman statuary, bas-reliefs, roaming centurions and handmaidens all look vaguely familiar to you, it's because you may have seen this quintessentially Las Vegas hotel in such movies as *Electric Horseman* and *Rain Man*. With 1,518 rooms, Caesars is not one of the largest hotels in the city, but it has always gone after quality rather than quantity. In recent years, the hotel has expanded its casino and added a lavish shopping mall, the Forum (*see* Chapter 5, Shopping). The restaurants are among the most expensive and opulent in town: along with the excellent Palace Court and Primavera and the showy Bacchanal (*see* Chapter 7, Dining, for all three), the hotel boasts six other restaurants, including an upscale Chinese eatery; Cleopatra's Barge lounge is one of a kind. The hotel is the home of world-class sporting events and top superstars, such as Julio Iglesias and Diana Ross.

Its Omnimax theater, a huge geodesic dome, shows movies specially made for the 70mm process. *3750 Las Vegas Blvd. S, 89109, tel. 702/731–7110 or 800/634–6661. 1,518 rooms and suites. Facilities: 9 restaurants, 2 swimming pools, 4 tennis courts, squash court, health spa, lounge, movie theater, showroom, shopping mall. AE, D, DC, MC, V.*

★ **ITT Sheraton Desert Inn Hotel & Country Club.** One of the classiest and best-laid-out in town, the DI was once the home and property of the late Howard Hughes. Hughes was staying on the ninth floor, so the story goes, when the hotel staff asked him to move out to make room for some high rollers. He promptly bought the place instead. This relatively small hotel, comprising three low-rise buildings, has always gone for an upscale clientele who like to play golf and gamble. If you get a room whose smoked-glass windows overlook the PGA championship golf course, you could almost forget you're in Las Vegas—no neon signs, tall buildings, or cigarette girls in the view (other rooms do face the Strip, however). Each year the hotel hosts three major Tour events: the Desert Inn–LPGA International, the Las Vegas Senior Classic (Senior PGA Tour), and the Las Vegas International (PGA Tour). Rooms have a Southwestern feel, many with separate dining or lounging areas; some suites even have private swimming pools. Top headliners perform in the Crystal Room Showroom. Among the three gourmet restaurants on the premises is HoWan (*see* Chapter 7, Dining); there are also two other casual dining rooms, one open 24 hours, on the grounds. *3145 Las Vegas Blvd. S, 89109, tel. 702/733–4444 or 800/634–6906. 821 rooms, including 95 suites. Facilities: 5 restaurants, 18-hole golf course, 10 tennis courts, spa, pool, outdoor jogging track, entertainment lounge, showroom. AE, D, DC, MC, V.*

Expensive– Very Expensive **Residence Inn by Marriott.** This town house–style all-suite hotel on nicely landscaped grounds is across the street from the Convention Center and a short cab ride away (1¼ miles) from the Strip. The studios and two-bedroom suites all have kitchens. Curbside parking is a plus. *3225 Paradise Rd., 89109, tel. 702/796–9300 or 800/331–3131. 144 studios, 48 2-bedroom suites. Facilities: complimentary breakfast, complimentary weekday dinner buffet, grocery shopping service. AE, D, DC, MC, V.*

Expensive **Alexis Park Resort Hotel.** Would businesspeople and couples come to a luxury hotel in Las Vegas that had no neon, no gaming tables, and no slots? The Alexis Park opened in 1984 and discovered that the answer was yes. Two miles from the convention center, this is a favorite spot for convention delegates who want a "normal" living experience during their business day. The individual buildings of the all-suite desert hotel are two-story, white-stucco blocks with red-tile roofs, all set in a water garden. Views are of either a rock pool or a lawn. Every room has a wet bar; some have fireplaces or Jacuzzis. *375 E. Harmon Ave., 89109, tel. 702/796–3300 or 800/582–2228. 500 suites. Facilities: 3*

Aladdin, **12**
Alexis Park, **10**
Bally's, **11**
Barbary Coast, **15**
Binion's Horseshoe, **40**
Caesars Palace, **14**
Circus Circus, **29**
El Cortez, **42**
Excalibur, **8**
Fitzgerald's, **39**
Flamingo Hilton
Las Vegas, **16**
Four Queens, **38**
Frontier, **25**
Gold Spike, **41**
Gold Strike, **2**
Golden Nugget, **37**
Hacienda, **3**
Harrah's, **19**
Imperial Palace, **18**
ITT Sheraton
Desert Inn, **24**
Lady Luck, **36**
Las Vegas Club, **35**
Las Vegas Hilton, **31**
Luxor, **5**
Maxim, **17**
MGM Grand, **9**
The Mirage, **20**
Motel 6, **6**
Plaza, **34**
Residence Inn by
Marriott, **23**
Rio Suites, **13**
Riviera, **30**
Royal Oasis, **4**
Sahara Las Vegas, **32**
Sam's Town, **43**
Sands, **22**
Stardust, **26**
Sun Harbor Budget
Suites, **27**
Treasure Island, **21**
Tropicana, **7**
Vegas World, **33**
Westward Ho, **28**
Whiskey Pete's, **1**

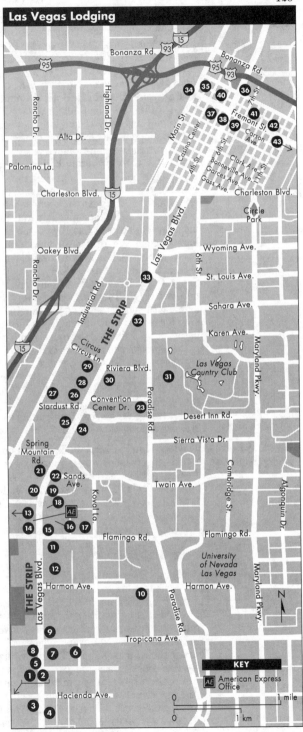

Las Vegas Lodging

restaurants, health spa, 2 tennis courts, 3 pools, 9-hole putting green, jogging track, lounge. AE, D, DC, MC, V.

Bally's Casino Resort. With nearly 3,000 rooms on the busiest corner of the Strip, the hotel calls itself "A City Within a City," and this is not much of an exaggeration. Bally's is the only hotel with two major showrooms: A superstar such as Tom Jones is featured in one, and the $10 million spectacular "Jubilee!" (*see* Chapter 9, Nightlife) is offered twice a night in the other. The hotel also has a huge casino; a comedy club; a 40-store shopping arcade, selling everything from fine furs to ice cream; 10 tennis courts; separate health spas for men and women; and an attractively landscaped outdoor pool. If the hotel's restaurants tend to be rather ephemeral—six of them are currently open—Bally's buffet is consistently one of the best in town. *3645 Las Vegas Blvd. S, 89109, tel. 702/739–4111 or 800/634–3434. 2,832 rooms, 265 suites. Facilities: 6 restaurants, 2 showrooms, 10 tennis courts, health spas, swimming pool, lounge, comedy club. AE, D, DC, MC, V.*

★ **Flamingo Hilton Las Vegas.** The Fabulous Flamingo that opened in 1946 with Jimmy Durante, Rose Marie, and Xavier Cugat as entertainers was a 98-room oasis with palm trees imported from California. The Flamingo has changed a lot since then: Today its five towers overlook a new 15-acre pool area where the original motor lodges once stood, and the showroom features a topless revue. In 1992 the casino gained a poker room and sports book, and the Crown Room buffet was expanded; a new 900-room tower is scheduled for completion in 1994. The Flamingo is pervasively pink, from the outside neon sign to the in-room vases and pens and the lobby carpeting. The spacious rooms in the towers offer expansive views of the Strip. The swimming pool area is one of the largest and prettiest in town, and, an unusual feature, the registration area is on the side of the hotel near the elevators, so you won't have to carry your luggage through the casino. Package rates for special tours keep this large hotel and casino bustling. *3555 Las Vegas Blvd. S, 89109, tel. 702/733–3111 or 800/732–2111. 3,334 rooms, 196 suites. Facilities: 8 restaurants, 2 swimming pools, Jacuzzi, health spa, 4 tennis courts, lounge, showroom, multilanguage services. AE, D, DC, MC, V.*

★ **Golden Nugget Hotel.** The Nugget was only a gambling hall with sawdust on the floors and no rooms when Steve Wynn took it over in the 1970s and decided to go after high rollers. Now red rugs flow over white marble, leading you to the lobby and a large public area with columns, etched-glass windows, and fresh flowers in gold-plated vases. Almost everything here is gold—the telephones, the slots, the elevators. The large, Victorian-style rooms have four-posters, period mirrors and furniture, and dining areas. In addition to the standard double rooms, the Nugget has 27 duplex suites—some with a personal room-service waiter—and six two-bedroom apartments, each decorated in a different style. A small showroom features singers and comedians.

The Nugget's one drawback is its downtown location. If you plan a lot of activities in Las Vegas, you'll have to endure the traffic—or taxi expense—between the Strip and downtown. *129 E. Fremont St., 89101, tel. 702/385–7111 or 800/634–3454. 1,805 rooms, 106 suites. Facilities: 5 restaurants, swimming pool, health club, lounge, showroom. AE, D, DC, MC, V.*

Las Vegas Hilton. Barbra Streisand opened this hotel with a four-week gig and was followed by Elvis Presley, who made the Hilton his official Las Vegas venue throughout the 1970s; you can still stay in the Elvis Suite on the 31st floor, where the King of Rock'n' Roll resided when he played here (his white jumpsuit is on display in front of the showroom). Though the Hilton, which is adjacent to the Las Vegas Convention Center, no longer holds the title of largest hotel in town, it's still a sight to see—best of all by standing at its foot and staring up at the 375-foot tower, 29 floors, and three wings. The rooms are spacious, with soft colors, large beds, and telephones in the lavatories; those on the higher floors have great views of the city. They can also be hard to find; the numbering system goes from hundreds to thousands and varies from wing to wing. But for all its size, the hotel functions remarkably smoothly: Elevators run properly, operators answer the phone promptly, and plenty of parking is available. The Hilton's Youth Hotel, a dormitory for kids ages 3 to 18, supervised by counselors who serve meals and snacks, is the only facility of its kind in the area. *3000 Paradise Rd., 89109, tel. 702/732–5111 or 800/732–7117. 2,950 rooms, 224 suites. Facilities: 13 restaurants, 6 tennis courts, health spa, swimming pool, putting green, youth hotel and lounge. AE, D, DC, MC, V.*

★ **The Mirage.** Steve Wynn's $630 million South Seas–theme resort is appropriately named. This desert property comprising a rain forest with 3,000 tropical plants, palm and banana trees, and lagoons; six Himalayan white tigers; a 53-foot-long aquarium filled with thousands of tropical fish, including baby sharks; six dolphins frolicking in the largest saltwater pool in the world; and a 50-foot waterfall that becomes an exploding volcano after dark seems at times to have been created by resident master illusionists Siegfried and Roy. Gleaming white marble and high-quality wood throughout the public areas add to the fantasy atmosphere. But there are many down-to-earth reasons to stay at the Mirage, not the least of which is the high quality of the service. The staff seems to actually like working here, and the hotel to want your business. And the accommodations are pleasant in all price ranges. Immaculate rooms feature bright colors and attractive if simple furnishings; make sure to get one (no extra charge) with an eye-popping view of the Strip, including the volcano. Suites, though pricey, are worth a special-occasion splurge: They feature Jacuzzi bathtubs, loads of amenities, hidden TVs that rise from out of nowhere, and enough space to throw a real party. The food in the hotel's buffet restaurant is a cut above the usual, and Moongate is the prettiest Chinese restaurant in town. *3400 Las Vegas Blvd. S, 89109, tel. 702/791–7111 or 800/ 627–6667. 2,825 rooms, 224 suites. Facilities: 9 restaurants, swimming pool, golf course, 4 tennis courts, exercise facility, lounge, shopping arcade. AE, D, DC, MC, V.*

Rio Suites Hotel and Casino. Opened in 1990, the Rio is the first all-suite hotel in Las Vegas with a casino. The striking blue-and-red, 21-story hotel is off the Strip (west of the I–15 freeway)—a good location if you prefer quieter surroundings—and has a Brazilian theme. While suites here don't have separate sitting rooms, they're spacious and feature extra-large sofas, sitting areas, and dining tables. *3700 W. Flamingo Rd., 89109, tel. 702/252–7777 or 800/888–1808. 430 suites. Facilities: 5 restaurants, sandy beach, swimming pool, fitness center, free shuttle to Strip, lounge. AE, D, DC, MC, V.*

Moderate **Aladdin Hotel and Casino.** In 1985, the Aladdin was purchased for $51.5 million by Ginsu Yasuda, the late Korean-born Japanese resident who liked to shoot craps in Las Vegas. He moved his family here, took over the penthouse, and sunk more millions into the hotel on a remodeling spree of the 1,100 rooms. Unfortunately, the hotel does not live up to the motto it adopted in those days, "Your wish is our command": Service can be less than swift here. The rooms are fairly standard, with low-key tan walls, dark-pink carpeting and bedspreads, and a view of the Strip. Elevators opposite the registration area make long walks unnecessary. The showroom has the only Country Western–style revue on the Strip, and, behind the hotel, the 10,000-seat Aladdin Theatre for the Performing Arts (*see* Chapter 9, Nightlife) has played host to some big-name artists. *3667 Las Vegas Blvd. S, 89109, tel. 702/736–0111 or 800/634–3428. 1,100 rooms, 44 suites. Facilities: 6 restaurants, shopping arcade, 2 swimming pools, 3 tennis courts, lounge, showroom. AE, D, DC, MC, V.*

★ **Barbary Coast Hotel and Casino.** The Barbary Coast has one of the most central locations in Las Vegas, across from Caesars and next door to the Flamingo Hilton and Bally's. It's a fun place with a San Francisco Gold Rush theme—the Victorian-style rooms have brass four-posters with canopies, old-fashioned lamps, lacy curtains, separate eating areas—and some of the best rates in town. The views are of the Strip or the Flamingo Hilton. Because there are only 200 rooms here, it's not always easy to get one. *3595 Las Vegas Blvd. S, 89109, tel. 702/737–7111 or 800/634–6755. 196 rooms, 12 suites. Facilities: 3 restaurants (including a McDonald's), lounge. AE, D, DC, MC, V.*

Binion's Horseshoe Hotel and Casino. You'll look in vain for the brilliant red neon sign of the old Mint Hotel on Fremont Street; it was taken down in 1988 when the Horseshoe's founder, Benny Binion, bought the Mint, tore down the walls between the two casinos, and created a larger Horseshoe. The new neon signs are a turquoise Horseshoe legend and, up top, a revolving neon horseshoe. Inside, staff members speak of the old Mint building as the "West" Horseshoe, the original Horseshoe as the "East" side. Before the expansion, the Horseshoe had just 80 rooms upstairs and they were hard to get. "We don't take reservations," Binion said once. "If I know you, you got a room. If I don't, you don't have a room." Today the 26-story hotel and casino, now run by Binion's son and daughter, has 300 rooms with some of the best views of downtown. These rooms are available to the public on a limited basis, though they are often reserved for the hotel's biggest gamblers. On the west side are modern, medium-size rooms decorated in light colors. The east side rooms, which you may never see, reflect the Western style of the Horseshoe: They have Victorian-style wallpaper and brass beds with quilted spreads. *128 E. Fremont St., 89101, tel. 702/382–1600 or 800/237–6537. 380 rooms. Facilities: 5 restaurants, pool, lounge. AE, DC, MC, V.*

★ **Excalibur Hotel/Casino.** Before they opened this spectacular 4,032-room Excalibur—the world's largest resort hotel—in 1990, Circus Circus execs visited the castles of England, Scotland, and Germany. The result might be described as King Arthur does Las Vegas. (A local "name-the-hotel" contest received many votes for Castle Castle.) The hotel's seven restaurants and 23-shop Medieval Village have an Arthurian theme, complete with strolling Renaissance performers, and the megaresort is the home of Las Vegas's most unusual entertainment extravaganza, "King Arthur's Tournament" (*see* Chapter 9, Nightlife). At a wedding chapel, you can tie the knot with all the trappings of King Arthur and Lady Guinevere. Merlin's Magic Motion Machine, a simulated thrill ride with a big screen, state-of-the-art sound, and synchronized seats, is pure modern Las Vegas, as is the 100,000-square-foot casino. The Excalibur is also notable for its good-value accommodations; the occupancy rate here often runs at 100%. *3850 Las Vegas Blvd. S, 89119, tel. 702/597–7777 or 800/937–7777. 4,032 rooms. Facilities: 7 restaurants, 2 swimming pools, shops, wedding chapel, theater, showroom. AE, DC, MC, V.*

Fitzgerald Hotel and Casino. The decor of this 34-story hotel (the tallest building in Nevada) perpetuates the Irish theme of the casino. The marquee is green, the bellmen sport green pants and green ties, the cocktail waitresses wear green dresses, and you'll walk to your room on—you guessed it—green carpeting. But when you reach your room, you'll find that the door is orange, the bedspreads tan, and the walls light brown—to complement the green curtains and carpets. The views are of Fremont Street or the neighboring Four Queens. *301 E. Fremont St., 89109, tel. 702/388–2400 or 800/274–5825. 650 rooms. Facilities: 3 restaurants, lounge. AE, D, DC, MC, V.*

Four Queens Hotel and Casino. This prominent downtown hotel has one amenity you'll find nowhere else in Las Vegas: A security guard stands at the elevator and asks to see your room key before you enter. The Queens rooms are furnished in New Orleans style with turn-of-the-century wallpaper, vintage lamps, four-posters, and views of Fremont Street, Fitzgerald, or the Golden Nugget. Jazz is performed in the French Quarter lounge on Monday evenings. *202 E. Fremont St., tel. 702/385–4011 or 800/634–6045. 720 rooms. Facilities: 2 restaurants, lounge. AE, DC, MC, V.*

Frontier Hotel. While the Frontier of today stands on the same property as the original 1942 hotel, it bears little resemblance to the old place, as depicted in mementos on the second-floor walls of the executive offices. In 1988, without disturbing the basic cowboy character of the place, a new owner lowered the room rates, reduced the gaming table minimums, and converted the showroom into a buffet. An Early West motif prevails, but the rooms have been upgraded and you won't find cactus or branding irons on the walls as in the original hotel. The medium-size rooms, decorated in earth tones, have separate dining areas and views of the Strip or the Frontier garden area. *3120 Las Vegas Blvd. S, 89109, tel. 702/794–8200 or 800/634–6966. 1,400 rooms. Facilities: 4 restaurants, swimming pool, putting green, 2 tennis courts, lounge. AE, D, DC, MC, V.*

Hacienda Hotel and Casino. One of the first hotels you see from the freeway if you're driving in from southern California, the Hacienda is a refreshing alternative to some of its bigger, more impersonal competitors up the Strip. In early 1991, 400 rooms were added and the casino space was doubled. A loud waterfall greets you when you enter the Spanish-style lobby. Rooms are small, with white walls, twin beds, and eating areas; the views take in Las Vegas Boulevard or the freeway. The showroom hosts an illusion act. The hotel's Little Church of the West, one of the oldest wedding chapels in town, was originally built in 1942 on the property of the Last Frontier Hotel. *3950 Las Vegas Blvd. S, 89119, tel. 702/739–8911 or 800/634–713. 985 rooms, 65 suites. Facilities: 3 restaurants, swimming pool, 6 tennis courts, showroom, wedding chapel, lounge, RV park. AE, D, DC, MC, V.*

Harrah's Hotel and Casino. You can't miss the 450-foot-long Mississippi River gambling boat affectionately known as the "Ship on the Strip"; even before you see it, you can hear it tooting its foghorn. Originally a Holiday Inn when it opened in 1973, it has sailed under Harrah's flag since 1992. While the casino is as red and bawdy-looking as it can be, the rooms are modest and have lavender doors, gray walls, blue bedspreads and matching curtains, and dark-wood furniture. Jackson Square shopping center outside the hotel furthers the New Orleans French Quarter theme, with such shops as Holiday Jazz, Louisiana Limited, and Cajun Spice. *3475 Las Vegas Blvd. S, 89109, tel. 702/369–5000 or 800/634–6765. 1,686 rooms, 39 suites. Facilities: 5 restaurants, swimming pool, health club, lounge, showroom. AE, D, DC, MC, V.*

Imperial Palace Hotel & Casino. The Imperial Palace was

the first hotel built in Las Vegas around an Oriental theme, featuring crystal, jade, and carved wood. Located in the heart of the Strip, it's home to one of Las Vegas's most popular long-running shows, "Legends in Concert" (*see* Chapter 9, Nightlife), and to one of Las Vegas's most popular tourist attractions, the Auto Collection (*see* Chapter 3, Exploring). The hotel offers eight restaurants and two buffets, the only multitiered sports book in Las Vegas, and its own wedding chapel. The hotel layout is somewhat confusing, and hallways to the rooms rather labyrinthine, but accomodations are pleasant. *3535 Las Vegas Blvd. S, 89109, tel. 702/731–3311 or 800/634–6441. 2,700 rooms. Facilities: 10 restaurants, swimming pool, doctor's office, shopping arcade, wedding chapel, lounge, antique-car museum, showroom. AE, DC, MC, V.*

Lady Luck Casino and Hotel. The addition of a 25-story, 400-room tower in 1989 made this the third-largest hotel property downtown. The new tower is across the street from the 17-story tower that opened in 1986, and visitors travel from the old Lady to the new Lady via a glass-enclosed pedestrian bridge on the third-floor level. Lady Luck has small, bright rooms with white walls and half-windows that look out on Ogden Street. *206 N. 3rd St., 89109, tel. 702/477–3000 or 800/634–6580. 800 rooms. Facilities: 4 restaurants, showroom, swimming pool. AE, D, DC, MC, V.*

Las Vegas Club Hotel and Casino. Here, a sports theme prevails everywhere but in the guest rooms. The coffee shop is the Dugout, the lobby walls display baseball and basketball photos and memorabilia, and a gift shop offers a wide selection of baseball shirts. The small rooms have a light-brown finish, the beds have small awnings, and the tiny half-windows overlook Fremont Street. *18 E. Fremont St., 89109, tel. 702/385–1664 or 800/634–6532. 224 rooms. Facilities: 2 restaurants, lounge. AE, DC, MC, V.*

Luxor. (Scheduled to open October 1993.) The folks at Circus Circus, who also developed Excalibur, are now busily at work on Luxor, 2,521-room, 30-story, pyramid-shape complex. Conceived as a vast archaeological dig where the mysteries of ancient Egypt are revealed as though in a state of excavation, Luxor will contain replicas of Egyptian artifacts, including a reproduction of King Tut's tomb. River Nile boats will transport hotel guests to elevators that travel up the 39-degree incline of the pyramid. Seven restaurants, a 1,200-seat arena, and an entertainment complex are on the drawing boards. *3900 Las Vegas Blvd. S, 89119, tel. 702/262–4000.*

Maxim Hotel and Casino. Situated just two blocks off the Strip, this is a good place to try when other establishments have no room. The Maxim's medium-size rooms are decorated in earth tones. Because the swimming pool—blue, with a big M on the bottom—is right on Flamingo Road, one of the busiest streets in town, you'll notice the exhaust fumes while you're in the water. *160 E. Flamingo Rd.,*

89109, tel. 702/731–4300 or 800/634–6987. 795 rooms. Facilities: 2 restaurants, swimming pool, lounge, showroom. AE, D, DC, MC, V.

MGM Grand Hotel and Theme Park. (Scheduled to open February 1994.) Construction is almost finished on a new 112-acre megaresort and movieland theme park, on the grounds of the former Tropicana golf course and Marina Hotel. The theme park (featuring shows, food, shops, and 12 rides) will be set in a re-creation of a movie studio's back lot. Four emerald-green, Wizard of Oz–theme towers, three of them 30 stories, will house 5,021 guest rooms, including 733 Hollywood-inspired suites. Eight eateries are planned (Chinese, Southwestern, Italian, seafood, and a steak house among them) plus a food court, a buffet, and a coffee shop. Also in the works are a health club, a swimming complex with three pools (plus slides and waterfalls), and tennis courts. A child-care center will offer supervised activities for youngsters. *3805 Las Vegas Blvd. S, 89109, tel. 702/891–1111 or 800/929–1111.*

Plaza Hotel. Those taking Amtrak to town will step off the train into the Plaza. One of the newer downtown hotels, opened in 1971, the Plaza anchors Fremont Street and can be seen in the center of nearly every photo of it. The hotel's roof is the base of activities for broadcasts of the Las Vegas New Year's celebrations. The Plaza almost always has a room, even during big conventions. A green decor and mirrors above the bed characterize the medium-size rooms. Be sure to ask for one overlooking Fremont Street; otherwise you'll have a view of the railroad tracks. *1 Main St., 89109, tel. 702/386–2110 or 800/634–6575. 1,037 rooms. Facilities: 3 restaurants, swimming pool, 4 tennis courts, wedding chapel, jogging track, lounge, Amtrak depot, showroom. AE, D, DC, MC, V.*

Riviera Hotel. Once upon a time there was a nice nine-story hotel-casino on the Strip that styled itself after the Miami resorts of the 1950s and tried to capture the feeling of the French Riviera. As time went on, an owner decided to expand by adding a tower. Then a new owner added another tower and enlarged the casino. Still another owner tacked on two more towers and moved the casino walls yet farther apart. It could be argued that one of them should have torn it all down and started from scratch, but what's done is done, and the Riviera won't be expanding again for a while (the last planned construction project, a new 40-story tower and amusement park, has been canceled indefinitely). Though the casino itself has become less of a maze since the completion of the last expansion in 1991 (it's now basically one huge room), it's still a ramble to locate the proper elevator to the correct tower to your room. Most of the accommodations are large, modern affairs with maroon bedspreads and carpeting, teak furniture, and dining areas (be sure to ask for a room overlooking the Strip). Four showrooms showcase female impersonators, a hot production show, a comedy club, and a topless dance revue. *2901 Las Vegas*

Blvd. S, 89109, tel. 702/734–5110 or 800/634–6753. 1,959 rooms, 150 suites. Facilities: 3 restaurants, swimming pool, health club, 2 tennis courts, 4 showrooms. AE, DC, MC, V.

Sahara Las Vegas Hotel. The oasis theme, established in 1952 when the Sahara opened for business and had statues of camels in the parking lot, still remains in this pleasant hotel, as does the familiar neon sign, the tallest freestanding sign in Las Vegas (222 feet high by 18 feet wide). Like many of its neighbors, the Sahara began as a small motor hotel and built itself up by adding towers, towers, and more towers. Unlike many of its neighbors, however, the Sahara has retained a small, gardenlike ambience. A walk through the lobby will take you past the pool, with its sunbathers and huts where you can sit and have a drink. The original rooms are small, in the motor-hotel style, with a dining area, a medium-size window, and utilitarian furniture; all the old garden rooms overlook the pool, greenery, and artificial grass. The tower rooms are larger, with king-size beds and mauve colors; they overlook the Strip or Paradise Road. *2535 Las Vegas Blvd. S, 89101, tel. 702/737–2111 or 800/634–6411. 1,961 rooms, 75 suites. Facilities: 5 restaurants, 2 swimming pools, health club, lounge, showroom. AE, D, DC, MC, V.*

Sands Hotel and Casino. This 750-room hotel, with its famous 16-story cylindrical tower poking up from the Strip like a periscope, is rich in history. The pool, shaped like a V (for Vegas), with a platform in the middle for sunbathers, was the setting for the classic 1950s Vegas publicity photograph that showed a group of fun-loving men and women shooting dice in it—truly a "floating" crap game. And in the swinging 1960s, the Sands was headquarters for Frank Sinatra, Sammy Davis, Jr., Dean Martin, Peter Lawford, and Joey Bishop, who came out here to make the quintessential Las Vegas film, *Ocean's 11*. The distinctive circular tower and casino underneath it were completed in 1967, though the original 11 low-rise 1950s buildings clustered around the pool remain. An 11-acre convention center opened here in 1990. Tower rooms are twice the size of garden rooms, with red bedspreads, walls, and curtains, and have views of the Strip and the Desert Inn. However, because of the shape, everything you do in this structure—such as finding the elevator or your room—takes you around in a circle. Presidents Kennedy, Nixon, and Reagan were guests in the Sands Presidential Suite. *3355 Las Vegas Blvd. S, 89109, tel. 702/733–5000 or 800/634–6901. 750 rooms. Facilities: 4 restaurants, 2 pools, putting green, 6 tennis courts, health club, lounge, showroom, convention center. AE, D, DC, MC, V.*

Stardust Hotel and Casino. The vision for the Stardust came from the mobster Tony Cornero, who in the 1930s had run gambling ships off the southern California coast; he owned a small club out on Boulder Highway and dreamed of building the biggest, classiest casino in town. He didn't live long enough to realize his dream, however; one morning, while shooting craps at the Desert Inn, he had a heart attack, dying with the dice in his hands. Today the Stardust belongs to the Boyd Group, the operators of middle-market hotels (Sam's Town, the Fremont, the California) that emphasize slots, low table minimums, and good deals on food. Just down the street from the Convention Center, the Stardust added a new casino and 32-story high rise in 1990, which more than doubled the number of its rooms. The tower rooms offer a great view of the Strip or the hotel garden and pool area. *3000 Las Vegas Blvd. S, 89109, tel. 702/732–6111 or 800/634–6757. 2,500 rooms. Facilities: 4 restaurants, swimming pool, health club, 2 tennis courts. AE, DC, MC, V.*

Treasure Island. (Scheduled to open in October 1993.) The developer of the Mirage is currently building a 3,000- room hotel and casino based on the stories of Robert Louis Stevenson. Designed to resemble a pirate's village, the hotel will wrap around Buccaneer Bay, where once an hour you can see pirates and sailors duke it out aboard *Hispaniola* and HMS *Sir Francis Drake*. Lush, South Seas landscaping and pirate treasure further the theme. Planned are five restaurants, boutiques, meeting spaces, and a spa and beauty salon. Also, Cirque du Soleil is scheduled to transfer there from the Mirage as soon as the hotel opens. *3300 Las Vegas Blvd. S, 89109, no tel. at press time.*

Tropicana Resort and Casino. The Tropicana ads refer to it as "the Island of Las Vegas," but in reality the property surrounds the water, rather than the water surrounding the property. Still, it is a beautifully landscaped hotel-casino, including 35-foot Easter Island–like sculptures; Polynesian totems; a longhouse bridge: waterfalls; and a meandering swimming pool boasting swim-up blackjack tables, swim-up bars, and a 110-foot-long waterslide. The theme of the Tropicana is, as you would expect, tropical, with colorful birds all over the place; rooms have rattan furnishings and flowered bedspreads. The hotel is also home to the longest-running show in Las Vegas, "Folies-Bergere" (*see* Chapter 9, Nightlife). *3801 Las Vegas Blvd. S, 89109, tel. 702/739–2222 or 800/634–4000. 1,708 rooms, 200 suites. Facilities: 7 restaurants, 3 swimming pools, 4 tennis courts, racquetball, health club, lounge, showroom. AE, D, DC, MC, V.*

Vegas World Hotel and Casino. As soon as you step inside, embodiments of the Vegas World motto, "The Sky's the Limit," are abundantly evident. Planets, astronauts, spacecraft, and moonscapes decorate the casino; fronting the registration desk, red and blue plastic columns send up bubbles, creating a kind of Star Wars meets Guy Lombardo look. The decor of the medium-size guest rooms is spacesuit silver, with matching bedspreads, curtains, and furniture; many of the rooms overlook the residences that border Las Vegas Boulevard. *2000 Las Vegas Blvd. S, 89109, tel. 702/ 382–2000 or 800/634–6277. 1,270 rooms. Facilities: 2 res-*

taurants, swimming pool, lounge, showroom. AE, D, DC, MC, V.

Inexpensive **Circus Circus.** You can *always* find a room at Circus Circus; if they don't have one for you, they'll locate one. But beware, this place is both a madhouse and a maze. Circus Circus has expanded several times over the years; now it can be hard to figure out where you're going, and you'll run into crowds of similarly confused people while you try. The registration area is in the front of the hotel, under the pink porte cochère, but the room elevators are all the way at the back, necessitating a long jostling stroll through the casino. Upstairs you'll find painted circus tents in the hallway and some of the most garishly appointed guest rooms in Las Vegas: bright-red carpets, matching red chairs, pink walls and, on one wall, red-, pink-, and blue-striped wallpaper. The casino attracts so many visitors that drivers will find it a major achievement just getting into the parking lot. On a Saturday night, the stretch of Las Vegas Boulevard leading up to Circus Circus is often gridlocked; the valet parking sign reads FULL (though you may be able to get help—for a toke) and the nearest parking space is halfway to Arizona. (If you spend a few minutes learning the back way in, from Industrial Rd., and locating alternative parking, you'll save yourself a lot of grief.) Circus Circus is a favorite of families: Parents can drop the kids off at the midway to play games or watch the circus acts while the adults hit the slots; five-minute circus acts are performed every 20 minutes from 11 AM to midnight. The most recent boon to families is Grand Slam Canyon, a 5-acre theme park opened in August 1993, offering a flume ride, a roller coaster, pools, beaches, mountains, waterfalls, and more. Some of the kitschiest gift shops in Vegas are at this hotel; you can buy Elvis decanters, $80 slot replicas, Vegas bells, toothpick holders, and thimbles here. *2880 Las Vegas Blvd. S, 89109, tel. 702/734–0410 or 800/634–3450. 2,793 rooms. Facilities: 5 restaurants, wedding chapel, carnival midway with live circus acts, RV park, 3 swimming pools. AE, D, DC, MC, V.*

El Cortez Hotel. Here is a good deal in lodging: a room for two in the downtown area for $23 a night—available on a walk-in basis only, and not on Saturday. The two floors of tiny rooms have twin beds, a small TV, and a narrow window with a view of Fremont Street. *600 E. Fremont St., 89109, tel. 702/ 385–5200 or 800/634–6703. 315 rooms. Facilities: 2 restaurants. AE, D, DC, MC, V.*

Gold Spike Hotel and Casino. Jackie Gaughan owns both El Cortez and the Gold Spike. The hotel is billed as "Las Vegas As It Used to Be," with penny slots, 40¢ live keno, and $1 blackjack tables. The Spike charges only $20 a night, every night, for a small, plain double room with twin beds, a nightstand, TV, and a view of East Ogden Avenue. A suite for $30 a night adds a four-poster, couch, and balcony. All rates include breakfast for each guest. *400 E. Ogden Ave.,*

89109, tel. 702/384–8444 or 800/634–6703. 110 rooms. Facilities: coffee shop. AE, D, DC, MC, V.

Sam's Town Hotel and Casino. Sam's Town is named for Sam Boyd, the pioneer gambler and owner who built a small grubstake into one of the largest casino companies—a closely held corporation of family and friends—in Nevada; he died in 1993 at the age of 86. His Boyd Group now owns Sam's, the Fremont, the California, and the Stardust in Las Vegas, and the Eldorado and new Joker's Wild in Henderson. This property is far from the center of activity and close to the desert, which gives its Old West decor some authenticity. Indeed, Sam's excels at perpetuating the Western theme: Everyone wears garters and string ties, the food is good, plentiful, and inexpensive, and there's a big Western-wear store on the property. It's one of the few local hotels where you can wake in the morning and look out at the desert mountains in the distance. And it's a nice drive to here from Hoover Dam and Lake Mead: Boulder Highway offers a more scenic back-road route to these attractions than the freeway. *5111 W. Boulder Hwy., 89109, tel. 702/456–7777 or 800/634–6371. 192 rooms, 6 suites. Facilities: 5 restaurants, swimming pool, bowling alley, lounge, RV park. AE, D, DC, MC, V.*

Out of Town Two casino hotels on Interstate 15 serve those traveling the Los Angeles to Las Vegas route who want a break from driving.

Inexpensive **Gold Strike Hotel and Gambling Hall.** Only 30 minutes from Las Vegas (off I–15 near the California-Nevada border), the Gold Strike has rooms for $31 a night and a weird white-and-orange facade that has to be seen in full daylight to be appreciated. The casino has a strong Old West ambience. *1 Main St., Jean 89019, tel. 702/477–5000 or 800/634–1359. 300 rooms. Facilities: 3 restaurants, pool, lounge. AE, D, DC, MC, V.*

Whiskey Pete's Casino and Hotel. That you can see the neon image of Pete at night while you're still 15 minutes away is an indication of how dark the desert is and how bright the sign. Inside you'll find a noisy, surprisingly busy, state-line casino (it straddles California and Nevada) with lounge bands, cheap food, and rooms for only $31. The rooms are large, with king-size beds, cable TV, direct-dial phone, and small bathrooms. When you're headed for Las Vegas from the west, an overnight stop at Pete's will leave you 45 minutes of driving time in the morning. *Box 93718, Las Vegas 89193, tel. 702/382–4388. 600 rooms. Facilities: 6 restaurants, swimming pool, lounge. AE, D, DC, MC, V.*

Motels

Motels offer you the opportunity to save some money and the chance to park just outside your room. Those who dread having to search for a parking space and then trek long distances through halls and casinos to reach their bed may prefer the compactness of the motel. Don't be concerned that staying in a motel will take you away from the action; all the motels listed here are near casinos, so when you have the gambling urge, you can cross the street and start dropping quarters.

Inexpensive **Motel 6.** Welcome to the largest Motel 6 in the United States, with 877 rooms, a pool, and a big neon sign. Rooms here look like those of any other Motel 6, but when travelers think in terms of cheap accommodations, they think of this chain, so the place tends to get booked up fast. *195 E. Tropicana Ave., 89109, tel. 702/798–0728. 877 rooms. Facilities: pool. AE, D, DC, MC, V.*

Royal Oasis. This is the quintessential 1960s Las Vegas motel: on a large piece of property at the south end of the Strip (across from the Hacienda) with "old-growth" landscaping, well-used rooms (a bit tattered around the edges), a friendly staff, and rates under $20 (under $30 on weekends). What sets the Royal Oasis apart is its no-reservations, first-come, first-served, policy. This is very handy for people who blow in without a room booked; it's also nice to know when you're settled into a room that you won't get asked to leave on Saturday night because the motel is sold out with reservations (a common occurrence in other places). Local calls are free. *4375 Las Vegas Blvd. S, tel. 702/739–9119. Facilities: pool, laundry. MC, V.*

Sun Harbor Budget Suites. An excellent and nearby alternative to the Westward Ho (often crowded with convention-eers, slot-club members, and tournament players) is this sprawling complex on the corner of Industrial and Stardust roads. Every room here is a minisuite, with a living/dining room, small separate bedroom, and full kitchenette; the TV fills an open space between the living room and bedroom. Weekly rates offer a good discount; rooms are least expensive on the second and third floors. The Frontier, Desert Inn, Stardust, Riviera, and Circus are all within walking distance. *1500 Stardust Rd., 89109, tel. 702/732–1500 or 800/752–1501. 639 rooms. Facilities: pool, spa. AE, MC, V.*

Westward Ho Motel and Casino. The largest motel in the world, with seven swimming pools and a casino, the Ho is strategically located between the Stardust and Circus Circus. The location is also a drawback, however: On Saturday night, this part of town is gridlocked, and returning to your room by car will take considerable time—unless you learn the shortcut from Industrial Road. *2900 Las Vegas Blvd. S, 89109, tel. 702/731–2900 or 800/634–6803. 1,000 rooms. Facilities: restaurant, 7 pools. MC, V.*

9 Nightlife

The very name "Las Vegas" has come to be synonymous with a certain style of showbiz ever since Jimmy Durante first headlined at Bugsy Siegel's Fabulous Flamingo Hotel in 1946 and "Minsky Goes to Paris" introduced topless showgirls at the Dunes in 1957. In those days, the lounges gave up-and-coming entertainers a chance to polish their acts on their way to the showrooms, where the camaraderie and informality lent an anything-can-happen-here-tonight air to the entertainment. Over the years, the Entertainment Capital of the World has weathered a number of changes in its stage presentations, policies, and prices, but one thing has remained consistent for the past nearly 50 years: style.

Headliners such as Frank Sinatra, Wayne Newton, Bill Cosby, Ann-Margret, Tom Jones, and Diana Ross still sell out the 1,200-seat showrooms. Extravagant revues like "Folies Bergere" and "Jubilee" still stage spectacular productions, with outrageous sets, costumes, variety acts, and song and dance. Young and exuberant shows like "Splash" and "Enter the Night" have modernized the spectacle, and illusionists, who started out as brief breaks for the major action, have elevated their status to exalted heights. Female and superstar impersonators, "dirty" dancers, comedians—all perpetuate the original style of entertainment that Las Vegas has popularized for the world.

Some traditions have changed in recent years, however. Several hotels have added afternoon performances to their show schedules—for example, the "Viva Las Vegas" revue presented weekday afternoons at the Sands. Certain hotels have eliminated nudity and foul language in the name of family entertainment, especially at early shows. Some hotels even encourage parents to bring their kids along by offering special prices for youngsters, and many showrooms have banned smoking. And the only hotels that still offer a dinner show today are the Flamingo Hilton, Sahara, and Excalibur.

In the not-so-old days, the shows were loss leaders, much as the buffets and hotel rooms are today: They were intended to draw patrons who would eventually wind up in the casino. Admission prices to shows were dirt cheap, and the programs were fairly short. Nowadays it may cost you $49 to see Wayne Newton, and a ticket to the biggest production, "Siegfried and Roy," will set you back $75. Yet many of the smaller shows have much lower prices; at press time, "Hanky Panky" at the San Remo was charging $12.95 and tickets to "American Superstars" at the Flamingo Hilton were $19.80. Las Vegas publicists are fond of pointing out that tickets, even to the top draws, are cheaper than those for Broadway productions—and two drinks are included.

There are several kinds of shows in Las Vegas. The major stars who appear in the "big rooms" are the headliners who command the $40 to $75 ticket prices and attract audiences of 1,000 to 1,500. The big-production spectaculars—90 minutes of singing, dancing, topless show girls, specialty acts, and special effects—are revues that are extremely popular with the increasing numbers of international tourists who have descended on the city over the last 15 years. Foreign visitors also seem to love magic shows; the two most popular performers in town are Siegfried and Roy—who make things disappear while saying hardly a word—so you don't have to understand English to enjoy them. The same is true for the revues, of course, which rely less on dialogue than on musical numbers and the ubiquitous topless showgirls, whose blatant charms can be appreciated in any language.

Getting into certain shows has become easier than it used to be. Many hotels now have a policy whereby all seats are reserved (pick up your ticket at a box office near the showroom). On the other hand, tickets to see "Siegfried and Roy" are distributed in a slightly different way. You have to appear at the box office (it opens at 6 AM) up to three days before the show, take a number, and wait. Tickets are distributed on a first-come, first-served basis (with preference given, of course, to high rollers and hotel guests). One strategy to bypass the long lines is to check with the box office just before it closes (around 4 PM); another is to appear a half hour before show time and see if there are any cancellations.

To attend a show that doesn't have tickets, the old rules apply. You need to make a reservation and then stand in line at the front door of the showroom for at least 30 minutes (and at least an hour for a popular show on a busy night). On weekends it can be tough getting in to see the top headliners and production revues. Crowds are large, lines are long, and the prime spots are reserved for comped players. Your chances of getting a seat are usually better when you're staying—and gambling—at the hotel. If you plan on spending a fair amount of time at the tables or slots, call VIP Services and find out what their requirements are for getting a comp, or at least a line pass (that allows you to go straight to the VIP entrance without waiting in line with the hoi polloi). Then be sure to have your play "rated" by the pit boss when you gamble in order to qualify for the privileges.

Once at the showroom door, you enter the frightening realm of maître d's (who assign the seats at the door) and captains (who show you to your seats). Many variables determine the quality of seats from which you'll watch the show: how early it is, how crowded it is, how assertive you are, how aloof the maître d' is, and whether or not you tip the seating personnel. If it's early, the showroom is empty, and the staff is friendly, you can often get the best seats (in the middle of the room, in a booth, on the second or third tier) simply by asking. If it's late, the room is packed, the maître d' has his hand out, and you don't tip, you'll probably be ushered to the corner table on the floor, crammed in with 15 other exiles. To ensure a good seat, arrive early and discreetly toke the maître d' (with bills or chips the denomination of which he can readily see; $15-$20 is usually sufficient); if your seats aren't satisfactory, slip the captain a few bucks and point to better ones. Once you've been seated at a table, before the show begins, you'll be asked to pay your bill, which covers two drinks. So as not to disrupt the show, at most places both drinks—which have to be identical—are brought to the table at the same time. (To get around this oddity, many people order a bottle of wine.) Regardless, don't forget to toke your server.

Information on current shows, including their reservation and seating policies, prices, suitability for children, and smoking restrictions, is available by calling or visiting the particular box offices, or in several local publications: The *Las Vegas Advisor* is available at its office (5280 S. Valley View, Las Vegas 89119, tel. 702/597–1884) for $5 ($45 per year); this monthly newsletter is invaluable for its up-to-the-minute information on Las Vegas dining, entertainment, gambling promotions, comps, news, and Top Ten Values. You can also pick up free copies of *Today in Las Vegas* and *What's On in Las Vegas* at hotels.

Las Vegas–Style Revues

Boy-lesque (Sahara Hotel and Casino, 2535 Las Vegas Blvd. S, tel. 702/737–2515). While this show has been around Las Vegas for more than 15 years, an all new version opened in 1992. The female impersonators, with their elaborate costumes and artful makeup, pay tribute to the leading ladies of Hollywood: Barbra Streisand, Cher, Madonna, Dolly Parton, and Diana Ross.

Cirque du Soleil (The Mirage Hotel and Casino, 3400 Las Vegas Blvd. S, tel. 702/793–7722; moving to Treasure Island in October 1993). This New Age circus is the premier family show in town, a uniquely memorable experience bound to please all ages. From the moment you enter the big top, you are intimately involved with this show. "Flounes" (clowns) mingle and fool with the audience as they're seated, and roving "devils" make trouble even before the show begins. The music is rousing and haunting, the acrobatics chilling, and the dance numbers inspiring. With only a single ring, the usual circus-type distractions are kept to a minimum, and there are no animals in the show. Except for Siegfried and Roy, this is the most expensive show ticket in town (half price for children), but it's worth every penny.

City Lites (The Flamingo Hilton and Tower, 3555 Las Vegas Blvd. S, tel. 702/733–3333). "City Lites" follows the basic revue formula: topless show girls, specialty act, singer, show girls, specialty act, show girls, finale. If you like Broadway musicals, "City Lites" is the show for you. You'll hear songs like "42nd Street," "Dames," "New York, New York," "Cabaret," and "Lullaby of Broadway" in this very nostalgic tribute to the Great White Way. (The name of the show comes from the song "City Lites," a tune featured in the Liza Minnelli vehicle *The Act*.) Besides old show tunes, "Lites" also features a sight that has to be seen to be believed: bare-breasted ice skaters wearing pink headdresses. In between the gals is comedy, magic by Joseph Gabriel, and the Garza Brothers, whose act consists of putting silver paint on their bodies and transforming themselves into human sculptures.

Crazy Girls (Riviera Hotel, 2901 Las Vegas Blvd. S, tel. 702/737–9301). This is the dirtiest show in town, and it was created to be that way. Unlike other shows, which feature a mixture of topless and clothed show girls, "Crazy" has a cast of women who wear practically nothing at all times. The basic formula is a chorus line of topless women who lip-sync songs, gyrate to taped music, sing, and do a little comedy. The show is designed to remind the audience of the Crazy Horse Saloon in Paris, which Crazy Girls' producers claim is dirtier than any Las Vegas show, including their own.

Enter the Night (Stardust Hotel and Casino, 3000 Las Vegas Blvd. S, tel. 702/732–6352). This recently opened show features Vladimir, the famous Russian aerialist who soars above the audience in a stunning ballet; ice-dancers Burt Lancon and Tricia Burton; and 30 show girls dressed in high-fashion style, performing intricate dance numbers. You'll get a taste of the latest theater technology, including computer-controlled scene changes, lighting, and music.

Folies Bergere (Tropicana Resort and Casino, 3801 Las Vegas Blvd. S, tel. 702/739–2411). This classic French topless revue is performed in a large showroom, with music from 100 to perhaps 40 years old, played at a ponderous pace. On the whole, it's the same standard stuff that "Folies" has been presenting since 1959: singers, dancers, comedians, jugglers, and a can-can finale.

Jubilee (Bally's Casino Resort, 3645 Las Vegas Blvd. S, tel. 702/739–4111). Donn Arden, who has been producing shows in Las Vegas since 1952, put together this spectacular stage tribute to Hollywood for the MGM Grand Hotel in 1981; it was all set to go when a devastating fire occurred. The show finally opened six months later and has been running ever since, even after the MGM Grand became Bally's. "Jubilee" is the largest show in town, with a cast of more than 100 performing in a showroom with 1,100 seats. It offers great special effects: The sinking of the *Titanic* is recreated; Samson destroys the temple, and the wreckage goes up in flames. Show girls parade about in the largest collection of feathers and bare breasts you've ever seen. The $5,000 headdresses weigh an average of 40 pounds each, and the costumes were designed by Hollywood veteran Bob Mackie, who is perhaps best known for the outrageous dresses he has invented for Cher. As is standard for a Donn Arden show, a tribute to the good old days includes songs made famous by Eddie Cantor, Al Jolson, Bing Crosby, and Judy Garland; a short classical ballet uses the music of Johann Strauss. Between the numbers, jugglers, magicians, and specialty performers do their thing in front of the curtain while the stagehands change the set. "Jubilee" is one Las Vegas spectacle that may also be a victim of its own size: The show is so large that it loses some of the live, up-close excitement you get with a show such as "City Lites."

King Arthur's Tournament (Excalibur Hotel and Casino, 3850 Las Vegas Blvd. S, tel. 702/597–7600). "King Arthur's Tournament" is Las Vegas's newest—and one of its most unusual—big shows. The musical retelling of the King Arthur legend incorporates a medieval jousting show. Costumed knights, beautiful ladies, and fast horses are preceded by a medieval dinner, which you eat with your fingers. It's a great bargain and a wonderful family show.

Legends in Concert (Imperial Palace Hotel and Casino, 3535 Las Vegas Blvd. S, tel. 702/794–3261). For those who like the old-time superstars and aren't content merely to watch them on videocassette, "Legends" features impersonators of Elvis Presley, Marilyn Monroe, Buddy Holly, Judy Garland, Louis Armstrong, Hank Williams, and, more recently, Liberace and Roy Orbison. (The rule used to be that only nonliving "legends" could be depicted in the show—the Liberace impersonator was added a few days after Mr. Showmanship died, and Roy Orbison was cloned in April 1989, four months after his death. But as of 1989 that rule was changed, clearing the way for impressions of Neil Diamond, Dolly Parton, and Madonna.) The show is basically wall-to-wall music (enlivened by multimedia images of the real stars and some show girls and boys dancing in the background); the finale features Elvis in his white jumpsuit, singing "Viva Las Vegas."

Melinda, the First Lady of Magic (Lady Luck Casino and Hotel, 206 N. 3rd St., tel. 702/477–3000). Beautiful blonde Melinda Saxe is the First (and *only*) Lady of Magic working in Las Vegas. Formerly a show girl in the old Siegfried and Roy extravaganza, Melinda aspired to create her own revue and succeeded. She's a pretty good magician, and the act features jugglers and unicyclists in addition to the magic. The early show is geared toward families.

Spellbound: A Concert of Illusion (Harrah's Hotel and Casino, 3475 Las Vegas Blvd. S, tel. 702/369–5222). As do most revues in Las Vegas, this one gives you a large dose of magic and illusion, along with comedy, dancing, and juggling. The headliners are Tim Kole and Jenny Lynn, a husband-and-wife team that specializes in transformation illusions; other acts include Sherry Lukas, who turns playing cards into doves and then the doves into poodles.

Splash (Riviera Hotel, 2901 Las Vegas Blvd. S, tel. 702/734–3901). This isn't a traditional Vegas T & A show in any sense. First of all, the large number of female dancers are clothed. Secondly, instead of wearing the usual show-girl costume of headdress, fishnet stockings, and feather boas, the "Splashgirls" dress as sea serpents, clams, mermaids, and other amphibious creatures. In time to the music, they jump into a 65,000-gallon water tank, climb out, dry off, and dance in front of fountains that spout from various parts of the stage. Not only do the dancers get wet, so do show goers in the front seats. The music in "Splash" is more contemporary than that of any other Vegas revue production; producer Jeff Kutash deliberately presents a Top 40 sound, hoping to appeal to younger audiences, and create a new wave, as it were, of Strip entertainment. "Splash" also features Shimada the Magician and motorcycle daredevils who whirl around inside a giant steel "Globe of Death." The finale is a 23-minute salute to Broadway and Hollywood, with medleys from *Cats*, *Little Shop of Horrors*, *A Chorus Line*, *Phantom of the Opera*, and *Dirty Dancing*.

Showroom Stars

Whenever you ask Las Vegas entertainment directors why their showrooms don't book more contemporary stars, they tell you that the Whitney Houstons, Bruce Springsteens, and Elton Johns won't play Vegas. Or they insist that the kind of audiences who come to Las Vegas wouldn't pay money to see Tone-Lōc, the Fine Young Cannibals, or Debbie Gibson. Las Vegas showrooms have become a tad more modern over the past few years: Eddie Murphy has played the Las Vegas Hilton, and other recent acts have included Randy Travis, Jeffrey Osborne, Gladys Knight, Natalie Cole, Barbara Mandrell, and Willie Nelson. The Grateful Dead have instituted a new tradition of playing three shows at the Silver Bowl over Memorial Day weekend; U2 played there as well in 1992. And in April 1993, Paul McCartney kicked off his North American tour at Bally's. In general, however, Las Vegas headliners are a curious mix of performers who haven't had a hit record in years (Engelbert Humperdinck, Paul Anka, the Four Seasons) and well-established personalities who could sell tickets anywhere (Frank Sinatra, Wayne Newton).

The "big rooms" of Vegas, where the headliners appear, are three in number: Bally's, Caesars Palace, and the Desert Inn. Performance schedules vary with the star and the season, but most performers appear at least Thursday through Sunday nights. The giveaway tourist magazines in hotels and gift shops will tell you what stars are in town and where and when they're performing during the week. The headliners who command the most attention in Las Vegas these days are:

Ann-Margret. In 1960 she was discovered in Las Vegas by George Burns, who hired her to open his show at the Sahara Hotel. Hollywood talent scouts saw her act there and signed her for starring parts in the films *Bye-Bye Birdie* and *Viva Las Vegas*, in which she costarred with Elvis Presley. Over the years, she has developed a must-see act that features many male dancers and irresistible energy.

One of the highest-paid performers today (earning a reported $285,000 a week), Ann-Margret, now in her fifties, puts on a fast-paced show combining lasers, film, and music.

Engelbert Humperdinck. When you go to see "The Hump" at the Las Vegas Hilton, where he performs frequently, you'll notice a large group of women up front. This is his fan club, a pack of women who travel all over the West to see him, no matter where. When he plays Las Vegas, they come for the weekend, they're first in line, and they see three or four shows, sitting together in the front row. Such is the devoted following for a man whose last hit, "After the Lovin'," was way back in 1977. On stage he delivers a friendly show, pleasing his audiences with such past hits as "Release Me," "There Goes My Everything," "The Last Waltz," and "Am I Easy to Forget?" Over the years, Humperdinck has seasoned into a fine performer, and recently he added a tap-dance segment, donning a top hat to sing Fred Astaire tunes.

Tom Jones. Another Las Vegas veteran who is getting better with age, Jones may still split his pants to please the blue-haired ladies, but he refuses to sing only his hits. Sure, he'll throw in "Green, Green Grass of Home" and "It's Not Unusual," but he also performs such current tunes as his own remake of Prince's "Kiss," Robert Cray's "Ain't Nothing But a Woman," and Paul Simon's "You Can Call Me Al."

Wayne Newton. Mr. Las Vegas, the Midnight Idol, the King of the Strip, Wayne Newton plays the Las Vegas Hilton 20 weeks a year and is in many ways the epitome of the Las Vegas headliner. A homegrown phenomenon, he has been performing here since his teens, when he did an act with his brother Jerry at the Fremont's Carnival Lounge. On stage, Newton gives it the Al Jolson treatment, working and sweating his way through two hours of show—singing, telling jokes, playing the guitar, violin, and trumpet. Whatever one thinks of the kind of music (and questionable financial decisions and libel lawsuits) Newton is known for, no one would dispute the fact that, after all these years, he knows how to entertain his audience. Seeing a Wayne Newton show is as much a part of the experience of visiting Las Vegas as gambling and Hoover Dam. You have to know that you've been part of a "very special" audience, and only the Wayne Man can tell you that.

Siegfried and Roy. A trip to Las Vegas isn't truly complete until you've seen the master illusionists Siegfried and Roy strut their stuff. As the stars of "Beyond Belief" at the Frontier from 1981 to 1988, they sold out every show over a seven-year run. They left to tour for a year and a half, but Steve Wynn then signed them to a $55.5 million contract to star at his new Mirage Hotel, where they opened with an entirely new show in February 1990. In their act, Siegfried and Roy have made elephants and motorcycles disappear and have levitated each other as well as the lions and tigers who are their roommates in Las Vegas. The current show includes a fire-breathing dragon, lasers, music written and recorded by Michael Jackson, plus a home video of the stars' pet tiger cubs.

Lounges

The lounges of the Las Vegas casino hotels were once places where such headliners as Frank, Dean, and the gang would go after their shows, taking a seat in the audience to laugh at the comedy antics of Shecky Greene or Don Rickles or to enjoy the music of Louis Prima and Keely Smith. Now the lounges have been reduced to small bars within the casino, where bands play Top 40 hits in front of small crowds pie-eyed from the slots. Virtually every casino has such a spot; all you need to do is buy a drink or two and you can listen to the music all night long. Two of the nicest lounges are at the Las Vegas Hilton and the Tropicana. And local, off-Strip casinos, such as Palace Station and Arizona Charlie's, often feature hot lounge acts.

Comedy Clubs

Since the demise of the days when comedians reigned in the casino lounges, comedy has suffered. It's thriving again, however, in the 1990s version of the Las Vegas lounge: the comedy club. There are three in town, and all are doing big business.

Catch a Rising Star (Bally's Casino Resort, 3645 Las Vegas Blvd. S, tel. 702/739–4111). Three comedians play week-long engagements here, in what was a movie theater when Bally's was the MGM Grand.
Comedy Stop (Tropicana Resort Casino, 3801 Las Vegas Blvd. S, tel. 702/739–2222). Three comedians play two shows nightly at this 400-seat showroom. The price of admission includes two drinks.
An Evening at the Improv (Riviera Hotel, 2901 Las Vegas Blvd. S, tel. 702/794–9300). Three shows a night, each with a different comic, fill the stage at the Riviera's small club in the Mardi Gras Center.

Dancing

Cleopatra's Barge offers dancing to rock bands on a big boat in the Caesars Palace casino. *Caesars Palace, 3570 Las Vegas Blvd. S, tel. 702/731–7110. Live band Wed.– Sun. 10 PM–4 AM.*
The Hop has the largest dance floor in the city. With live music every night, a nice mixed crowd gathers. *1650 E. Tropicana Ave., tel. 702/736–2020. Open Wed.–Sun., 8 PM–6 AM.*
Shark Club is a dark, trendy, young club on three levels,

each with a dance floor and live music. *75 E. Harmon Ave., tel. 702/795–7525. Open nightly 7 PM–dawn.*

Fine Arts

If your tastes in shows tend toward the low key and cultural, you can call the Allied Arts Council (3750 S. Maryland Pkwy., tel. 702/731–5419) for the local theater, dance, music, and fine arts performances scheduled for the dates of their trip.

Music

Concerts   A number of large stadiums in town host individual artists or groups whose audience can't be contained in a club: The Grateful Dead and Paul McCartney, for example, are among those who have performed at the 31,000-seat outdoor **Sam Boyd Silver Bowl** (off Boulder Hwy. on Russel Rd., tel. 702/895-3900). The **Thomas and Mack Center** (Tropicana Ave. at Swenson St., tel. 702/895–3900) is the indoor equivalent of the Silver Bowl. The 10,000-seat **Aladdin Theatre for the Performing Arts** (in the back of the Aladdin Hotel, 3667 Las Vegas Blvd. S, tel. 702/736–0250) occasionally features major artists and touring companies that don't generally work Las Vegas showrooms—the likes of Fleetwood Mac, Tina Turner, and Anita Baker.

Country and   **Dance Hall and Saloon** offers live Country and Western music
Western   every night except Tuesday, when big-band tapes play. Country-and-western dance lessons are given free on Sunday, Monday, Wednesday, and Thursday at 6:30 PM. *Gold Coast Hotel, 4000 W. Flamingo Rd., tel. 702/ 367–7111. Open Tues. 7:30–11:30 PM, hours vary other nights.*
Western Dance Hall is another spot for country-and-western dancing to live bands. You can expect to hear renditions of recent country hits by George Strait, Randy Travis, and Garth Brooks. *Sam's Town Hotel and Casino, 5111 Boulder Hwy., tel. 702/456–7777. Open nightly 7:30 PM–5 AM.*

Jazz   The French Quarter room in the **Four Queens Casino** (202 E. Fremont St., tel. 702/385–4011) has live jazz Monday and many other evenings as well. New Orleans jazz plays nightly in the lounge of the **Bourbon Street Casino** (120 E. Flamingo Rd., tel. 702/737–7200).

Movies

A lot of movies play Las Vegas—there are 12 theaters and 67 screens in town—but you won't see film marquees on the Strip. The easiest cinemas to find are the **Gold Coast Twin** (4000 W. Flamingo Rd., tel. 702/367– 7111), which is at the Gold Coast Hotel and Casino, a couple of blocks west of the Strip; and the **Parkway 3** (3768 S. Maryland Pkwy., tel. 702/734–8151), near the Boulevard Shopping Mall, a short trek from the Strip.

Caesars Palace Omnimax Theatre (3570 Las Vegas Blvd. S, tel. 702/731–7901) shows movies every day in a big, shiny dome outside its casino; the immense screen shows 70mm movies. Films available in this format usually have appealing scientific or natural history subjects such as travel on a space shuttle or exploring the Grand Canyon; "The Fires of Kuwait," on the ecological disaster in the Persian Gulf, ran in 1993. If you've never seen a film this way, you owe it to yourself to have a look, for the larger-than-life images are breathtaking.

Merlin's Magic Motion Machine (Excalibur, 3859 Las Vegas Blvd. S, tel. 702/597–7777), the only "virtual reality" experience in Las Vegas, takes visitors on a wild, three-minute simulated joyride via roller coaster, toboggan, or run-away train. The large screen, intense sound system, and moving seats synchronized to the action on the screen work with the headset-induced images to take you temporarily into another world.

Strip Club

Olympic Gardens (1531 Las Vegas Blvd. S, tel. 702/385–8987), open 24 hours, is by far the swankiest strip joint in town. The dancers are real crowd pleasers and the patrons are out for good (more or less) clean fun. And women oglers get equal time here: A separate entrance in the rear leads to a back room with male strippers.

10 Reno and Lake Tahoe

Reno

Smaller, less crowded, friendlier, and prettier than Las Vegas, Reno is one of the great secret vacation destinations in the West. Like Las Vegas, Reno was first put on the map as a railroad station; Reno's action, however, remains downtown, on either side of the famous Arch, only a few minutes on foot from both the railroad station and the scenic Truckee River, which runs through town roughly parallel to the tracks. The casinos here have more amicable dealers, lower table minimums, and some vintage slot machines from the 1950s. Some Reno casinos also provide entire nonsmoking areas.

Reno and its sister city, Sparks (elevation: roughly 4,500 feet), preside over Truckee Meadows, a large valley blocked on the west by the mighty Sierra Nevada and on the east by the Virginia Range of Comstock Lode fame. The Truckee River originates at Lake Tahoe, one of the largest and most beautiful mountain lakes in the world, only 45 minutes from Reno. It then runs down the sheer eastern scarp of the Sierra, passes through Reno and Sparks, traverses spectacular Truckee Canyon in the Virginia Range, and finally empties into Pyramid Lake, a stunning watery apparition in the desert. A score of world-class ski resorts are within an hour of Reno, as are Virginia City, the best-preserved mining ghost town in the west, and Carson City, capital of Nevada.

Western Nevada, this section of the state, is surrounded by the Great Basin Desert. Its climate is continental: mild, dry, breezy. The average annual high temperature is just under 70 degrees; the low is just over 32 degrees. Rarely does the temperature climb as high as the high 90s in the summer or fall as low as single the digits in the winter. The sun shines more than 300 days a year.

The first permanent settlement in the area was Mormon Station, east of Lake Tahoe, in what is Genoa today. Yet Nevada was known for little more than its hot deserts until June 1859, when gold was found in Virginia City. The Comstock Lode, one of the richest bodies of gold and silver ore ever discovered, drew so many people to the area that Nevada became a territory in 1861 and a state in 1864. Virginia City is said to have had 25 saloons before it had 4,000 residents. In 1863 a young reporter on Virginia City's *Territorial Enterprise*, Samuel Clemens, signed his name "Mark Twain" for the first time in writing about the legislature in Carson City.

Reno's beginnings were in 1859, when Charles Fuller built a toll bridge across the Truckee River. Two years later Myron Lake bought the bridge, rebuilt the trading station, and added an inn and tavern. About four blocks up the street from where Lake's businesses once were is today's bustling Virginia Street and the Reno Arch. After the railroad came through town in 1868—to connect with the Virginia and Truckee railroad that carried the silver from the Comstock in Virginia City—the first building lot was sold and the city named in honor of General Jesse Reno, a northern Civil War hero. The present-day Reno Arch, with its legend, THE BIGGEST LITTLE CITY IN THE WORLD, is the fourth since 1926, when the first arch commemorated the passage of Victory Highway, one of the first transcontinental thoroughfares, through town.

Gambling came to northern Nevada in 1868 when the railroad reached Reno. By 1910 gaming had been outlawed throughout the state, but by 1930 lawmakers were being urged to legalize it again as a source of income for the state treasury. In 1931 the gambling bill was signed into law.

Raymond "Pappy" Smith, a carnival entrepreneur, came to Reno in the mid-1930s and called upon his carnie experience to usher gambling from the back room to the front. He opened Harold's Club right on Virginia Street: brightly lit, inviting, legitimate. Among his many innovations, most of which are still standard operating procedure for casinos today, were free drinks and other liberal complimentaries, a never-ending variety of gambling promotions, eye-in-the-sky catwalks, women dealers, and a massive national advertising campaign that went a long way toward making casinos palatable to the masses. William Harrah copied Pappy's techniques, but upped the ante by sparing no expense toward creating an impeccable, classy atmosphere.

Because the first major casinos were opened in Reno, by the early 1950s it had come to be known as the gambling capital of the state. The area was also known as a divorce haven. Nevada law permits divorces to residents of the state, and residency can be attained by living in the state for six consecutive weeks. For many years, before divorce laws elsewhere were liberalized, married women came to northern Nevada dude ranches, vacationed under the sun for six weeks, and left for home as single women.

In the mid-1950s, Reno took one look at the growth of Las Vegas, shuddered, and installed a "red line" around downtown beyond which no casinos could be built—thus limiting the expansion of gambling for another 25 years. It was only in 1979 that the line was erased and Reno began to look the way it does today. Del Webb's Reno Sahara (now the Flamingo Hilton), Circus Circus, Sundowner, Comstock, Peppermill, and MGM Grand (now Reno Hilton) were all built then.

Nowadays, Reno attracts a little more than 6 million visitors a year, many from northern California, the Pacific Northwest, and western Canada. After years of neglect and stagnation, downtown Reno is undergoing some improvement: two high-rise parking structures have recently been built, and the National Bowling Stadium, the only one of its kind in the country, is scheduled to open in early 1995.

Important Addresses and Numbers

Tourist **Reno-Sparks Convention and Visitors Authority** (4590
Information S.Virginia St., Reno, NV 89504, tel. 702/827–7647 or 800/ 367–7366).
Reno-Sparks Visitor Center (275 N. Virginia St., tel. 702/ 329–3558) is open weekdays 9–4:30, Saturdays 9–4, and June–August, Sundays 10–3.

Emergencies Police, fire, ambulance (tel. 911).

Hospital **Washoe Medical Center** (77 Pringle Way at Mill St., tel. 702/
Emergency 328–4140) and **St. Mary's Regional Medical Center** (235 W.
Rooms 6th St., tel. 702/789–3188) have 24-hour medical service.

Pharmacy **Shopko** (6139 S. Virginia St., tel. 702/852–0700) is open weekdays 9–9; Saturday 9–6; Sunday 10–6.

Getting Around

Reno, accessible by air, rail, and road, has a small central visitor core. Most major hotels are on or near Virginia Street, and the majority of the gambling action is within a four-block radius of downtown (with the notable exceptions of the Reno Hilton, Peppermill, Clarion, and John Ascuaga's Nugget in Sparks). A car will come in handy for those who want to hike, ski, or visit Virginia City, Lake Tahoe, or Pyramid Lake. A number of bus companies serve the area, making it easy to arrange nearby excursions.

By Plane **Reno-Cannon International Airport** (tel. 702/328–6400), on the east side of the city, serves western Nevada. The airport is a 10-minute drive from downtown. There is no commercial airline service to Carson City, the state capital.

America West (tel. 800/348-2777), **American** (tel. 800/433–7300), **Continental** (tel. 800/231–0856), **Delta** (tel. 800/221–1212), **Reno Air** (tel. 800/736–6247), **Southwest** (tel. 800/435–9792), **United** (tel. 800/241–6522), and **USAir** (tel. 800/428–4322) are the principal airlines that fly into Reno.

Airport **Citifare Bus 24** runs between the airport and the downtown
Transportation bus center every 25 minutes. **Airport Minibus** (tel. 702/786–3700) has service to Reno and surrounding areas. All major hotels offer courtesy shuttles from the airport.

By Car To reach downtown Reno from the airport, take Route 395N to Interstate 80, head west on I–80, and get off at the N.Virginia exit.

By Taxi **Reno-Sparks Cab Co.** (tel. 702/333–3333), **Whittlesea Checker Taxi** (tel. 702/323–0503 or 702/322–2222), and **Yellow Deluxe Cab Co.** (tel. 702/355–5555) serve the Reno area. The base charge is $1.50 plus $1.40 per mile.

By Train **Amtrak** (tel. 800/872–7245) provides daily service on the *California Zephyr*, westbound to San Francisco in the morning and eastbound toward Chicago in the evening. The passenger trains stop at 135 E. Commercial Row, right in the middle of downtown, snarling traffic—an amusing reminder that Reno is Reno thanks to the railroad.

By Bus **Greyhound Lines** (155 Stevenson St., tel. 702/322–2970) offers nationwide service, with frequent runs to the San Francisco Bay Area and other points in California.

Citifare (4th and Center Sts., tel. 702/348–7433) operates local buses in Reno 24 hours a day. The fare is 75¢.

Guided Tours

General-Interest **Sierra Nevada Stage Lines/Gray Line Tours** (2570 Tacchino
Tours St., tel. 702/329–2877 or 800/822–6009) has daily tours in Reno and from Reno to Virginia City and Lake Tahoe. Passengers are picked up at, and returned to, their hotels.

Exploring Reno

Numbers in the margin correspond with points of interest on the Reno map.

Reno's climate, much milder than that of Las Vegas, lures visitors year-round. In winter people come to the area to ski and gamble; in summer they come to enjoy the scenery and gamble. No matter what the season, laying a bet is the number-one activity in downtown Reno, and a tour of the city is principally a tour of the casinos, which are located on and near Virginia Street.

Casinos **Club Cal-Neva** (38 E. 2nd St., at Virginia St., tel. 702/323–
❶ 1046). Cal-Neva is a raucous, two-story gambling hall (there's no hotel) with an emphasis on slots surrounded by large railroad-car facades. The gaming tables have some of the lowest minimums in Nevada, and feature Top Deck Blackjack, a blackjack variation that can pay 17 to 1. The Reno Cal-Neva, which has no relation to the lodge of the same name at Crystal Bay at north Lake Tahoe, also houses Reno's largest and busiest race and sports book (the managers also run books at four other casinos) and its biggest keno game. Warren Nelson, one of the owners of Cal-Neva, has been around Reno gambling since the earliest days; he modernized the ancient Chinese game of keno by adding horse race terminology and Ping-Pong balls.

❷ **Harrah's** (219 N. Center St., tel. 702/786–3232 or 800/648–3773). Opened by Bill Harrah in 1937 as The Tango Club, Harrah's is the second-oldest casino in Reno. This is the snazziest joint in town, the house where the biggest entertainers play and the wealthy come for upscale treatment. To Harrah's credit, you can still find the occasional $1 blackjack table, nickel slot, friendly people, and friendly service

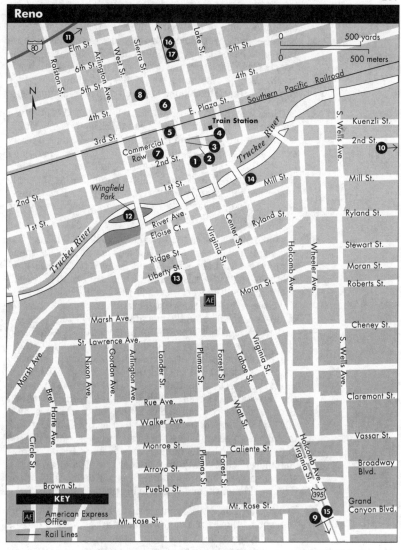

Circus Circus, **8**

Club Cal-Neva, **1**

Eldorado, **6**

Fitzgerald, **5**

Flamingo Hilton, **7**

Fleischmann Planetarium, **16**

Harold's, **4**

Harrah's, **2**

John Ascuaga's Nugget, **11**

Liberty Belle Saloon, **15**

The National Automobile Museum, **14**

Nevada Club, **3**

Nevada Historical Society, **17**

Nevada Museum of Art, **13**

Peppermill, **9**

Reno Hilton, **10**

Wingfield Park, **12**

here. Large and sprawling, Harrah's is composed of two buildings—one to the east and one to the west of Center Street—that cover almost two city blocks and house three casinos. The building east of Center Street features the Sports Casino (with a new large sports book), a children's arcade, a high-rise hotel, and a 420-seat showroom, plus Harrah's Steak House, one of the city's best restaurants.

❸ **Nevada Club** (224 N. Virginia St., tel. 702/329–1721). If you want to step into a time machine that can show you what life was like in the 1950s, you'll love the Nevada Club. Virtually every slot here is a 1950s reel classic. Pull the handle and line up three cherries or three bells, and you might win a classic hot rod. The Nevada Club's minimums at the table games are consistently the lowest in town, and fans of burgers, flapjacks, shakes, and penny slots should enjoy the 1940s-style diner, Kilroy's, on the second floor.

❹ **Harold's** (250 N. Virginia St., tel. 702/329–0881). This was the first major casino in Nevada, begun by Raymond "Pappy" Smith and his son Harold in 1935. It was the establishment that advertised HAROLD'S CLUB OR BUST on billboards around the world, even at the North Pole. Out front you'll see one of the prettiest murals in town, a portrayal of pioneers camped out in the mountains, with flowing blue water separating them from the Indians on the opposite bank. Harold's, the legend says, is dedicated in all humility to those who blazed the trail. Harold's has no hotel rooms, just casino space, restaurants, and a collection of more than 500 historic guns, the oldest dating to the 1500s. In the hallway between the Nevada and Harold's (both are owned by the Fitzgerald Group and they're connected on the second floor) is an exhibit of the USS *Nevada* World War II battleship. Harold's Club is the best place in the state to shoot craps, since it's the only casino with the Long Hands Meter, a kind of dice "odometer" that counts the number of rolls and amount of time a shooter has going. The "Long Hands" rolls of the day, week, month, and year win big prizes.

❺ **Fitzgerald** (255 N. Virginia St., tel. 702/785–3300). The concept of the Fitz, now extended to Las Vegas, had its start in Reno, where the original stands proudly on Virginia Street opposite Harold's. The center of the city's St. Patrick's Day celebration (when the Arch's hundreds of bulbs are replaced with all-green lights), the large, green casino is the home of good luck, Irish themes, and leprechauns. On the second floor, in the Lucky Forest, patrons can walk wishing steps, rub the belly of Ho-Tei (the god of good fortune), kiss the only Blarney stones to leave Ireland, and touch a lucky horseshoe. But don't be conned— more people lose here than win every day, or the Fitz would have closed long ago.

❻ **Eldorado** (345 N. Virginia St., tel. 702/786–5700). This property has been in the Carano family for three generations, and the Eldorado Hotel and Casino has grown into one of the two ritziest downtown establishments, competing with Harrah's for top honors. The casino is always rammin' and jammin', and boasts the world's largest roulette table. The restaurants are among the best in Reno, and the buffet is consistently voted number one; Choices, a food court extraordinaire, even puts most of the ones in Las Vegas to shame. The Caranos own their own California winery, and Greg Carano, the marketing director, was a quarterback for the Dallas Cowboys in the 1980s.

7 **Flamingo Hilton** (255 N. Sierra St., tel. 702/322–1111). What was originally Del Webb's Sahara in the 1970s, and the Reno Hilton for much of the 1980s, was transformed into the Flamingo Hilton in 1989. A multimillion-dollar remodeling brought a carbon copy of the Las Vegas Flamingo to the Biggest Little City in the World. The large, pink-feather neon signs that hang outside cast a bright-pink neon glow in the casino, and the tables include a few $2 minimums, but mostly $3 or more. The Flamingo has a small wing on Virginia Street, with some slots, a bar, and a fine Chinese restaurant, but the main operation is a block west on Sierra Street. The Sunday brunch at the Top of the Hilton, the bar and Continental restaurant on the 24th floor, is the most popular in town.

8 **Circus Circus** (500 N. Sierra St., tel. 702/329–0711). At the northern end of Virginia Street stands the familiar large neon clown. This version of Circus Circus (both sign and casino) is smaller than that in Las Vegas, but it's just as kitschy and crowded. For visitors with children, Circus Circus is a required stop. Complete with circus acts, clowns, games, funhouse mirrors, a snack bar, and a cheap buffet, the midway (overlooking the casino floor) is open from 10 AM–midnight.

9 **Peppermill** (2707 S. Virginia St., tel. 702/826–2121). Those who prefer the gaudy, glitzy craziness of Las Vegas to the more sedate Reno scene will love the Peppermill. In terms of both noise and decor, this is the loudest casino in town. Neon signs sit atop each section of the room, the dealers wear shiny vests that sparkle in the neon light, and the Peppermill's trademark silk plants, flowers, and trees appear in profusion, especially in the buffet.

10 **Reno Hilton** (2500 E. 2nd St., tel. 702/789–2000). To get the full effect of a grand casino, walk through the doors of the newest Hilton. Built as the MGM Grand and sold to Bally's in 1986, this 2,001-room monster was taken over by Hilton Hotels in August 1992. The 100,000-square-foot casino would be a giant in Las Vegas, so it's doubly overwhelming in Reno. The entertainers here, too, are on a grand scale, appearing in the largest showroom in town, the 2,000-seat Ziegfeld Theater. A ritzy shopping arcade is on the lower floors, along with an intimate movie theater left over from the original Grand, and a computer golf course. The bowling alley and big ballrooms are on the second level. Tennis

courts, a big swimming pool, a spa, a 452-space RV park,
parking for 6,000 cars, and a large concrete-based reflect-
ing pool occupy the rest of the property.

⑪ **John Ascuaga's Nugget** (1100 Nugget Ave., Sparks, tel.702/
356–3300). John Ascuaga's Nugget is the anchor of Sparks,
Nevada, Reno's sister city, founded in 1905 as a railroad
maintenance town. John A's, as it's locally known, was one
of four Nuggets opened in western Nevada in the mid-1950s
by Dick Graves, an Idaho restaurateur. The Sparks Nugget, eventually purchased by one of Graves's general managers, John Ascuaga, has expanded continually since it
opened, until today I–80 runs directly over the casino, and
there are 1,000 rooms, a beautiful indoor recreation area
(fifth floor), a 750-seat headliner room that features the
Nugget's own two elephants, and five restaurants. The
Nugget also boasts one of the largest exotic tropical fish
tanks in the world outside of a museum, set up behind the
extremely long casino bar. While you're here, take a stroll
around Victoria Square on the street out front, which has
an Old England theme.

Other   For a breath of fresh air and relief from the casinos and
Attractions crowds, walk about four blocks west along the Truckee Riv-
⑫   er until you reach **Wingfield Park.** From here you can catch
a glimpse of the river and its environs.

⑬ South of Wingfield Park, the **Nevada Museum of Art** features an array of traveling exhibits, from the Old Masters
to contemporary lithographs, and usually has one show featuring Nevada artists or history. The museum also has a
nice gift shop. *160 W. Liberty, tel. 702/329–3333. Admission: $3 adults, $1.50 students and visitors over 49. Open
Tues.–Sat. 10–4, Sun. noon–4.*

⑭ At Mill and Lake streets, you'll find **The National Automobile Museum.** Only a shell of what it once was, when William
Harrah was alive and owned it, this collection still features
more than 220 antique and classic automobiles. Harrah began buying vintage autos in 1948 with the purchase of a
1911 Maxwell and a 1911 Ford. When Holiday Inn bought
the company in 1986, many of the jewels were sold, a number of them to Ralph Engelstad of the Imperial Palace
in Las Vegas, where they are now displayed at its Auto Collection. Among those that remain are Elvis Presley's
1973 Cadillac Eldorado, John Wayne's 1953 Corvette, and
Al Jolson's Cadillac. All the cars are displayed in clever
period-piece galleries inside a gorgeous new $10 million
museum building. There's also a 22-minute multimedia pre-
sentation in the theater, a café right on the Truckee River,
and a gift shop full of automobile paraphernalia. *Mill and
Lake Sts., tel. 702/333–9300. Admission: $7.50 adults,
$6.50 senior citizens over 61, $2.50 children 6–18. Open daily 9:30–5:30; closed Thanksgiving and Christmas.*

If your Great American Love Affair is not with cars, but
⑮ with slot machines, be sure not to miss the **Liberty Belle Saloon** (4250 S. Virginia St., in front of the Convention Center, tel. 702/825–1776). This popular bar and grill is owned
by the Fey brothers, grandsons of Charlie Fey, who in-
vented the modern-day slot in the late 19th century, and au-
thors of the definitive reference book on the history of the
machines. Exhibits here display antique machines, including Fey's first, along with descriptions of the evolution of
the technology. The Liberty Belle is not only fascinating,
but it's also a fine place to eat and drink. It's open Monday
through Friday for lunch and dinner, on weekends for dinner only. The bar generally stays open till 11:30 PM.

To explore Reno further, head north on Virginia Street until
you reach the University of Nevada's Reno campus. The university, founded in Elko, Nevada, in 1874, moved to Reno in
1885 and now enrolls more than 11,000 students. Best known
for its business and mining schools, the Reno campus sprawls
over more than 200 acres.

⑯ On the campus is the **Fleischmann Planetarium,** with a 6-
foot-diameter model of the earth and moon, computer-
based exhibits, an observatory, a telescope, and science
quiz games. In the meteorite collection is one meteor that
you can handle. The planetarium programs special shows
that change periodically. *1650 Virginia St., tel. 702/784–
4812. Admission: $5 adults, $3.50 children under 13 and
senior citizens. Children under 6 not admitted to evening
shows. Open weekdays from 8 AM, weekends from 10:30 AM.*

⑰ At the northern end of the university grounds, the **Nevada
Historical Society** has much to satisfy the visitor interested
in Nevada's past. A permanent exhibit surveys mining activities, gambling, the Victorian era, and Native Americans. Additional special exhibits change regularly. Native
American artifacts, beadwork, and basketry are also on
display, and a research library that specializes in Nevada
and the Great Basin is open to the public. *1650 N. Virginia
St., tel. 702/688–1190. Admission free (donations accepted). Museum open Mon.–Sat. 10–5. Research library
open Tues.–Sat. noon–4.*

What to See and Do With Children

Circus Circus. This is one of Reno's big kiddie attractions.
Styled like its sister hotel in Las Vegas, the mezzanine midway is the place for free circus acts and carnival games.
Grab a couple of rolls of quarters downstairs in the casino,
then set the older children loose (the younger kids get
quickly overwhelmed), and hope that they don't win one of
the huge stuffed-animal prizes, which you'll have to carry
till you get home! *500 N. Sierra St., tel. 702/329–0711. Midway open daily 10 AM–midnight.*

The Great Basin Adventure. A covered children's history park, the Great Basin has seven exhibits that include a mining area, log ride, dinosaur pit, and children's petting zoo. Next door, The Wilbur May Museum has a fine display of wild animals and exotic artifacts from around the world. The whole complex is surrounded by Rancho San Rafael Park, the largest in the metropolitan area. *1502 Washington St., Reno, tel. 702/785–4319. Admission: $2 adults, $1 children and senior citizens over 62. Open mid-June–Sept., Tues.–Sun. 10–5.*

Idlewild Park. One of the oldest parks near downtown, dating back to 1926 when the first Reno Arch was installed on Virginia Street, Idlewild has lots of big trees, ducks and geese, a rose garden, picnic areas, and a small amusement park with a mini–roller coaster and other kiddie rides. *Idlewild Drive (take W. 1st or 2nd to Riverside, then cross the river and head right on Idlewild). Admission: $3 for five rides. May–Sept. open daily 11–6; Oct.–Apr. open 11–6 weekends and holidays only.*

Oxbow Nature Study Area. Do the kids' legs need stretching? Take them to this unusual city park by the river. A series of paths meanders through and around an oxbow (former channel) of the Truckee River. Decks, overlooks, narrative signs, and an interpretive center make this a great place for learning about Reno's river and water system. *Dickerson Rd. (head out W. 2nd; bear left on Dickerson; follow it to the end), tel. 702/785–2260. Park is open during daylight hours; call ahead for hours of interpretive center.*

Wild Island. This 11-acre water park features the slides and body flumes, and there's a kiddie wading area. A 36-hole miniature golf course includes a haunted house and a 41-foot castle. *250 Wild Island Ct., Sparks, tel. 702/359–2927. Admission: $13.50 adults, $9.95 children 4–9. Golf course admission: $5.95 for 36 holes, $3.95 for 18 holes. Open Memorial Day–Labor Day, daily 11–7; Sept., weekends 11–5.*

Wedding Chapels

Like Las Vegas, the Reno area is flush with wedding chapels that take advantage of Nevada's liberal marriage laws. A marriage license can be obtained in the state of Nevada without a blood test or waiting period, and it's valid anywhere in the state. A license may be obtained for $35 (cash only) at the Marriage Bureau in the Washoe County Courthouse (S. Virginia and Court Sts., tel. 702/328–3275) for anyone 18 years of age or older. Legal ID with proof of age is required. Couples age 16–18 can obtain marriage licenses with their parents' or a legal guardian's consent, given in person or in writing (and notarized) to the county clerk. The bureau is open 8 AM to midnight.

Civil marriages in Reno and Sparks are performed at the office of the **Commissioner of Civil Marriages** (195 S. Sierra St.). Witnesses are provided for the couple as part of the $35 package.

Many wedding chapels in Reno offer quick weddings that cost approximately $35 for the service (photos, music, and food are extra), plus a $10 filing fee and a $25 donation to the minister. Three wedding chapels on Virginia Street are: **Cupid's Chapel of Love** (629 N. Virginia St., tel. 702/323–2930), **Reno Wedding Chapel** (655 N. Virginia St., tel. 702/323–5818), and **Wedding Bells Chapel** (642 N. Sierra St., tel. 702/329–0909).

Shopping

Harold's Club Antique Slots (250 N. Virginia St., tel. 702/329–0881). Want to take home a classic slot machine? That can be arranged on the mezzanine level of Harold's, where prices begin at around $600.

Meadowood Mall (Virginia St. at McCarran Blvd., tel. 702/827–8450). Located in fast-growing southwest Reno, Meadowood is anchored by Macy's and J. C. Penney. Stores run the gamut from clothing to sporting goods, candy to luggage. Macy's is divided in two—with menswear and housewares in one store and women's apparel and accessories in the other.

Park Lane Mall (310 Plumb La. at Virginia St., tel. 702/825–7878). Closest mall to downtown Reno, Park Lane is anchored by Sears and Weinstock's and located between downtown Reno and the airport. In addition to the department stores, there are shops selling toys, jewelry, men's and women's apparel, and books, and an interesting Nevada store that carries only locally related items, as well as fast-food restaurants.

Parker's Western Wear (151 N. Sierra St., tel. 702/323–4481). This is the oldest and certainly the largest Western shop in town. Established in 1919, Parker's is an old-fashioned shop with hardwood floors, autographed celebrity photos on the wall, and large stocks of jeans, boots, shirts, jackets, and other cowboy and cowgirl duds.

Southwest Pavilion (8100 block of Virginia St.). A bit of a drive from downtown, this boutique-style shopping center is worth the trip if you're looking for upscale clothing, shoes, jewelry, or gifts. A number of shops here also feature Southwestern clothing and jewelry.

Sports and Fitness

Ballooning Reno hosts one of the biggest hot-air balloon races in the country in early September. One company that provides rides and weddings is **Zephyr Balloons** (Box 268, Reno, tel. 702/329–1700).

Biking This being the land of big hills and mountains, mountain biking seems to be the preferred mode of cycling, yet one can take leisurely rides through Reno along the paths that follow the Truckee River. Bicycle and Rollerblade rentals are available at **Bobo Sheehan's Ski Co.** (1200 S. Wells Ave., tel. 702/786–5111) and **Reno Bicycle Center** (809 W. 4th St., tel. 702/323–1221).

Golf When it comes to teeing off, Reno cannot match the year-round sunny desert terrain of Las Vegas, yet several 18-hole courses are in the area. These courses operate seasonally, most of them closing in the winter, so it would be wise to phone ahead before planning a visit to **Lakeridge Golf Course** (1200 Razor Back Rd., Reno, tel. 702/825–2200), **Wildcreek Golf Course** (3500 Sullivan La., Sparks, tel. 702/673–3100), or **Glenbrook Golf Course** (Hwy. 50, Glenbrook, tel. 702/749–5201).

Hiking Many hiking trails have been established in the Sierra Nevadas. Detailed information about hiking in the Reno–Carson City area is available from the **Carson Ranger District, U.S. Forest Service** (tel. 702/882–2766).

Trails **Mt. Rose.** One of the highest peaks hereabouts, Mt. Rose offers panoramas of Lake Tahoe, the Sierra Nevadas, and Reno. The trailhead of the 5-mile trail is located at the Mt. Rose summit on the right side of Highway 431, en route to Lake Tahoe from Reno, where you'll find a dirt road next to the maintenance building.

Jones Creek, Whites Creek. This 8-mile, moderate-to-difficult loop ascends to two creeks along a fire road and a jeep trail. You can pick up the trail at Galena Creek Park's north picnic area along Highway 431, about 15 miles from Reno.

Skiing Most of the good skiing is in the Lake Tahoe area. **Mount Rose Ski Area** (off Hwy. 431, 22222 Mount Rose Hwy., Reno 89511, tel. 702/849–0704), the closest resort to Reno—only 25 minutes by car—has 43 runs. Its summit is 9,700 feet, its base 8,260 feet.

Ski rentals are available at **Alpine Sports** (112 W. Moana La., Reno, tel. 702/825–8803) and **Bobo Sheehan's Ski Co.** (1200 S. Wells Ave., Reno, tel. 702/786–5111).

Tennis **Lakeridge Tennis Club** (6000 Plumas St., Reno, tel. 702/827–4500) has 14 outdoor courts and four indoor courts open to the public; it's a $15 court fee for all-day use. The **Reno Hilton** (2500 E. 2nd St., Reno, tel. 702/789–2000) has three outdoor courts and five indoor courts; rates are $6 an hour for outdoor courts, $20 an hour for indoor courts.

Windsurfing One of the thrills of coming to the Reno and Lake Tahoe area is partaking in the sport of windsurfing. Near Reno, the most popular spot for this activity is on Little Washoe

Lake. Lessons and rental equipment are available at **Alpine Sports** (112 W. Moana La., Reno, tel. 702/825–8803), and **High Sierra Sports** (6431 S. Virginia St., Reno, tel. 702/851–0200).

Dining

The number of restaurants in the Reno area is certainly smaller than that in Las Vegas, but the kinds of dining opportunities are similar: hotel restaurants, buffets, and coffee shops, in addition to some independent steak houses and ethnic eateries. Restaurants are listed in order of their price category.

Category	Cost*
Very Expensive	over $18
Expensive	$15–$18
Moderate	$7–$15
Inexpensive	under $7

Average cost of a three-course dinner, per person, excluding drinks, service, and 7% sales tax.

The following credit card abbreviations are used: AE, American Express; D, Discover Card; DC, Diners Club; MC, MasterCard; and V, Visa.

Harrah's Steak House. Located within the usually busy Harrah's casino, this dark, romantic restaurant has no view of slot machines to disrupt the warm ambience of the luxurious red booths and candlelight. Burgers, BLTs, and chicken sandwiches are available for lunch; veal steaks, chops, chicken, and fish are offered at dinner. *219 N. Center St. at Virginia St., tel. 702/786–3232. Reservations advised. Dress: casual, but no shorts. AE, D, DC, MC, V. Very Expensive.*

19th Hole Restaurant. One of the top rooms in town, the 19th Hole gets raves from locals as much for its outstanding setting as for its well-prepared Continental fare. This upscale, special-occasion restaurant is located right on the Lakeridge golf course, atop a hill: At night, seated in the plush red chairs, you can see the lights of Reno through picture windows; at lunchtime you can watch golfers at play, the mountains in the background. The lunch menu consists of sandwiches and burgers; seafood, steaks, and chicken are featured at dinner. All entrées come with the soup du jour or salad and a vegetable. *1200 Razor Back Rd., tel. 702/825–1250. Reservations advised. Dress: casual. AE, MC, V. Very Expensive.*

Rapscallion Seafood House & Bar. Steaks and pastas are available at this clubby restaurant, with lots of dark wood and private booths, but the specialty here is fish: Up to 30 varieties of fresh seafood appear on the menu daily. Among

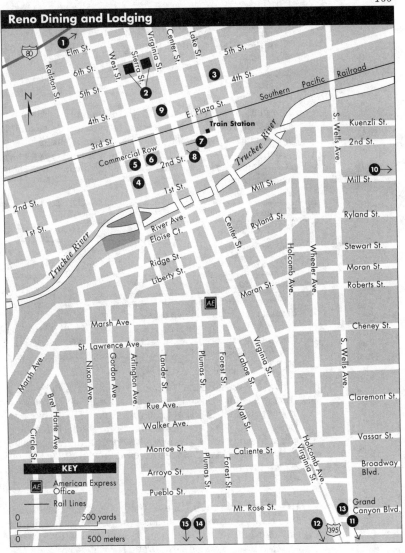

Reno Dining and Lodging

Café de Thai, **11**

Circus Circus, **2**

Comstock Hotel, **4**

Eldorado, **9**

Flamingo Hilton, **6**

General Store
(Nugget), **1**

Harrah's, **8**

Harrah's Steak
House, **8**

John Ascuaga's
Nugget, **1**

La Strada, **9**

Louis' Basque
Corner, **3**

19th Hole
Restaurant, **14**

Palais de Jade, **15**

Peppermill Hotel, **12**

Presidential Car, **7**

Rapscallion Seafood
House & Bar, **13**

Reno Hilton, **10**

Rivoli's, **5**

Trader Dick's, **1**

the popular dishes are calamari Rapscallion, deep-fried squid served with scallions and mushrooms, and Rapscallion stew, a concoction that includes a variety of shellfish as well as fish fillets, leeks, tomatoes, garlic, and white wine. Salads, burgers, fish, and steak sandwiches are available at lunch. The service is extremely efficient, with impeccable timing. *1555 S. Wells Ave., tel. 702/323–1211. Reservations advised for dinner. Dress: casual. AE, MC, V. Very Expensive.*

★ **La Strada.** This exceptional Italian restaurant is designed to reflect its name, which means a small street in an Italian market. The Carano family, which owns the casino, imported a special wood-fired brick oven from Italy for baking and an Italian chef who knows his stuff. His wild-mushroom ravioli is especially good, and all the pastas are handmade. *345 N. Virginia St. at 4th St., tel. 702/786–7297. Reservations advised. Dress: casual, but no shorts. AE, D, DC, MC, V. Moderate–Expensive.*

Rivoli's. Here is another Italian restaurant, but with a difference—the owner sings opera as he dishes up his specialties. The restaurant is small and intimate, right downtown but not in a hotel, and the food is terrific, with pasta, veal, and seafood specialties. The Rivoli has been a successful little trattoria since 1965. *221 W. 2nd St., tel. 702/784–9792. Reservations recommended. Closed Sun. and Mon. Dress: casual, but no shorts. MC, V. Dinner only. Moderate–Expensive.*

Presidential Car. The gourmet comp room for the high rollers of Harold's Club, the Presidential Car is another dining room with a view: Large picture windows look out on the spectacular night lights of Reno. The place has a private-railroad-car feel, with ornately scrolled tin ceilings and dark-wood chandeliers. Although it's primarily a steak house, this restaurant also does veal, fish, and chicken well. It's known above all for its desserts, luring local chocoholics with a fatally rich Death By Chocolate. *Harold's Club, Commercial Row and N. Virginia St., tel. 702/329–0881. Reservations advised. Dress: casual. AE, D, MC, V. Moderate–Expensive.*

Trader Dick's. This restaurant in John Ascuaga's Nugget features Polynesian cuisine in a low lit, South Seas–style atmosphere. Tropically clad servers bring out tropically prepared (i.e., dominated by sweet-and-sour sauces) beef, chicken, and seafood; a 6,000-gallon aquarium filled with—what else?—tropical fish sits above the back bar. If you're in the middle of dinner and a gong sounds, that means it's someone's birthday (the waiters sing a robust rendition of "Happy Birthday"). *1100 Nugget Ave., Sparks, tel. 702/356–3300 or 800/648–1177. Reservations advised. Dress: casual, but no tank tops. AE, D, DC, MC, V. Moderate–Expensive.*

John Ascuaga's Nugget. Although the buffets here are slightly more expensive than usual ($7 for lunch and $11 for dinner), they're consistently voted the best in town in local polls. There's a nice variety of fresh steam-table dishes, as well as an abundance of salads and desserts baked on the premises; the bread is particularly tasty. *1100 Nugget Ave., Sparks, tel. 702/356–3300 or 800/648–1177. Reservations advised 1 hour before buffet begins. Lunch 11–2; dinner 5–10. Dress: casual. AE, D, MC, V. Moderate.*

Louis' Basque Corner. The Basque tradition is very strong in northern Nevada; every good-size town north of Tonopah has at least one family-style Basque restaurant (and rooming house). The Basque hotel is a remnant of a time when tough solo shepherds roamed the mountains with their flocks during the summer, then spent the winters in the towns. At Louis's, the hearty peasant fare typical of the Basque region is served at long tables (you'll probably sit with strangers). The dinner price is all inclusive and you'll find yourself facing huge portions of soup, salad, Basque beans, French fries, and a choice of beef, lamb, or seafood entrées—along with a glass of wine and dessert. Be sure to try the Basque special cocktail, Picon Punch, a potent mix of liquors that'll quickly put you into the lively spirit of this place. *301 E. 4th St., tel. 702/323–7203. Reservations accepted for 10 or more. Dress: casual. AE, DC, MC, V. Moderate.*

★ **Café de Thai.** What the Café de Thai—a fancied-up hole-in-the-wall in a strip mall—lacks in atmosphere, it more than makes up for in food. Everything cooked up by Sakul Cheosakul, a Thai national who trained at the Culinary Institute, is exquisitely prepared. His creative menu includes excellent satay and papaya salad appetizers; hot-and-sour shrimp soup; and Oriental sausage salad. Traditional rice noodle dishes (pad Thai and the like) are also offered. The wok preparations are superb and reasonably priced: Try the garlic pepper pork, peanut beef, or basil chicken. The curries are spicy, but not incendiary. Service is attentive yet unobtrusive. *3314 S. McCarran Ave., (Mira Loma Shopping Center), tel. 702/829–8424. Reservations recommended. Dress: casual. AE, DC, MC, V. Inexpensive–Moderate.*

General Store. One of the better coffee shops in town is the General Store at the Nugget, a large, Barbary Coast–style setting. Open 24 hours, it offers an extensive children's menu along with your basic coffee-shop fare: burgers, chicken-fried steak, Jell-O salads. The fine fresh-baked bread is a plus. *1100 Nugget Ave., Sparks, tel. 702/356–3300 or 800/648–1177. No reservations. Dress: casual. AE, D, DC, MC, V. Inexpensive–Moderate.*

★ **Palais de Jade.** The ritziest Chinese restaurant in Reno is in a tasteful black-and-white room, understated and elegant. The dishes tends toward fancy Cantonese, with the mu shu, cashew, and kung pao you've come to know, along with some scallop and lobster preparations and Szechuan specials. The food is delicious, and the servers seem genuinely happy to see you—and treat you accordingly well. *960 W. Moana Ave., tel. 702/827–JADE. Reservations recom-*

*mended. Dress: casual. AE, DC, MC, V. Inexpensive–
Moderate.*

Lodging

Reno's 20,000 hotel and motel rooms serve roughly 7 million
visitors a year. As in Las Vegas, many of the hotels in Reno
are huge: The Reno Hilton, the largest by far, has 2,000
rooms, Circus Circus has 1,625, John Ascuaga's Nugget has
1,000; the room count at other hotels tends to be in the hundreds. Generally speaking, high season is the summer, low
season is the winter. Rooms can be especially difficult to
book on short notice between May and October, when local
events such as Hot August Nights, the Reno Air and Balloon races, the Reno Rodeo, and the Reno State Fair take
place one right after another. On the other hand, on weekdays in winter, hotels and motels practically give away
their rooms; they're still not as inexpensive as Las Vegas's
lodgings during slow times, but almost. Any time of year,
however, it's always best to call as far ahead as possible and
ask about any package deals that the large hotels may be
offering.

Category	Cost*
Very Expensive	over $80
Expensive	$60–$80
Moderate	$50–$60
Inexpensive	under $50

**All prices are for a standard double room, excluding service
charge and 8% tax.*

The following credit card abbreviations are used: AE,
American Express; D, Discover Card; DC, Diners Club;
MC, MasterCard; and V, Visa.

Eldorado. Recently expanded to compete with the best of
Reno's big hotel casinos, the family-owned Eldorado is
known for its fine food and attention to detail. Although it's
located right in the central gambling district,the hotel offers rooms that overlook the mountains on all sides. Valet
parking is available, and a large new parking structure has
just been completed across Sierra Street, with overhead
walkways into the hotel. *345 N. Virginia St., tel. 702/786–
5700 or 800/648–5966. 800 units. Facilities: 8 restaurants,
lounge, cabaret, pool. AE, D, DC, MC, V. Expensive–Very
Expensive.*

Flamingo Hilton. When the old Reno Hilton became the
Flamingo Hilton in 1990, it was was spruced up and given a
new casino, new neon signs, new restaurants, and remodeled rooms. The green-and-white accomodations are medium-size, and have mountain views from either side of the
hotel. On July 4, 1993, a new million dollar neon sign lit up

the entryway to this hotel, which is one block west of Virginia Street. *255 N. Sierra St., 89501, tel. 702/322–1111 or 800/648–4882. 604 units. Facilities: 4 restaurants, lounge, AE, D, DC, MC, V. Expensive–Very Expensive.*

Harrah's. One of the most luxurious hotels in downtown Reno, Harrah's has large rooms decorated in blues and mauves, with king-size beds and quilted bedspreads. Both sides of the hotel offer picture windows with views of the mountains. Because the lobby is on the second floor, you'll have to lug your bags through the casino. Full-scale production revues with show girls and comedians are staged in Harrah's showroom. *219 N. Center St. at Virginia St., tel. 702/788–3773 or 800/648–3773. 565 units. Facilities: 4 restaurants, showroom, pool, health club. AE, MC, V. Expensive–Very Expensive.*

Reno Hilton. While most of Reno's hotels are downtown (only the Peppermill, Clarion, and John A's Nugget are not), the Hilton is out near the airport, thrust up in the middle of the metro area, alone and proud, surrounded by a huge parking lot and little else of interest. The former Bally's was bought by Hilton in 1992 for a bargain-basement $82 million and received a new paint job and face-lift. Bally's, which owned the resort for five years, redecorated some rooms in earth tones; others remain Las Vegas–style gaudy, with green or orange color schemes and king-size beds. Some picture windows offer spectacular views of the mountains. The tallest (27 floors) hotel in Reno, the Hilton also has the largest casino, 100,000 square feet of tables and slots, and a large shopping arcade downstairs. *2500 E. 2nd St., 89595, tel. 702/789–2000 or 800/648–5080. 2,001 units. Facilities: 7 restaurants, lounge, tennis courts, pool, 24-hour bowling alley, shopping arcade, health club, indoor golf course, movie theater, wedding chapel, showroom. AE, DC, MC, V. Expensive–Very Expensive.*

John Ascuaga's Nugget. Don't let the out-of-the-way location in downtown Sparks put you off; the Nugget has a lot going for it, including some of the largest and most luxurious rooms in town—and at lower rates than Harrah's. Also, the stunning new recreation area on the fifth floor of the tower provides indoor swimming and hot-tubbing year-round. Another nice touch is that the elevators are adjacent to the front desk, thereby eliminating long, baggage-laden treks through the casino. Kids will enjoy seeing Bertha and Angel, the elephants who live in a habitat in front of the employee parking lots; the "girls" parade between the showroom and their home each night, and sun themselves at various times during the day outside their house. The ELEPHANT CROSSING sign at the street is a good photo op. *1100 Nugget Ave., Sparks 89431, tel. 702/356–3300 or 800/648–1177. 983 units. Facilities: 7 restaurants, indoor pool, showroom, lounge. AE, DC, MC, V. Inexpensive–Very Expensive.*

Comstock Hotel. Two blocks west of Virginia Street is one of the many Nevada casinos that aim to re-create the Old

West. Here the subject is the mining activity of the 1890s in nearby Virginia City. The small and conservative rooms have Victorian-style furnishings and views of the mountains or the city. *200 W. 2nd St., 89501, tel. 702/329–1880 or 800/648–4866. 310 units. Facilities: 2 restaurants, deli, pool, lounge. MC, V. Moderate–Expensive.*

Peppermill Hotel. The home of Reno's most colorful casino has plush, sedate rooms upstairs in various color schemes. While the Peppermill is 3 miles from downtown, it's near the shopping centers, and local residents love it. The fireside lounge and the slots regularly win top honors in the *Reno Gazette–Journal*'s "Best of Reno" awards. *2707 S. Virginia St., tel. 702/826–2121 or 800/648–6992. 633 rooms. Facilities: 4 restaurants, outdoor pool, lounge. AE, D, DC, MC, V. Moderate.*

Circus Circus. Although this is a smaller version of the giant Las Vegas property, it still has two sprawling towers, connected by a monorail. The marquee promises: ROOMS AVAILABLE. IF NOT, WE'LL PLACE YOU. If you do get a room here—and these are easily the most inexpensive rooms in a major downtown Reno hotel—you'll find the small, orange-walled accommodations, with two queen beds, as garish as those at the Las Vegas Circus Circus; here, though, some have views of the mountains. *500 N. Sierra St. at Virginia St., 89503, tel. 702/329–0711 or 800/648–5010. 1,625 units. Facilities: 3 restaurants, lounge, free circus acts, carnival midway for children. AE, DC, MC, V. Inexpensive.*

Nightlife

Reno's nightlife is much less frenzied than that of Las Vegas. There are only four showrooms. The **Ziegfeld Theater** at the Reno Hilton (2500 E. 2nd St., tel. 702/789–2000) is the biggest, with seating for 2,000. The entertainment alternates among headliners, such as George Carlin, Smokey Robinson, and Tony Bennett, rock bands like the Allman Brothers and Santana, and production shows such as "Spellbound." The 750-seat **Celebrity Room** at John Ascuaga's Nugget (1100 Nugget Ave., Sparks, tel. 702/356–3300) features country stars: Michael Martin Murphy, Juice Newton, the Bellamy Brothers, and Exile. **Sammy's Showroom** at Harrah's (219 N. Center St., tel. 702/788–3773) now has the only two minirevues in Reno: "Stagestruck," a celebration of Broadway, and "High Voltage," an eclectic dance and comedy cabaret. The 600-seat **Showroom** at the Flamingo Hilton (255 N. Sierra St., tel. 702/322–1111) currently is presenting "American Superstars," a high-glitz impersonator show.

Just for Laughs (Reno Hilton, tel. 702/789–2285), the only comedy club in town, has one show (8 PM) on weekdays, two shows (8 and 10:30) Friday night, and three shows (7, 9, and 11) Saturday.

Popular nightclubs for drinking and dancing to rock music with the locals include **Delmar Station** (700 S. Virginia St., tel. 702/322-7200), **Ice House Saloon** (310 Spokane Ave., tel. 702/786-8858), and the **Lime Lite** (50 E. Grove St., tel. 702/829-0448). The best place to dance to country music is at **Baldini's Casino** (865 S. Rock Blvd., Sparks, tel. 702/358-0116).

Excursions from Reno

A rewarding side trip from Reno, Virginia City is one of the largest and best-preserved 19th-century mining towns anywhere, attracting hundreds of thousands of visitors a year. Clinging precariously to the slope of Mt. Davidson, the little town is a time capsule of the Wild West, complete with boardwalks, saloons, and mine barons' mansions. Similarly, Carson City, one of the smallest state capitals in the country (and one of the few with no scheduled airline service) is well worth a visit. Among its attractions are fine 100-year-old stone buildings, the best museum in the state, several casinos, the State Capitol, a number of handsome 19th-century mansions on shady back streets, and the governor's residence.

Virginia City

Getting There From Reno, head 8 miles south on U.S. 395. Then take the Highway 341 turnoff and proceed 20 miles through the scenic Virginia Range to Virginia City. Geiger Overlook just before the summit provides a spectacular view of Truckee Meadows.

Exploring Virginia City *Numbers in the margin correspond with points of interest on the Virginia City map.*

The Comstock Lode remains one of the largest gold and silver deposits ever discovered; in today's dollars, with today's technologies, the Comstock would be worth in the tens of billions. The boomtown of Virginia City was built right atop the lode, which was mined from the hard rock under Mt. Davidson from thousands of miles of tunnels reaching a depth of 3,500 feet. The heyday of the boom lasted nearly 20 years, from 1860 till 1880. At that time, Virginia City boasted 30,000 residents, six churches, 110 saloons, and the only elevator in existence between Chicago and San Francisco. Half the town burned to the ground in 1875; only a few buildings still standing originate from an earlier date.

Unlike thousands of boomtowns throughout the American west, Virginia City was never rendered a total ghost town. Its die-hard residents, proximity to Carson City and Reno, and on-again off-again mining kept it alive for the nearly forgotten 75 years between final *borrasca* (bust) and its rediscovery in the 1950s. Though only 800 people now call Virginia City home, the town's proud citizens, some of them descendants of the first settlers, preserve their Wild West heritage like a treasured family heirloom.

The town is small, with only one commercial business street, and ideal for walking. Most visitors will stroll for a couple of hours on C Street, take a 35-minute railroad ride, look for souvenirs, and grab a bite to eat before going on to Carson City. But do explore a bit of B Street (uphill) and D Street (downhill) for the town behind the town.

● To orient yourself, you might well begin at the Virginia City **Chamber of Commerce** (C St., across from the post office, tel. 702/847–0311).Here you can pick up brochures, maps, and tips on what to see in town.

Samuel Clemens, then in his twenties, lived in Virginia City for a couple of years and reported on the local excitement, often utilizing the techniques of frontier journalism—wild exaggeration, satire, and ribaldry–for the *Territorial Enterprise*. It was here that he first used the name "Mark Twain," and later he wrote of those early days in *Roughing* ● *It*. His memory lives on in the **Mark Twain Museum,** where you'll find his copy desk, typewriter, an original printing press, and other artifacts. *C St., tel. 702/847–0525. Admission: $1 adults, 50¢ children, under 12 free. Open daily 10–5.*

One block south, at the corner of C and Taylor Streets, a ● second museum devoted to the writer, the **Mark Twain Museum of Memories,** commemorates Twain's time in Virginia City through many period items and exhibits on Virginia City history. *C and Taylor Sts., tel. 702/847–0454. Admission: Donation suggested. Open year-round, daily 9:30–5, with extended hours in summer.*

For a thirst quencher and a taste of Old West "hospitality," ● consider the **Bucket of Blood Saloon** (1 S. C St., tel. 702/847–0322), the host to many a Friday night brawl back in 1876 (which is how it got its name). Today it offers drinks and gaming, a wonderful view of the mountains, and a piano-banjo duo that plays the old tunes. The original 30-foot wood bar still stands, along with old pictures, guns, bottles, and swords. The world's largest dice machine (a $1 slot that flips and reads the dice, then pays off according to the odds) is not only one of a kind, but the best gambling experience in Virginia City, which has no tables, only slots. The Bucket of Blood T-shirt is a classic.

● Another Old West establishment, the **Delta Saloon** (C St., tel. 702/847–0789), is home to the "suicide table," a faro table later converted to a blackjack table. Three of the various owners of this item were said to have taken their lives when they were wiped out financially in the games played on it. The suicide table is at the same time the most hyped and humdrum sight in town. The nearby shrine to the Bonanza Kings, who unearthed the largest and richest vein of them all, is far more interesting. The rest of the joint is

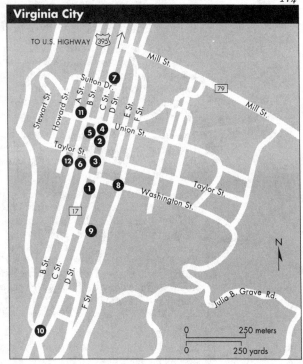

nicely remodeled, especially the upstairs hallway and ball-rooms.

6 Another historic Old West watering hole, the **Ponderosa Saloon** hosts a rear tunnel that meanders more than 300 feet into a restored portion of the Best and Belcher mine. A guided tour through this passageway offers a graphic display of the horrendous working conditions under which the Comstock miners labored. It's now a constant 52 degrees in the tunnel, around 60 degrees lower than the searing temperatures to which the men were subjected—along with steam, poison gases, and primitive technology—when they descended into the mine. The tour lasts 30 minutes, so if you chill easily, bring a sweater. *106 S. C St., tel. 702/847–0757. Admission: $3 adults, $1.50 children. Open daily 10–5.*

For further insight into local history, walk north to the intersection of C Street and Sutton Drive, where you'll find
7 **The Way It Was Museum.** A 16-minute color video describes the history of the Comstock Lode, and the museum holds an extensive collection of mining artifacts, among them a working model of an early water-powered stamp mill (used to crush the ore from which silver and gold was extracted), costumed mannequins, mining equipment, and a blacksmith shop. *C St. and Sutton Dr., tel. 702/847–0766. Admission: $2. Open daily 10–6.*

Turn now, and walk southeast toward F and Washington streets and the celebrated old **Virginia and Truckee Railroad.** In its heyday, as many as 45 trains arrived and departed daily between Virginia and Carson cities and Reno. Completed in 1869, the line hauled millions of dollars in gold and silver ore from the Comstock mines. Today the steampowered train makes 35-minute rail trips nine times a day through the old mining area. Passengers have the choice of riding in the open car or in the partially covered car. *Washington and F Sts., tel. 702/847–0380. Admission: $4 adults, $2 children 5–12, $8 all-day pass. Open daily Memorial Day–Sept., weekends only in Oct.; first ride at 10:30, last ride at 5:45.*

Head over to D Street to visit the history-rich **Mackay Mansion,** built in 1860 by the Gould and Curry Mining Co. John Mackay (pronounced MAK-kee), one of the Comstock's richest mining barons, took control of Gould and Curry and this house in 1874. The mansion is one of the area's oldest homes and includes an old mine vault. Tours of this beautifully restored Victorian-style home are offered. *129 D St., tel. 702/847–0173. Admission: $3 adults, children under 8 free. Open daily 10–5.*

Now go south on D Street until it curves toward C Street. Built in 1876, the **Fourth Ward School** is one of the nation's few schools of this size and type left standing. The four-story building was meant to accommodate 1,026 students, and it remained a school until 1936. Visitors can now enjoy an exhibit called "A Comstock Lesson," two classrooms restored to their original state, and a gift shop. *C St., tel. 702/ 847–0975. Donation requested. Open May 15–Oct. 31, daily 10–5.*

On the corner of B and Union streets, you'll find **Piper's Opera House,** host to such legendary actors as Maude Adams and David Belasco. Restored in 1969 by John Piper's greatgrandaughter, the theater operates on and off (mostly off, lately) as a museum. *N. B and Union Sts., tel. 702/847– 0433. Admission: $2 adults, children under 10 free. Open daily 11–4.*

A block south of the Opera House is **the Castle,** the best-restored mansion not only in Virginia City but in all of Nevada. Built in 1868 by a mine superintendent, the Castle was untouched by the big fire of 1875, and was sold only twice, with all its furnishings included. Thus, the museum part of the house (the rear half is occupied by the owners) has a fine collection of the original European antiques, including furniture, lamps, mirrors, wallpaper, shutters. *D St. just south of Taylor, no phone. Admission: $2.50. Open 11-4 daily.*

Carson City

Getting There For the trip to Carson City, head south on Highway 341 from Virginia City, turn west on U.S. 50, and continue for about 3 miles until you come to U.S. 395. You can also get to Carson directly from Reno by traveling south for 40 miles on U.S. 395.

Exploring Carson City Carson City was founded in 1858 by Abraham Curry, one of Nevada's great pioneers and visionaries, who bought Eagle Valley, a large patch of desert and a small trading post, for $1,000. Curry immediately laid out a town site for a state capital, even though "Nevada" was not yet a state, nor even a territory. In fact, it was still part of the Latter-day Saints' (Mormons') vast Utah Territory and had only a few hundred people living in it. Curry's amazing foresight was validated less than a year later when silver was discovered nearby in the Virginia Range. Within four years, Nevada had become a state. Curry's town site, named Carson City after famed western explorer Kit Carson, was indeed its capital.

Today, Carson City, a beautiful old town with 40,000 residents, has a vitality beyond its population numbers. Because two major highways—U.S. 50 and U.S. 395—both pass through the center of town, the streets are always lively. This is the place where gambling and easy divorces were legalized in 1931, where brothel prostitution has never been declared fully illegal (except in Clark, Washoe, and Douglas counties), and from where Nevada has fought its numerous battles with the federal government over the regulation of gambling, wilderness areas, and a high-level nuclear-waste repository. If Reno is the Biggest Little City in the World, then Carson City might just be the Biggest Little Town in the World.

A visit to the **Nevada State Museum**—the former Carson Mint, across from the Carson Nugget Casino—will brief you on local history. During the Civil War era, in an attempt to raise money for the Union, Congress authorized the hasty construction of this mint, where some $50 million in silver and gold was coined from 1870 to 1893. A complete set of Carson City–minted coins is now on display, reflecting this financial period in the building's history. Also featured are exhibits on early mining days; complete silver service from the USS *Nevada*, an early 20th-century battleship; the handiwork of Dat So La Lee, a Washoe Indian whose willow baskets are considered the finest in the world; and a maze of mining tunnels and exhibits in the basement. The gift shop is well stocked with Nevada books and souvenirs. *600 N. Carson St., tel. 702/687–4810. Admission: $2 adults. Open daily 8:30–4:30; closed Thanksgiving, Christmas, and New Year's Day.*

While you're in the town center, be sure to take a self-guided tour of the **State Capitol.** With its impressive dome, large green lawn, Alaskan-marble halls, and interesting murals, this is easily one of the prettiest capitols in the country. Portraits of Nevada's governors line the walls. A small museum on the second floor has the finest and most eclectic display of artifacts in the state, including a photographic history of the building itself and an exhibit of all the state symbols. While the governor still maintains an office here, most governmental activity takes place across the street, in the newer legislative building. *101 N. Carson St., tel. 702/687–5030. Admission free. Open daily 8–5 for self-guided tours.*

About 2 miles south of the capital complex, off U.S. 395, the **Nevada State Railroad Museum** features beautifully restored antique rolling stock of the Virginia & Truckee Railroad. An old locomotive and passenger car do a loop around the property during summer months. *2180 S. Carson St., tel. 702/687–6953. Admission: $1 adults, under 18 free. Open Wed.–Sun. 8–4:30.*

The **Carson City Chamber of Commerce** maintains its office nearby, and sells souvenirs, T-shirts, and maps for self-guided tours of local sites, government buildings, and 26 historically significant or interesting homes in the area. *1900 S. Carson St., tel. 702/882–1565. Open Mon.–Fri. 8–5 year-round, Sat. and Sun. 10–3 May–Dec.*

Lake Tahoe

An oasis amid Nevada's arid deserts, Lake Tahoe's vast expanse of crystal-blue water surrounded by rugged mountain peaks and dense forests of Ponderosa pines has become a favorite playground for natives and tourists alike. Tahoe offers some of the country's best downhill ski resorts in the winter, boating and fishing in the summer, and casino entertainment 24 hours a day, every day of the year.

Although the California/Nevada border officially divides the lake from north to south, Lake Tahoe's character also reflects an east/west split. The woodsier north shore has a few scattered casinos on the Nevada side and rustic condominiums on the California side, whereas the more developed south shore has 18-story luxury casinos clustered on the Nevada state line and blocks of small motels and restaurants on the California side. A scenic road circling Tahoe offers stunning vistas of lake, forest, and mountain.

Important Addresses and Numbers

Tourist Information **Lake Tahoe Visitors Authority** (Box 16299, South Lake Tahoe 95706, tel. 916/544–5050 or 800/288–2463) provides information and lodging reservations for the south shore.

For those who are driving a car around the lake, **Lake Tahoe Visitors Center** (Taylor Creek, tel. in season, 916/573–

2674; off season, 916/573–2600), operated by the U.S. Forest Service, offers a free cassette player and a tape that tells about points of interest along the way. It's open daily June–September, weekends in October.

Tahoe North Visitors and Convention Bureau (Box 5578, Tahoe City 96145, tel. 916/583–3494 or 800/824–6348, fax 916/581–4081) provides information and lodging reservations for the California north shore.

Incline Village/Crystal Bay Visitors & Convention Bureau (969 Tahoe Blvd., Incline Village 89451, tel. 702/831–4440 or 800/468–2463) stocks information on the Nevada north shore.

Lake Tahoe Hotline (tel. 916/542–INFO).

Ski Phone (tel. 415/864–6440) offers around-the-clock ski reports and weather information.

Road Conditions (tel. 916/577–3550, 702/793–1313, or 415/557–3755).

Emergencies Dial 911 for **police** or **ambulance** in an emergency, or call the **California Highway Patrol** (tel. 916/587–3510) or the **Nevada Highway Patrol** (tel. 702/793–1313).

Arriving and Departing

By Plane **Tahoe Casino Express** (tel. 702/785–2424 or 800/446–6128) provides service from the Reno airport (*see* Getting Around Reno, *above*) to Lake Tahoe's south shore casinos; **Aero-Trans** (tel. 702/786–2376) and **Reno-Tahoe Connection** (tel. 702/825–3900) serve the north shore.

By Car The major route is I–80, which cuts through the Sierra Nevada about 14 miles north of the lake; from there CA 89 and CA 267 reach the north shore. U.S. 50 is the more direct highway to the south shore. U.S. 395 runs 35 miles south from Reno to Carson City; U.S. 50 to the lake intersects with U.S. 395 at the south end of town. NV 431 connects the south end of Reno to the north end of the lake in 35 miles.

By Train There is an **Amtrak** station in Truckee (tel. 800/231–RAIL).

By Bus **Greyhound** (tel. 916/587–3822, 916/587–3822, or 800/531–2222) stops in Truckee and South Lake Tahoe.

Getting Around

By Car The scenic 72-mile highway around the lake is marked Route 89 on the southwest and west, Route 28 on the north and northeast shores, and U.S. 50 on the southeast. It takes about three hours to drive, but allow plenty of extra time—heavy traffic on busy holiday weekends can prolong the trip, and there are frequent road repairs in summer.

In winter, sections of Route 89 may be closed, making it impossible to complete the circular drive—call 916/577–3550 to check road conditions. I–80, U.S. 50, and U.S. 395 are all-weather highways, but there may be delays during major storms. Carry tire chains from October to May (car-rental agencies provide them with rental cars).

By Bus **South Tahoe Area Ground Express** (STAGE, tel. 916/573–2080) runs 24 hours along U.S. 50 and through the neighborhoods of South Lake Tahoe. On the lake's west and north shores, **Tahoe Area Regional Transit** (TART, tel. 916/581–6365 or 800/736–6365) runs between Tahoma (from Meeks Bay in summer) and Incline Village daily 6:30–6:30. Free shuttle buses run among the casinos, major ski resorts, and motels of South Lake Tahoe.

By Taxi **Sierra Taxi** (tel. 916/577–8888) serves all of Tahoe Basin. On the south shore, call **Yellow Cab** (tel. 800/332–9090) or **Lake Tahoe Taxi** (tel. 916/546–4444). On the north shore, try **North Shore Taxi** (tel. 916/546–3181) or **Truckee Taxi Service** (tel. 916/587–6336).

Guided Tours

Orientation Tours **Gray Line** (tel. 702/329–1147 or 800/822–6009) runs daily tours to Emerald Bay, South Lake Tahoe, Carson City, and Virginia City. Other tour providers are **Showboat Lines** (Box 12119, Zephyr Cove 89448, tel. 702/588–6688) and **Tahoe Limousine Service** (Box 9909, South Lake Tahoe 96158, tel. 916/577–2727 or 800/334–1826).

Air Tours **CalVada Seaplanes Inc.** (tel. 916/525–7143) provides rides over the lake for $43–$77 per person, depending on the length of the trip.

Boat Tours The *Tahoe Queen* (tel. 916/541–3364 or 800/23–TAHOE) is a glass-bottom stern-wheeler that makes 2½-hour lake cruises year-round from Ski Run Marina off U.S. 50 in South Lake Tahoe; sunset and dinner cruises are also offered. Fares are $14–$18 adults, $5–$9.50 children; in winter, the boat shuttles skiers to north-shore ski areas on weekdays for $18 round-trip.

Exploring Lake Tahoe

This tour covers the Nevada side of Lake Tahoe, traveling from north to south.

Numbers in the margin correspond with points of interest on the Lake Tahoe map.

To reach Lake Tahoe from Reno, drive south on U.S. 395 to Highway 431 (the Mt. Rose road), and take it over the summit (8,911 feet) and down to Highway 28.

❶ Two miles north on Highway 28, **Crystal Bay** is Nevada's northernmost community on Lake Tahoe's shores. Don't expect the flash of Las Vegas or the "biggest little city" atmosphere of Reno. Crystal Bay has more of a small-town,

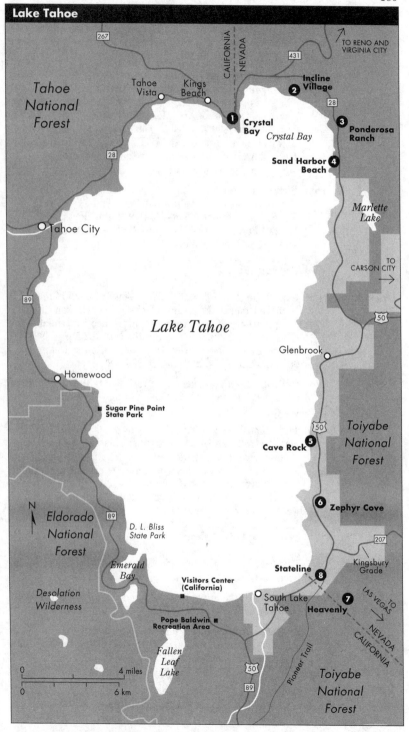

Lake Tahoe

267

TO RENO AND
VIRGINIA CITY

431

Tahoe
National
Forest

Tahoe Vista   Kings Beach

CALIFORNIA
NEVADA

② Incline
Village

① Crystal
Bay

Crystal Bay

28

③ Ponderosa
Ranch

28

Sand Harbor
Beach ④

*Marlette
Lake*

Tahoe City

TO
CARSON CITY →

89

50

Lake Tahoe

Glenbrook

Homewood

■ Sugar Pine Point
State Park

50

Cave Rock ⑤

*Toiyabe
National
Forest*

N

89

*Eldorado
National
Forest*

*D. L. Bliss
State Park*

⑥ Zephyr Cove

207

Kingsbury
Grade

*Emerald
Bay*

Visitors Center
(California)

Stateline ⑧

*Desolation
Wilderness*

South Lake
Tahoe

⑦
Heavenly

TO
LAS VEGAS →

NEVADA
CALIFORNIA

■ Pope Baldwin
Recreation Area

Pioneer Trail

*Fallen
Leaf
Lake*

0   4 miles

0   6 km

50

89

*Toiyabe
National
Forest*

outdoorsy feel. The **Cal-Neva Lodge** (2 Stateline Rd., Crystal Bay, tel. 702/832–4000) is one of the area's most popular casinos. In the 1950s, Frank Sinatra co-owned this casino/hotel, until he was seen in the company of a prominent gangster. The Nevada Gaming Control Board forced Sinatra to sell his share in the property, on the grounds that it was illegal for gaming licensees to hobnob with known mobsters. Today, the exterior of the Cal-Neva has a dated, '50s look, but it is undergoing a complete renovation. Inside, a spacious, mountain-lodge sitting room with an immense stone fireplace and a stuffed deer and elk create an Old West feel.

② Just a few miles south on Highway 28 is **Incline Village,** one of Tahoe's most attractive communities, with affluent lakeshore homes, contemporary redwood condominiums, and inviting shopping areas, as well plenty of outdoor diversions—hiking and biking trails and the area's greatest concentration of tennis courts. A new **Recreation Center** (980 Incline Way, tel. 702/832–1300) features an eight-lane swimming pool, a cardiovascular-fitness area, and a health-food bar. The **Hyatt Lake Tahoe** (Country Club Dr. at Lakeshore, tel. 702/831–1111 or 800/233–1234), Incline's only casino, offers gambling in an elegant setting, first-rate guest rooms, and a lakeshore dinner restaurant.

Fans of the longtime television series *Bonanza* can visit the ③ **Ponderosa Ranch,** at the southeast edge of Incline Village on Highway 28. The Cartwrights' home is set in a Hollywood-style Western town, complete with a Pettin' Farm, Moonshine Shootin' Gallery, and Hossburgers. There's also a self-guided nature trail, free pony rides for children, and, if you're here from 8 to 9:30 in the morning, a breakfast hayride. *Tel. 702/831–0691. Admission: $7.50 adults, $5.50 children 5–11, hayride $2. Open late April–Oct., daily 9:30–5.*

Traveling south along the east side of the lake, you'll come ④ across **Sand Harbor Beach,** a popular recreation area that often reaches capacity by 11 AM on weekends. In July the beach hosts a pop-music festival; in August it's the site of a Shakespeare festival (tel. 916/583–9048) in which performances take place on the beach under the stars.

Next you will meet U.S. 50 and wind through the forests along the lakeshore. The road passes through one of Tahoe's ⑤ landmarks, **Cave Rock,** a tunnel cut through 25 yards of stone (it's one of only two tunnels in all of Nevada). Tahoe Tessie, the local version of the Loch Ness monster, is reputed to live in a cavern below. About 6 miles south of Cave ⑥ Rock, you'll come to **Zephyr Cove,** a tiny resort with a beach, marina, campground, picnic area, historic log lodge, and nearby riding stables. From late April to early November, the MS *Dixie* sails from here to Emerald Bay, one of the most beautiful spots on the lake. *Tel. 702/588–3508. Fare:*

$12–$31 adults, $4–$9.50 children 4–12, including meals. Breakfast, cocktail, and dinner cruises.

A short distance past Zephyr Cove, just before the towering casinos and neon lights of Stateline, Kingsbury Grade (Rte. 207) goes off to the left (east). This was originally a toll road used by wagon trains to get over the Sierras' crest. **7** Now it leads to the Nevada side of **Heavenly** (tel. 916/541–1330 or 800/243–2836), America's largest ski resort, with all levels of terrain on both the California and Nevada sides of the mountain. Whether you're a skier or not, you'll want to ride 2,000 feet up on the 50-passenger **Heavenly Tram,** which runs part way up the mountain, to 8,200 feet. There you'll find a memorable view of Lake Tahoe and the Nevada desert. *Tel. 702/586–7000. Round-trip tram fare: $10.50 adults, $6.50 senior citizens and children under 12. Tram runs June–Sept., daily 10–10; Nov.–May, daily 9–4.*

Past Heavenly, Kingsbury Grade continues east. It's a steep and winding road down to Carson Valley, with spectacular views all along the way. At the bottom of Rte. 207, turn left on Foothill Road (Rte. 206), which leads past **Walley's Hot Springs Resort** (2001 Foothill Rd., tel. 702/782–8155), a small lodge with natural hot-spring pools (admission: $10). Beyond the resort you'll soon come to **Genoa,** the oldest settlement in Nevada, which hosts two good museums, Mormon Station State Park, and the state's oldest saloon, the Genoa Bar—all on the main street.

If you don't turn off at Kingsbury Grade, when you arrive in **8** **Stateline** park in one of the hotel lots, and walk. Five casinos are clustered together within one long block just east of the California/Nevada state border.

Harvey's Resort Hotel and Casino (tel. 702/588–2411 or 800/648–3361) is where gambling in Lake Tahoe all began. The hub of this towering casino is the original Wagon Wheel Saloon and Gambling Hall, established in 1944 by Harvey Gross. At the time, it was a six-stool counter with three slot machines and a 24-hour gas pump, the only service between Placerville and Carson City. Today, Tahoe's largest resort offers well-appointed rooms, eight restaurants, 10 cocktail lounges, and a complete health spa. Games include blackjack, craps, pai gow, roulette, baccarat, and many slot machines. Free "Party Aces" classes give tips on the table games on the hour every day from noon to 6.

A pedestrian walkway beneath Highway 50 connects Harvey's to **Harrah's Casino/Hotel Lake Tahoe** (tel. 702/588–6606 or 800/648–3773). This luxurious hotel offers spacious rooms with views of the lake and the mountains. Top-name entertainment is offered in the South Shore Room and Stateline Cabaret. Gamblers will enjoy the more than 150 table games, including blackjack, craps, baccarat, keno, roulette, poker, big six, pai gow, and bingo, as well as more than 1,500 slot machines. Harrah's also offers free classes in the table games. While parents gamble, kids can play video games in the supervised children's arcade downstairs.

Harrah's operates a second casino, **Bill's** (tel. 702/588–2455), next door. Open to the street, Bill's is comparatively low-key, with generally lower table minimums, a McDonald's restaurant, and 10-cent popcorn. Bill's is strictly a fun gaming house, not a hotel, and may be less intimidating to novice gamblers.

Caesars Tahoe Resort (Hwy. 50, tel. 702/588–3515 or 800/648–3353), on the other hand, attracts the high rollers. Roman details are subtle but prevalent in the casino, from laurel-wreath designs in the carpet to the waitresses' toga-style dresses. Games include craps, twenty-one, roulette, big six, roulette, baccarat, sic bo, pai gow, and, of course, hundreds of slot machines. Caesars also offers a race and sports book. Top-name entertainment is featured in the 1,500-seat Circus Maximus and the Cabaret.

The **Lake Tahoe Horizon Casino Resort** (tel. 702/588–6211 or 800/322–7723) is across the street from Caesars, and is shaking off its dated Western interior for a rich, contemporary look. In a bid to attract upscale patrons, the $15 million renovation follows a French beaux-arts design, with cream-colored marble and mirrors. Games include blackjack, craps, roulette, keno, mini-baccarat, and many slot machines. The Golden Cabaret features adult revues and production shows.

What to See and Do with Children

With its wealth of outdoor recreation, Lake Tahoe is an easy place to keep children and teenagers entertained. All the ski areas offer children's ski programs and most have child-care facilities. Although children are not allowed in the casinos' gambling areas, all these establishments have game arcades and some, like the Hyatt Regency in Incline Village, offer special youth-oriented activities all day. Among the lake's attractions, the **Ponderosa Ranch** (*see* Exploring Lake Tahoe, *above*) is usually a big hit with kids.

Commons Beach in the middle of Tahoe City has a playground for children. The **North Tahoe Beach Center** has a 26-foot hot tub, open year-round; in summer, the heat is turned down until 1 PM for youngsters. The beach has an enclosed swim area and four sand volleyball courts. This popular spot for families has a barbecue and picnic area, a fitness center, windsurfing, boat rental and tours, a snack bar, and a clubhouse with games. *Daily fee: $6 adults, $3 children. 7860 N. Lake Blvd. Kings Beach, tel. 916/546–2566.*

In summer the **Lake Tahoe Visitors Center** (*see* Important Numbers and Addresses, *above*) sets up discovery walks and nighttime campfires, with singing and marshmallow roasts.

Off the Beaten Track

Donner Memorial State Park (off I–80, 2 mi w. of Truckee) commemorates the Donner Party, a group of 89 westward-bound pioneers who were trapped here in the winter of 1846–47 in snow 22 feet deep. Only 47 survived, some by cannibalism and others by eating animal hides. The Immigrant Museum offers a slide show hourly about the Donner Party's plight. Additional displays relate the history of other settlers and of railroad development through the Sierras. *Tel. 916/587–3841. Admission: $2 adults, $1 children 6–17. Open Dec.–Aug., daily 10–4; Sept.–Nov., daily 10–noon, 1–4. Closed major holidays.*

Old West facades line the main street of nearby **Truckee,** a favorite stopover for people traveling from the San Francisco Bay area to the north shore of Lake Tahoe. Fine-art galleries and upscale boutiques are plentiful, but you will also find low-key diners, discount skiwear, and an old-fashioned five-and-dime store. For a map outlining a walking tour of historic Truckee, stop by the information booth in the Amtrak depot.

Shopping

In South Lake Tahoe there's some good shopping south of town at the intersection of Routes 50 and 89, at the **Factory Outlet Stores.** In Tahoe City, try **Boatworks Mall** (780 N. Lake Blvd.), **Cobblestone Mall** (475 N. Lake Blvd.), and the **Roundhouse Mall** (700 N. Lake Blvd.).

Participant Sports

For most of the popular sports at Lake Tahoe, summer or winter, you won't have to bring much equipment with you. Bicycles and boats are readily available for rent at Lake Tahoe. Golf clubs can be rented at several area courses. All of the major ski resorts have rental shops.

Boating Lake Tahoe draws boat, waterski, and jet-ski enthusiasts. Keep in mind that the water at Lake Tahoe is always cold— you'll need a wetsuit. **North Tahoe Marina** (7360 N. Lake Blvd., Tahoe Vista, tel. 916/546–8248) rents power boats, ski boats,waterski equipment, and private party boats. It also offers fishing charters. **Zephyr Cove Resort** (4 miles north of the south shore casinos, in Zephyr Cove, tel. 702/588–3833) features power boats, ski boats, Jet Skis, parasailing, and fishing charters.

Golf These courses in the Lake Tahoe area have food facilities, pro shops, cart rentals, and putting greens.

Edgewood Tahoe (U.S. 50 and Lake Pkwy., behind Horizon Casino, Stateline, tel. 702/588–3566) is an 18-hole, par-72 course with a driving range. Carts are mandatory.

Incline Championship (955 Fairway Blvd., Incline Village, tel. 702/832–1144) is another 18-hole, par-72 course with a driving range. Carts are mandatory.

Incline Executive (690 Wilson Way, Incline Village, tel. 702/832–1150) has 18 holes but is much easier: Par is 58.

Lake Tahoe Golf Course (U.S. 50 between South Lake Tahoe Airport and Meyers, tel. 916/577–0788) has 18 holes, par 71, and a driving range.

Northstar-at-Tahoe (Rte. 267 between Truckee and Kings Beach, tel. 916/562–2490) has 18 holes, par 72, with a driving range.

Old Brockway Golf Course (Rtes. 267 and 28, Kings Beach, tel. 916/546–9909) is a nine-hole, par-35 course.

Resort at Squaw Creek Golf Course (400 Squaw Creek Rd., Olympic Valley, tel. 916/583–6300) is an 18-hole championship course designed by Robert Trent Jones, Jr.

Tahoe City Golf Course (Rte. 28, Tahoe City, tel. 916/583–1516) is a nine-hole, par-33 course.

Tahoe Paradise Golf Course (Rte. 50 near Meyers, South Lake Tahoe, tel. 916/577–2121) has 18 holes, par 66.

Hiking and Camping **Desolation Wilderness,** a 63,473-acre preserve of granite peaks, glacial valleys, subalpine forests, the Rubicon River, and more than 50 lakes, offers hiking, fishing, and camping. Trails begin outside the wilderness preserve; Meeks Bay and Echo Lake are two starting points. Permits (free) are required for access and can be obtained from the **U.S. Forest Service's Lake Tahoe Visitors Center** (*see* Important Addresses and Numbers, *above*), the **Desolation Wilderness** headquarters (870 Emerald Bay Rd., Suite 1, South Lake Tahoe 96150, tel. 916/573–2600 or 916/573–2674), and the **El Dorado National Forest** (tel. 916/644–6048).

D. L. Bliss State Park (tel. 916/525–7277), near Emerald Bay, has 168 family campsites; the fee is $14 per campsite. There's a $5 day-use fee for entering the park; the park is closed in winter.

Skiing The Tahoe Basin ski resorts offer the largest concentration of skiing in the country: 15 downhill ski resorts and 11 cross-country ski centers, with more cross-country skiing available on thousands of acres of public forests and parklands. The major resorts are listed below, but other, smaller places also offer excellent skiing. To save money, look for ski packages offered by lodges and resorts; some include interchangeable lift tickets that allow you to try different slopes. Midweek packages are usually lower in price. **Ski Lake Tahoe Association** (tel. 702/588–8598) furnishes information on skiing in the area. Free shuttle-bus service is available between most ski resorts and hotels and lodges.

Downhill Skiing **Alpine Meadows Ski Area** is a ski cruiser's paradise, with skiing from two peaks—Ward, a great open bowl, and Scott, for tree-lined runs. All main runs are groomed nightly. Alpine has some of Tahoe's most reliable skiing conditions and an excellent snowmaking system; it's usually the first in the area to open each November and the last to close, in May or even June. The base lodge contains rentals, a cafeteria, restaurant-lounge, bar, bakery, sports shop, handicapped and regular ski schools, and a children's snow school; there's also an area for overnight RV parking. Beginner runs are close to the base lodge. Ski from every lift; there are no "transportation" lifts. *6 mi northwest of Tahoe City off Rte. 89, 13 mi south of I-80, Box 5279, Tahoe City, NV 96145, tel. 916/583-4232; snow phone, tel. 916/581-8374; information, 800/441-4423; fax 916/583-0963.*

Diamond Peak has a fun, family atmosphere with many special programs and affordable rates. A learn-to-ski package, including rentals, lesson, and lift ticket, is $29; a parent-child ski package is $37, with each additional child's lift ticket $5. There is a half-pipe run just for snowboarding. Snowmaking covers 80% of the mountain, and runs are well-groomed nightly. The ride up mile-long Crystal chair rewards you with one of the best views of the lake from any ski area. Diamond Peak is less crowded than some of the larger areas, and it offers free shuttles to lodging in nearby Incline Village. There's Nordic skiing here, too (*see* Cross-Country Skiing, *below*). *1210 Ski Way, Incline Village, NV 89450, off Rte. 28 (Country Club Dr. to Ski Way), tel. 702/832-1177 or 800/468-2463, fax 702/832-1281.*

Heavenly Ski Resort gives skiers plenty of choices. Go up the Heavenly Tram on the California side (*see* Exploring Lake Tahoe, *above*) to ski the imposing face of Gunbarrel or the gentler runs at the top, or ride the Sky Express high-speed quad chair to the summit and choose wide cruising runs or steep tree skiing. Or drive over the Kingsbury Grade to the Boulder or Stagecoach lodges and stay on the Nevada-side runs, which are usually less crowded. Snowmaking covers both sides, top to bottom, for generally good conditions. The ski school, like everything else at Heavenly, is large and offers a program for everyone, beginner to expert. *Ski Run Blvd., Box 2180, Stateline, NV 89449, tel. 916/541-1330 or 800/243-2836; snow information, tel. 916/541-7544; fax 916/541-2643.*

Kirkwood Ski Resort lies 36 miles south of Lake Tahoe in an Alpine-village setting, surrounded by incredible mountain scenery. Most of the runs off the top are rated expert only, but intermediate and beginning skiers have their own vast bowl, where they can ski through trees or wide-open spaces. This is a destination resort, with 120 condominiums, several shops, and restaurants in the base village, overnight RV parking, and a shuttle bus to Lake Tahoe. There's snowboarding on all runs, with lessons, rentals, and sales available. (For Nordic skiing, *see* Cross-Country Skiing, *below.) Rte. 88, Box 1, Kirkwood, NV 95646, tel. 209/258–6000; lodging information, 209/258–7000; snow information, 209/258–3000; fax 209/258–8899.*

Northstar-at-Tahoe is the Sierras' most complete destination resort, with lots of activity in summer and winter. The center of action is the picturesque Village Mall, a concentration of restaurants, shops, recreation facilities, and lodging options from hotel rooms to condos and houses. Two northeast-facing, wind-protected bowls offer some of the best powder skiing around, including steep chutes and long cruising runs. Top to bottom snowmaking and intense grooming assure good conditions. There's a half-pipe run for snow boarding, as well as lessons, rentals, and sales. (For Nordic skiing, *see* Cross-Country Skiing, *below.) Off Rte. 267 between Truckee and North Shore, Box 129, Truckee, NV 96160, lodging reservations, tel. 916/562–1010 or 800/533–6787; snow information, 916/562–1330; fax 916/587–0214.*

Squaw Valley USA was the site of 1960 Olympics. The immense resort has changed significantly since then, but the skiing is still first class, with steep chutes and cornices on six Sierra peaks. Beginners delight in riding the tram to the top, where there is a huge plateau of gentle runs. At the top of the tram you can reach the Bath and Tennis Club in the recently renovated lodge with impressive views from its restaurants, bars, and outdoor ice-skating pavilion. Base facilities are clustered around the Village Mall, with shops, dining, condos, hotels, and lodges. The valley golf course doubles as a cross-country ski facility (*see* Cross Country Skiing, *below*). On the other side of the golf course is the new Resort at Squaw Creek, with its own run and quad chair lift that runs to Squaw's ski terrain. *Rte. 89, 5 mi northwest of Tahoe City, Squaw Valley USA, NV 96146, tel. 916/583–6985; reservations, 800/545–4350; snow information, 916/583–6955; fax 916/583–6985.*

Cross-Country Skiing With 11 areas to choose from on mountaintops and in valleys, this is a Nordic skier's paradise. For the ultimate in groomed conditions, there is America's largest cross-country ski resort, **Royal Gorge** (Box 1100, Soda Springs, CA 95728, tel. 916/426–3871), which offers 317 kilometers of 18-foot-wide track for all abilities, 81 trails on 9,000 acres, two ski schools, and 10 warming huts, as well as four cafés, two hotels, and a hot tub and sauna.

Diamond Peak at Ski Incline (tel. 702/832–3249) has 35 kilometers of groomed track with skating lanes. The trail system goes from 7,400 feet to 9,100 feet with endless wilderness to explore. The entrance is off Route 431.

Kirkwood Ski Resort (*see* Downhill Skiing, *above*) has 80 kilometers of groomed-track skiing, with skating lanes, instruction, and rentals.

Northstar-at-Tahoe (*see* Downhill Skiing, *above*) gives cross-country skiers access to Alpine ski slopes for telemarking and also provides 65 kilometers of groomed, tracked trails with a wide skating lane. There's a ski shop, rentals, and instruction.

Skiers who want to tour the backcountry should check with the **U.S. Forest Service** (tel. 916/587–3558) prior to entering the wilderness.

Sledding and Snowmobiling There are five public **Sno-Park** areas in the vicinity, some for snowmobiling and cross-country skiing, as well as sledding. All are maintained by the Department of Parks and Recreation; an advance permit is required. Call the parks department at 916/322–8993 or contact the Lake Tahoe Visitor Center (*see* Exploring Lake Tahoe, *above*).

Several companies in the area offer snowmobile tours. **Snowmobiling Unlimited** (Box 1591, Tahoe City 96145, tel. 916/583–5858), one of the area's oldest operators, offers guided tours and rentals, as well as a track to zoom around on, for $25 per half hour.

Swimming There are 36 public beaches on Lake Tahoe. Swimming is permitted at many of them, but since Tahoe is a high mountain lake with fairly rugged winters, only the hardiest will be interested, except in midsummer. Even then the water warms to only 68°F. Lifeguards are on duty at some of the swimming beaches, and yellow buoys mark safe areas where motorboats are not permitted. Opening and closing dates for beaches vary with the climate and available park-service personnel. There may be a parking fee of $1 or $2.

Dining

At all Tahoe restaurants, make advance reservations for weekends, and plan to wait for the coffee shops and buffets that don't take reservations. Because Tahoe is a resort area, dress tends to be casual, even in the more expensive restaurants.

Category	Cost*
Very Expensive	over $30
Expensive	$20–$30
Moderate	$16–$20
Inexpensive	under $16

*Average cost of a three-course dinner, per person, not including 7% sales tax, service, or drinks

North Tahoe Area

Hugo's. A Hyatt restaurant, this is the best place on the north shore to come for dining with a view. Located on the lakeshore in a wooded setting, it is a short, pleasant walk from the hotel. Specialties are duck, fresh fish, and steak. Dinner includes an extensive, all-you-can-eat salad buffet and dessert bar. *Country Club Dr. at Lakeshore, Incline Village, tel. 702/831–1111. Reservations recommended. AE, D, DC, MC, V. Dinner and Sunday brunch only. Expensive–Very Expensive.*

★ **The Soule Domain.** A cozy, romantic, 1927 pine-log cabin with stone fireplace is the setting for some of Lake Tahoe's most creative and delicious dinners. Chef/owner Charles Edward Soule IV uses fresh foods and herbs to create such specialties as filet mignon with shiitake mushrooms, Gorgonzola, and brandy or tuna grilled with papaya-mango salsa. *Across from the Tahoe Biltmore, Crystal Bay, tel. 916/546–7529. Reservations recommended. AE, DC, MC, V. Dinner only. Moderate–Expensive.*

Lake View Dining Room. Eggs, burgers, salads, and steaks are served 24 hours a day in summer, and from early morning until late night the rest of the year, before a wide lakeside view in the Cal-Neva Casino. *2 Stateline Rd., Crystal Bay, tel. 702/832–4000. Reservations unnecessary. AE, D, DC, MC, V. Inexpensive–Moderate.*

Sierra Cafe. Located downstairs in the Hyatt, this coffee shop has a touch of elegance. Padded, burgundy-leather booths, upholstered chairs, a large brick fireplace, and an abundance of greenery add to the ambience. You can order from the menu, or go for the Sierra's buffet. This is the place to bring the kids if you're staying at the Hyatt. *Country Club Dr. at Lakeshore, Incline Village, tel. 702/831–1111. No reservations. AE, D, DC, MC, V. Open daily 24 hours. Inexpensive.*

South Tahoe Area

The Summit. On the 16th floor of Harrah's, in the former Star Suite (once the home-away-from-home of visiting royalty and celebrities), this intimate restaurant offers romantic dining with spectacular views of Lake Tahoe. A tuxedo-clad pianist plays the grand by candlelight while a fire crackles in the immense hearth. The creative menu includes quail with prune sauce for an appetizer; artfully presented salads; lamb, venison, or seafood entrées with delicate sauces; and such sensuous desserts as soufflé with vanilla cream sauce. *Harrah's Hotel/Casino, Stateline, tel. 702/588–6606 or 800/648–3773. Reservations recommended. Jacket and tie required. AE, DC, MC, V. Very Expensive.*

Empress Court. Plush velvet booths, etched-glass partitions, and linen tablecloths prove that "elegant Chinese" is not an oxymoron. Empress Court serves traditional Chinese dishes as well as such specialties as grilled squab salad, seasoned deep-fried pork ribs, and satay beef. Even the fortune cookies—dribbled with sweet chocolate—look impressive. *Caesars Tahoe Resort, Hwy. 50, Stateline, NV*

89449, tel. 702/588–3515 or 800/648–3353. Reservations advised. AE, DC, MC, V. Expensive–Very Expensive.

Sage Room Steak House. In the center of Harvey's casino, this romantic restaurant is far removed from the flashing lights and slot machine jangles. Elegant but unpretentious service is the rule, with Steak Diana and Bananas Foster flamed tableside. Specialties include Dungeness-crab cocktail, black-bean soup, filet mignon, beef Wellington, and an award-winning wine list. *Box 128, Stateline, NV 89449, tel. 702/588–2411 or 800/648–3361. Reservations advised. AE, D, DC, MC, V. Moderate–Expensive.*

El Vaquero. Harvey's Mexican restaurant is downstairs, in the hotel's shopping arcade, far from the slots and gaming tables. Decorated with wrought iron, a fountain, and tiles, giving an authentic Old Mexico feel, El Vaquero serves traditional Mexican fare, such as carne asada, enchiladas, and chimichangas. *Box 128, Stateline, NV 89449, tel. 702/588–2411 or 800/648–3361. Reservations advised. AE, D, DC, MC, V. Inexpensive.*

Sierra. Harrah's casual coffee shop is pleasantly decorated with upholstered booths, brass lanterns on the walls, and lots of greenery. Hearty dinners—most less than $10—include old-fashioned meat loaf, Cajun catfish, ravioli, and sandwiches. Asia, a dimly lit section at the back, offers Chinese, Vietnamese, Korean, and other Pacific Rim specialties. *Harrah's, Hwy. 50 and Stateline, South Lake Tahoe, tel. 702/588–6611. No reservations. Dress: casual. AE, D, DC, MC, V. Inexpensive.*

Lodging

In addition to the Nevada casino/hotels described here, many small, less expensive motels are clustered on the California side of Lake Tahoe's south shore. Free shuttle buses provide convenient access between south shore motels and casinos. Some inexpensive choices in the area include **Lakeside Inn** (Hwy. 50 at Kingsbury Grade, tel. 702/588–7777), the only lowrise casino in Stateline, and a short car ride from the main hotels at the border; **Tropicana Lodge** (4132 Cedar Ave., off Stateline Ave., tel. 916/541–3911), the quintessential California resort motel, clean and cheap; and **Day's Inn** (3530 Lake Tahoe Blvd., one mi. west of Stateline, tel. 916/544–3445), which offers good rates and no surprises.

Category	Cost*
Very Expensive	over $100
Expensive	$75–$100
Moderate	$50–$75
Inexpensive	under $50

All prices are for a standard double room, not including 8% tax and service charge.

North Tahoe Area

Hyatt Lake Tahoe. At this elegant, four-star resort, all of the guest rooms have a view of the lake. Blond-wood furniture, oversize beds with lots of extra pillows, warm color schemes, and minibars lend the guest rooms an understated luxury. The hotel is a block from a private beach, where guests can enjoy Jet Ski and speedboat rentals and a lakeside restaurant. The casino is classy, not flashy, offering all the traditional games plus a sports book and live entertainment. Camp Hyatt (for ages 3–12) and Rock Hyatt (for ages 13–17) offer supervised indoor and outdoor games, meals, movies, and sightseeing throughout the summer and on weekends and holidays year-round. *Country Club Dr. at Lakeshore, Incline Village 89450, tel. 702/ 831–1111 or 800/233–1234. 460 units. Facilities: 2 restaurants, 24-hour café, health club, tennis courts, lake, pool, 24-hour room service. AE, D, DC, MC, V. Very Expensive.*

Cal-Neva Lodge Resort Hotel/Casino. Recent renovations have transformed Cal-Neva's standard hotel rooms into upscale accommodations, with Country French armoires and dressers and floral bedspreads. All rooms have lake views. This hotel/casino is a five-minute walk from Lake Tahoe's shores. *2 Stateline Rd., Crystal Bay 89402, tel. 702/832– 4000 or 800/225–6382. 220 rooms. Facilities: 2 restaurants, pool, tennis courts, health club and spa, exercise room, Jacuzzi, masseuse. AE, DC, MC, V. Expensive–Very Expensive.*

Tahoe Biltmore. Across the street from the Cal-Neva Lodge, the Biltmore is a bargain for those seeking an alternative to the bustle of South Lake Tahoe and the expense of the Hyatt. Room rates average $59 in the high season (and can get as low as $24), and the lake isn't far off. Built in 1946, this '50s-style resort features dark wood and has a rustic-lodge feel, but don't expect it to be as nice or well kept as its more expensive neighbor. The large, smoky casino offers table games such as poker and keno, and lots of slots. *5 Hwy. 28, Crystal Bay 89402, tel. 702/831–0660 or 800/245–8667. 86 rooms. Facilities: restaurant, pool. AE, D, DC, MC, V. Inexpensive–Moderate.*

South Tahoe Area

Caesars Tahoe. For easy access to the registration desk, enter through the doors nearest valet parking. Once upstairs, you'll find faux Corinthian columns in the hallway and plush rooms, some recently redecorated in gray, mauve, and mint green. Most rooms have round Roman tubs. The pool is indoors, with a waterfall and a swim tunnel through a manmade rock. *Box 5800, Stateline 89449, tel. 702/588–3515 or 800/648–3353. 440 units. Facilities: 5 restaurants, showroom, lounge, pool, tennis courts, health club, nightclub. AE, DC, MC, V. Very Expensive.*

Harrah's Casino/Hotel Lake Tahoe. The most ostentatiously luxurious hotel on the south shore, Harrah's provides spacious, comfortable rooms, most offering superb views of the lake and mountains. Each guest room comes with a minibar and two full bathrooms—and each bathroom has its own color TV and telephone. Downstairs are a heated indoor pool, two hot tubs, and a complete health club. *Box 8, Stateline 89449, tel. 702/588–6606 or 800/648–3773. 534 rooms. Facilities: 7 restaurants, pool, 2 hot tubs, health club, valet parking, 24-hour room and valet service, pet kennel. AE, DC, MC, V. Very Expensive.*

Harvey's Resort Hotel/Casino. This family-owned hotel is Tahoe's largest resort. The reception area is one flight down from the casino, completely removed from the frenetic gaming atmosphere. The rooms are elegantly but comfortably furnished in "American traditional" with Colonial and French Provincial accents, featuring soft color schemes and marble-tiled baths. Most rooms have excellent lake and mountain views. Llewellyn's, Harvey's 19th-floor restaurant, offers fine dining with panoramic views. *Box 128, Stateline 89449, tel. 702/588–2411 or 800/648–3361. 717 rooms. Facilities: 8 restaurants, 10 cocktail lounges, convention center, tennis, valet parking, garage, health spa. AE, DC, MC, V. Expensive–Very Expensive.*

Horizon Casino/Resort. Formerly the Old West–style High Sierra, this hotel underwent a $15 million renovation in a bid to attract upscale patrons; the casino and lobby now sport a beaux-arts look, with Italian-marble floors, brass highlights, and lots of mirrors. Games include blackjack, craps, roulette, keno, mini-baccarat, and slot machines. The Grand Lake Theater offers top-name entertainment, and the Golden Cabaret features revues, magicians, and smaller-scale production numbers. The hotel's restaurants include Le Grande Buffet, Continental cuisine at Josh's, and bistro sandwiches and specialty coffees at the 24-hour Four Seasons cafeteria. *Box C, Stateline, 89449, tel. 702/588–6211, outside NV 800/322–7723. 539 rooms. Facilities: 3 restaurants, pool, wading pool, 3 hot tubs. AE, DC, MC, V. Moderate–Very Expensive.*

Nightlife

You will find top-name entertainment and production shows at the casinos. The Circus Maximus at Caesars Tahoe and the South Shore Room, a 950-seat theater at Harrah's, are as large as some Broadway houses. Typical headliners include David Copperfield, the Moody Blues, and Diana Ross.

Sometimes there are two performances a night in the big showrooms, and reservations are almost always required for superstars. Cocktail shows usually run $20–$40, including tax and one drink. Smaller casino cabarets sometimes have a cover charge or drink minimum. At Harrah's Stateline Cabaret, the $11 cover includes two drinks and the show. Casino lounges have no cover charges, and they feature jazz and pop musicians; the last set usually ends at 2:30 or 3 AM.

Lounges around the lake often offer pop and country music singers and musicians, and in winter the ski resorts do the same. **Turtles** (tel. 916/544–5400) is a fun spot for dancing in the brand-new, luxurious Embassy Suites, just across the state line from Harrah's; a DJ spins Top 40 tunes and oldies. Summer alternatives are outdoor music events, from chamber quartets to jazz bands and rock performers, at Sand Harbor (Hwy. 28, 5 mi. south of Incline Village, tel. 916/583–9048) and the Lake Tahoe Visitors Center amphitheater (Hwy. 89, 6 mi. north of junction of Hwy. 89 and Hwy. 50, tel. 916/573–2674 in summer, 916/573–2600 rest of the year); summer at Sand Harbor also includes the Sand Harbor Shakespeare Festival (tel. 916/583–9048).

194

Index

Fodor's Travel Guides

Available at bookstores everywhere, or call 1–800–533–6478, 24 hours a day.

U.S. Guides

Alaska

Arizona

Boston

California

Cape Cod, Martha's Vineyard, Nantucket

The Carolinas & the Georgia Coast

Chicago

Colorado

Florida

Hawaii

Las Vegas, Reno, Tahoe

Los Angeles

Maine, Vermont, New Hampshire

Maui

Miami & the Keys

New England

New Orleans

New York City

Pacific North Coast

Philadelphia & the Pennsylvania Dutch Country

The Rockies

San Diego

San Francisco

Santa Fe, Taos, Albuquerque

Seattle & Vancouver

The South

The U.S. & British Virgin Islands

The Upper Great Lakes Region

USA

Vacations in New York State

Vacations on the Jersey Shore

Virginia & Maryland

Waikiki

Walt Disney World and the Orlando Area

Washington, D.C.

Foreign Guides

Acapulco, Ixtapa, Zihuatanejo

Australia & New Zealand

Austria

The Bahamas

Baja & Mexico's Pacific Coast Resorts

Barbados

Berlin

Bermuda

Brazil

Brittany & Normandy

Budapest

Canada

Cancun, Cozumel, Yucatan Peninsula

Caribbean

China

Costa Rica, Belize, Guatemala

The Czech Republic & Slovakia

Eastern Europe

Egypt

Euro Disney

Europe

Europe's Great Cities

Florence & Tuscany

France

Germany

Great Britain

Greece

The Himalayan Countries

Hong Kong

India

Ireland

Israel

Italy

Japan

Kenya & Tanzania

Korea

London

Madrid & Barcelona

Mexico

Montreal & Quebec City

Morocco

Moscow & St. Petersburg

The Netherlands, Belgium & Luxembourg

New Zealand

Norway

Nova Scotia, Prince Edward Island & New Brunswick

Paris

Portugal

Provence & the Riviera

Rome

Russia & the Baltic Countries

Scandinavia

Scotland

Singapore

South America

Southeast Asia

Spain

Sweden

Switzerland

Thailand

Tokyo

Toronto

Turkey

Vienna & the Danube Valley

Yugoslavia

WHEREVER YOU TRAVEL, *H*ELP IS NEVER FAR AWAY.

From planning your trip to providing travel assistance along the way, American Express® Travel Service Offices* are always there to help.

Nevada

LAS VEGAS

American Express Travel Service
Caesar's Palace
3570 Las Vegas Blvd. South
(702) 731-7705

Mickey Cole Travel Service, Inc.
Gold Coast Hotel & Casino
4000 West Flamingo Road
(702) 876-1410

RENO

Deluxe Travel, Ltd.
102 California Avenue
(702) 323-4644

Deluxe Travel, Ltd.
Reno Connon Int'l. Airport
2000 East Plumb Lane
(702) 322-0927

STATELINE

Deluxe Travel, Ltd.
Caesar's Tahoe Hotel & Casino
55 Highway 50
(702) 588-6616

For the office nearest you, call 1-800-YES-AMEX.

INTRODUCING

Fodor's
WORLDVIEW
TRAVEL UPDATE

**AT LAST, YOUR OWN PERSONALIZED
LIST OF WHAT'S GOING ON IN THE
CITIES YOU'RE VISITING.**

**KEYED TO THE DAYS WHEN YOU'RE
THERE, CUSTOMIZED FOR YOUR
INTERESTS, AND SENT TO YOU
BEFORE YOU LEAVE HOME.**

**EXCLUSIVE FOR PURCHASERS OF
FODOR'S GUIDES...**

Fodor's WORLDVIEW
TRAVEL UPDATE

Introducing a revolutionary way to get customized, time-sensitive travel information just before your trip.

Now you can obtain detailed information about what's going on in each city you'll be visiting <u>before</u> you leave home—up-to-the-minute, objective information about the events and activities that interest you most.

Your Itinerary:
Customized reports available for 160 destinations

This is a special offer for purchasers of Fodor's guides – a customized Travel Update to fit your specific interests and your itinerary.

Travel Updates contain the kind of time-sensitive insider information you can get only from local contacts – or from city magazines and newspapers once you arrive. But now you can have the same information before you leave for your trip.

The choice is yours: current art exhibits, theater, music festivals and special concerts, sporting events, antiques and flower shows, shopping, fitness, and more.

The information comes from hundreds of correspondents and thousands of sources worldwide. Updated continuously, it's like having your own personal concierge or friend in the city.

You specify the cities and when you'll be there. We'll do the rest — personalizing the information for you the way no guidebook can.

It's the perfect extension to your Fodor's guide and the best way to make the most of your valuable travel time.

Reg
The
in th,
domain
tion as
worthwhil
the perform
Tickets are u
venue. Alter
mances are cand
given. For more i.
Open-Air Theatre,
NW1 4NP Open Ai
Tel: 935-5756. Ends: 9-
International Air Tattoo
Held biennially, the world
military air display inc
demostra-
tions, milita
bands

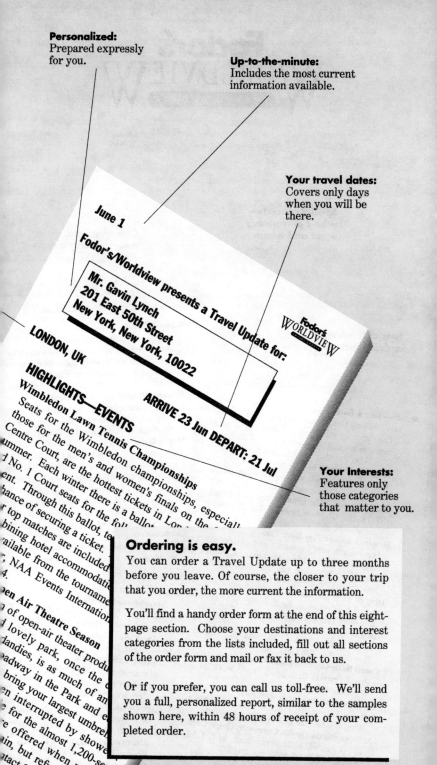

Personalized:
Prepared expressly
for you.

Up-to-the-minute:
Includes the most current
information available.

Your travel dates:
Covers only days
when you will be
there.

June 1

Fodor's/Worldview presents a Travel Update for:

Mr. Gavin Lynch
201 East 50th Street
New York, New York, 10022

Fodor's
WORLDVIEW

LONDON, UK

ARRIVE 23 Jun DEPART: 21 Jul

HIGHLIGHTS—EVENTS

Wimbledon Lawn Tennis Championships
Seats for the Wimbledon championships, especiall
those for the men's and women's finals on the
Centre Court, are the hottest tickets in Lon
summer. Each winter there is a ballo
No. 1 Court seats for the fo
ent. Through this ballot, te
hance of securing a ticket.
top matches are included
bining hotel accommodati
vailable from the tourname
; NAA Events Internation
4.

en Air Theatre Season
of open-air theater produ
lovely park, once the
dandies, is as much of an
adway in the Park and e
bring your largest umbrel
en interrupted by showe
e for the almost 1,200-seat
e offered when perfor-
ain, but refunds are not
tact Sheila Benjamin
gent's Park, L
gent's P

Your Interests:
Features only
those categories
that matter to you.

Ordering is easy.

You can order a Travel Update up to three months
before you leave. Of course, the closer to your trip
that you order, the more current the information.

You'll find a handy order form at the end of this eight-
page section. Choose your destinations and interest
categories from the lists included, fill out all sections
of the order form and mail or fax it back to us.

Or if you prefer, you can call us toll-free. We'll send
you a full, personalized report, similar to the samples
shown here, within 48 hours of receipt of your completed order.

Special concerts—
who's performing
what and where

One-of-a-kind,
one-time-only events

Special interest,
in-depth listings

Children — Events
Angel Canal Festival
The festivities include a children's funfair, entertainers, a boat rally and displays on the water. Regent's Canal. Islington. N1. Tube: Angel. Tel: 267 9100. 11:30am-5:30pm. 7/04.
Blackheath Summer Kite Festival
Stunt kite displays with parachuting teddy bears and trade stands. Free admission. SE3. BR: Blackheath. 10am. 6/27.
Megabugs
Children will delight in this infestation of giant robotic insects, including a praying mantic 60 times life size. Mon-Sat 10am-6pm; Sun 11am-6pm. Admission 4.50 pounds. Natural History Museum, Cromwell Road. SW7. Tube: South Kensington. Tel: 938 9123. Ends 10/01.
Childminders
This establishment employs only women, providing nurses and qualified nannies to

Music — Jazz & Blues
Tito Puente's Golden Men of Latin Jazz
The father of mambo and Cuban rumba king comes to town. Royal Festival Hall. South Bank. SE1. Tube: Waterloo. Tel: 928 8800. 8pm. 7/15.
Georgie Fame and The New York Band
Riding a popular tide with his latest album, the smoky-voiced Fame and his keyboard are on a tour yet again. The Grand. Clapham Junction. SW11. BR: Clapham Junction. Tel: 738 9000. 7:30pm. 7/07.
Jacques Loussier Play Bach Trio
The French jazz classicist and colleagues. Kenwood Lakeside. Hampstead Lane. Kenwood. NW3. Tube: Golders Green, then bus 210. Tel: 413 1443. 7pm. 7/10.
Tony Bennett and Ronnie Scott
Royal Festival Hall. South Bank. SE1. Tube: Waterloo. Tel: 928 8800. 8pm. 7/11.
Santana
Royal Festival Hall. South Bank. SE1. Tube: Waterloo. Tel: 928 8800. 8pm. 7/12.
Count Basie Orchestra and Nancy Wilson Trio
Royal Festival Hall. South Bank. SE1. Tube: Waterloo. Tel: 928 8800. 8pm. 7/14.
King Pleasure and the Biscuit Boys
Royal Festival Hall. South Bank. SE1. Tube: Waterloo. Tel: 928 8800. 6:30 and 9pm. 7/16.
Al Green and the London Community Gospel Choir
Royal Festival Hall. South Bank. SE1. Tube: Waterloo. Tel: 928 8800. 8pm. 7/13.
BB King and Linda Hopkins
Mother of the blues and successor to Bessie Smith, Hopkins meets up with "Blues Boy" King. Royal Festival Hall. South Bank. SE1. 6:30 and 9pm.

Music — Classical
Marylebone Sinfonia
Kenneth Gowen conducts music by Puccini and Rossini. Queen Elizabeth Hall. South Bank. SE1. Tube: Waterloo. Tel: 928 8800. 7:45pm. 7/16.
London Philharmonic
Franz Welser-Moest and George Benjamin conduct selections by Alexander Goehr, Messiaen, and some of Benjamin's own compositions. Queen Elizabeth Hall. South Bank. SE1. Tube: Waterloo. Tel: 928 8800. 8pm.
London Pro Arte Orchestra and Forest Choir
Murray Stewart conducts selections by Rossini, Haydn and Jonathan Willcocks. Queen Elizabeth Hall. South Bank. SE1. Tube: Waterloo. Tel: 928 8800. 7:45pm.
Kensington Symphony Orchestra
Russell Keable conducts Dvorak's South Bank.

Here's what you get . . .

Detailed information about what's going on — precisely when you'll be there.

Show openings during your visit

Reviews by local critics

Exhibitions & Shows—Antique & Flower

Westminster Antiques Fair

Over 50 stands with pre-1830 furniture and other Victorian and earlier items. Thu-Fri 11am-8pm; Sat-Sun 11am-6pm. Admission 4 pounds, children free. Old Royal Horticultural Hall. Vincent Square. SW1. Tel: 0444/48 25 14. 6-24 thru 6/27.

Royal Horticultural Society Flower Show

The show includes displays of carnations, summer fruit and vegetables. Tue 11am-7pm; Wed 10am-5pm. Admission Tue 4 pounds, Wed 2 pounds. Royal Horticultural Halls. Greycoat Street and Vincent Square. SW1. Tube: Victoria. 7/20 thru 7/21.

mpton Court Palace International Flower Show

Major international garden and flower show king place in conjunction with the British

Theater — Musical

Sunset Boulevard

In June, the four Andrew Lloyd Webber musicals which dominated London's stages in the 1980s (Cats, Starlight Express, Phantom of the Opera and Aspects of Love) are joined by the composer's latest work, a show rumored to have his best music to date. The 1950 Billy Wilder film about a helpless young writer who is drawn into the world of a possessive, aging silent screen star offers rich opportunities for Webber's evolving style. Soaring, aching melodies, lush technical effects and psychological thrills are all expected. Patti Lupone stars. Mon-Sat at 8pm; matinee Thu-Sat at 3pm. In-person sales only at the box office; credit card bookings, Tel: 344 0055. Admission 15-32.50 pounds. Adelphi Theatre. The Strand. WC2. Tube: Charing Cross. Tel: 836 7611. Starts: 6/21

Leonardo A Portrait of Love

A new musical about the great Renaissance arti and inventor comes in for a London premier tested by a brief run at Oxford's Old Fire Stati autumn. The work explores the relations Vinci and the woman '

Spectator Sports — Other Sports

Greyhound Racing: Wembley Stadium

This dog track offers good views of greyhound racing held on Mon, Wed and Fri. No credit cards. Stadium Way. Wembley. HA9. Tube: Wembley Park. Tel: 902 8833.

Benson & Hedges Cricket Cup Final

Lord's Cricket Ground. St. John's Wood Road. NW8. Tube: St. John's Wood. Tel: 289 1611. 11am. 7/10.

siness-Fax & Overnight Mail

Post Office, Trafalgar Square Branch

Offers a network of fax services, the Intelpost system, throughout the country and abroad. Mon-Sat 8am-8pm, Sun 9am-5pm. William IV Street. WC2. Tube: Charing Cross. Tel: 930 95

Alberquerque • Atlanta • Atlantic City • Ne
Baltimore • Boston • Chicago • Cincinnati
Cleveland • Dallas/Ft.Worth • Denver • De
• Houston • Kansas City • Las Vegas • Los
Angeles • Memphis • Miami • Milwaukee •
New Orleans • New York City • Orlando •
Springs • Philadelphia • Phoenix • Pittsburg
Portland • Salt Lake • San Antonio • San Di
San Franc
Oslo • Wash
Hawaii • Kaua
Ex
Ber

Fodor's WORLDVIEW TRAVEL UPDATE

Antigua & B
Gorda • Barbados • Dominica • Porte
cia • St. Vincent • Trinidad &Tobago
ymans • Puerto Plata • Santo Doming
Aruba • Bonaire • Curacao • St. Mac
ec City • Montreal • Ottawa • Toron
Vancouver • Guadeloupe • Martiniqu
elemy • St. Martin • Kingston • Ixta
o Bay • Negril • Ocho Rios • Ponce
n • Grand Turk • Providenciales • S
St. John • St. Thomas • Acapulco •
& Isla Mujeres • Cozumel • Guadal
a • Los Cabos • Manzinillo • Mazatl
City • Monterrey • Oaxaca • Puerto
do • Puerto Vallarta • Veracruz • Ix
dam • Athens • Barcelon

Interest Categories

For your personalized Travel Update, choose the categories you're most interested in from this list. Every Travel Update automatically provides you with *Event Highlights* – the best of what's happening during the dates of your trip.

1.	**Business Services**	Fax & Overnight Mail, Computer Rentals, Photocopying, Secretarial , Messenger, Translation Services

Dining

2.	**All Day Dining**	Breakfast & Brunch, Cafes & Tea Rooms, Late-Night Dining
3.	**Local Cuisine**	In Every Price Range—from Budget Restaurants to the Special Splurge
4.	**European Cuisine**	Continental, French, Italian
5.	**Asian Cuisine**	Chinese, Far Eastern, Japanese, Indian
6.	**Americas Cuisine**	American, Mexican & Latin
7.	**Nightlife**	Bars, Dance Clubs, Comedy Clubs, Pubs & Beer Halls
8.	**Entertainment**	Theater—Drama, Musicals, Dance, Ticket Agencies
9.	**Music**	Classical, Traditional & Ethnic, Jazz & Blues, Pop, Rock
10.	**Children's Activities**	Events, Attractions
11.	**Tours**	Local Tours, Day Trips, Overnight Excursions, Cruises
12.	**Exhibitions, Festivals & Shows**	Antiques & Flower, History & Cultural, Art Exhibitions, Fairs & Craft Shows, Music & Art Festivals
13.	**Shopping**	Districts & Malls, Markets, Regional Specialities
14.	**Fitness**	Bicycling, Health Clubs, Hiking, Jogging
15.	**Recreational Sports**	Boating/Sailing, Fishing, Ice Skating, Skiing, Snorkeling/Scuba, Swimming
16.	**Spectator Sports**	Auto Racing, Baseball, Basketball, Football, Horse Racing, Ice Hockey, Soccer

Please note that interest category content will vary by season, destination, and length of stay.

Destinations

The Fodor's/Worldview Travel Update covers more than 160 destinations worldwide. Choose the destinations that match your itinerary from this list. (Choose bulleted destinations only.)

United States (Mainland)
- Albuquerque
- Atlanta
- Atlantic City
- Baltimore
- Boston
- Chicago
- Cincinnati
- Cleveland
- Dallas/Ft. Worth
- Denver
- Detroit
- Houston
- Kansas City
- Las Vegas
- Los Angeles
- Memphis
- Miami
- Milwaukee
- Minneapolis/ St. Paul
- New Orleans
- New York City
- Orlando
- Palm Springs
- Philadelphia
- Phoenix
- Pittsburgh
- Portland
- St. Louis
- Salt Lake City
- San Antonio
- San Diego
- San Francisco
- Seattle
- Tampa
- Washington, DC

Alaska
- Alaskan Destinations

Hawaii
- Honolulu
- Island of Hawaii
- Kauai
- Maui

Canada
- Quebec City
- Montreal
- Ottawa
- Toronto
- Vancouver

Bahamas
- Abacos
- Eleuthera/ Harbour Island
- Exumas
- Freeport
- Nassau & Paradise Island

Bermuda
- Bermuda Countryside
- Hamilton

British Leeward Islands
- Anguilla
- Antigua & Barbuda
- Montserrat
- St. Kitts & Nevis

British Virgin Islands
- Tortola & Virgin Gorda

British Windward Islands
- Barbados
- Dominica
- Grenada
- St. Lucia
- St. Vincent
- Trinidad & Tobago

Cayman Islands
- The Caymans

Dominican Republic
- Puerto Plata
- Santo Domingo

Dutch Leeward Islands
- Aruba
- Bonaire
- Curacao

Dutch Windward Island
- St. Maarten/ St. Martin

French West Indies
- Guadeloupe
- Martinique
- St. Barthelemy

Jamaica
- Kingston
- Montego Bay
- Negril
- Ocho Rios

Puerto Rico
- Ponce
- San Juan

Turks & Caicos
- Grand Turk
- Providenciales

U.S. Virgin Islands
- St. Croix
- St. John
- St. Thomas

Mexico
- Acapulco
- Cancun & Isla Mujeres
- Cozumel
- Guadalajara
- Ixtapa & Zihuatanejo
- Los Cabos
- Manzanillo
- Mazatlan
- Mexico City
- Monterrey
- Oaxaca
- Puerto Escondido
- Puerto Vallarta
- Veracruz

Europe
- Amsterdam
- Athens
- Barcelona
- Berlin
- Brussels
- Budapest
- Copenhagen
- Dublin
- Edinburgh
- Florence
- Frankfurt
- French Riviera
- Geneva
- Glasgow
- Interlaken
- Istanbul
- Lausanne
- Lisbon
- London
- Madrid
- Milan
- Moscow
- Munich
- Oslo
- Paris
- Prague
- Provence
- Rome
- Salzburg
- St. Petersburg
- Stockholm
- Venice
- Vienna
- Zurich

Pacific Rim Australia & New Zealand
- Auckland
- Melbourne
- Sydney

China
- Beijing
- Guangzhou
- Shanghai

Japan
- Kyoto
- Nagoya
- Osaka
- Tokyo
- Yokohama

Other
- Bangkok
- Hong Kong & Macau
- Manila
- Seoul
- Singapore
- Taipei

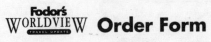
Order Form

THIS TRAVEL UPDATE IS FOR (Please print):

Name

Address

City   State   ZIP

Country   Tel # (   )   -

Title of this Fodor's guide:

Store and location where guide was purchased:

INDICATE YOUR DESTINATIONS/DATES: Write in below the destinations you want to order. Then fill in your arrival and departure dates for each destination.

		Month	Day		Month	Day
(Sample) LONDON	From:	6 /	21	To:	6 /	30
1	From:	/		To:	/	
2	From:	/		To:	/	
3	From:	/		To:	/	

You can order up to three destinations per Travel Update. Only destinations listed on the previous page are applicable. Maximum amount of time covered by a Travel Update cannot exceed 30 days.

CHOOSE YOUR INTERESTS: Select up to eight categories from the list of interest categories shown on the previous page and circle the numbers below:

1   2   3   4   5   6   7   8   9   10   11   12   13   14   15   16

CHOOSE HOW YOU WANT YOUR TRAVEL UPDATE DELIVERED (Check one):

❑ Please mail my Travel Update to the address above **OR**

❑ Fax it to me at **Fax #** (   )   -

DELIVERY CHARGE (Check one)

	Within U.S. & Canada	Outside U.S. & Canada
First Class Mail	❑ $2.50	❑ $5.00
Fax	❑ $5.00	❑ $10.00
Priority Delivery	❑ $15.00	❑ $27.00

All orders will be sent within 48 hours of receipt of a completed order form.

ADD UP YOUR ORDER HERE. *SPECIAL OFFER FOR FODOR'S PURCHASERS ONLY!*

	Suggested Retail Price	Your Price	This Order
First destination ordered	$13.95	$ 7.95	$ 7.95
Second destination (if applicable)	$ 9.95	$ 4.95	+
Third destination (if applicable)	$ 9.95	$ 4.95	+
Plus delivery charge from above			+
		TOTAL:	$

METHOD OF PAYMENT (Check one):   ❑ AmEx   ❑ MC   ❑ Visa   ❑ Discover
❑ Personal Check   ❑ Money Order

Make check or money order payable to: Fodor's Worldview Travel Update

Credit Card #   **Expiration Date:**

Authorized Signature

SEND THIS COMPLETED FORM TO:
Fodor's Worldview Travel Update, 114 Sansome Street, Suite 700, San Francisco, CA 94104

OR CALL OR FAX US 24-HOURS A DAY
Telephone **1-800-799-9609** • Fax **1-800-799-9619** (From within the U.S. & Canada)
(Outside the U.S. & Canada: Telephone 415-616-9988 • Fax 415-616-9989)

(Please have this guide in front of you when you call so we can verify purchase.)

Offer valid until 12/31/94.